RETAINING AND TRANSITIONING BUSINESSES IN COMMUNITIES

This edited collection presents successful business succession planning in smaller rural communities where profit margins are low, markets are shrinking, and there are few potential buyers. Finding innovative ways to successfully transition these businesses to new owners is at the heart of community and economic development efforts if many of these communities are to thrive in the future. Chapters outline options for successfully transitioning businesses that have worked in Canada, England, and the U.S. The book explores a variety of alternative approaches to transitioning small businesses to new owners using a different ownership model. A common theme running through these approaches is that employees and/or members of the community are engaged in working with or possibly owning the business in some cases. The book's discussions are not prescriptive, recommending specific models or strategies. Instead, they provide valuable insights into viable alternatives and suggest additional resource materials. This book is essential for academics, policymakers, and practitioners working on community and economic development issues, especially in areas with aging populations.

Norman Walzer is professor of economics emeritus and founding director of the Illinois Institute for Rural Affairs, at Western Illinois University. He also is past president of the Community Development Society.

Christopher D. Merrett is dean for Innovation and Economic Development, director of the Illinois Institute for Rural Affairs, and program chair for the Master of Arts in Community and Economic Development at Western Illinois University.

Community Development Research and Practice Series

Other books in the series:

Democracy as Creative Practice
Weaving a Culture of Community Life
Tom Borrup and Andrew Zitcer

Community Development and Schools
Conflict, Power, and Promise
Mildred E. Warner, Jason Reece and Xue Zhang

Community Change in Action
A Roadmap for Students
Sarah L. Young and Carly L. Redding

Retaining and Transitioning Businesses in Communities
Strategies in a New Era
Norman Walzer and Christopher D. Merrett

For more information about this series, please visit: https://www.routledge.com/Community-Development-Research-and-Practice-Series/book-series/CDRP

"One of the most critical challenges facing both rural and urban communities is the retention and transitioning of local businesses. This book is incredibly timely as it addresses these conditions in a post-pandemic world that has significantly reframed how businesses can operate, despite geography or other conditions that previously would have threatened retention and transition. In response to these unprecedented conditions, Norman Walzer and Christopher Merrett provide invaluable insights into the opportunities, challenges, critical needs, and careful considerations needed to revitalize local businesses and economies in a variety of settings. It is a must-read to help business owners, policy makers, practitioners, and others make businesses and communities stronger."

Mark Brennan, *Professor of Community Development and UNESCO Chair for Community and Leadership Development, Penn State University*

"With nearly 3 million business owners approaching retirement causing the largest transfer of wealth ever in the United States, this book couldn't be more timely. Retiring owners must consider alternative ownership approaches (including employee ownership) and the editors have gathered a 'who's who' of experts that provide incredibly easy to understand, yet in-depth, information on all forms of employee ownership and other alternatives to a traditional third-party sale. It is a must read for business owners, advisors, and community leaders concerned with keeping good jobs local and rewarding the employees who have helped produce the profits."

Steve Storkan, *Executive Director, Employee Ownership Expansion Network*

"Companies usually are owned by private individuals, or by external shareholders. However, they can be owned by their customers, employees, local communities, or other stakeholders (such as with producer co-operatives), or by some combination of these stakeholders. Such alternative, or 'mutual' ownership, is sometimes criticised as being unable to scale up, particularly globally, as easily as privately and shareholder owned companies can. This book focusses on what is good especially in rural areas and small towns. In these cases, it is a positive advantage if businesses remain relatively small scale and locally rooted. Thus, for these areas, when it comes to business succession, selling the company to its employees or customers makes perfect sense."

Jonathon Michie, *Director, Oxford Centre on Mutual & Co-owned Business and President, Kellogg College, Oxford*

"*Retaining and Transitioning Businesses in Communities* is an insightful, must-read exploration of how employee ownership models—ESOPs, EOTs, worker cooperatives, and community-supported enterprises—can safeguard businesses during ownership transitions. The focus on rural and smaller communities demonstrates how these strategies not only preserve local economies but also foster resilience and long-term sustainability. This timely work is a powerful resource for those passionate about building inclusive, transformative businesses that empower communities and reshape the future of ownership. An essential addition to the conversation on the power of employee ownership."

James de le Vingne, *CEO, UK Employee Ownership Association*

"Retiring small business owners with no family successors are selling to their workers, securing family wealth and creating a huge employee share ownership sector in the US economy. What a positive development: this is the best book to read about it."

Joseph R. Blasi, *J. Robert Beyster Distinguished Professor and Director, Institute for the Study of Employee Ownership and Profit Sharing, Rutgers University*

RETAINING AND TRANSITIONING BUSINESSES IN COMMUNITIES

Strategies in a New Era

Edited by Norman Walzer and Christopher D. Merrett

Routledge
Taylor & Francis Group
NEW YORK AND LONDON

Designed cover image: Getty Images

First published 2025
by Routledge
605 Third Avenue, New York, NY 10158

and by Routledge
4 Park Square, Milton Park, Abingdon, Oxon, OX14 4RN

Routledge is an imprint of the Taylor & Francis Group, an informa business

ISBN: 978-1-032-80563-4 (hbk)
ISBN: 978-1-032-80562-7 (pbk)
ISBN: 978-1-003-49746-2 (ebk)

DOI: 10.4324/9781003497462

Typeset in Times New Roman
by SPi Technologies India Pvt Ltd (Straive)

To help retiring business owners and community leaders find successful ways to preserve essential services during demographic changes.

CONTENTS

FIGURES

TABLES

ABOUT THE CONTRIBUTORS

Todd Barman is the Downtown Development Specialist at the University of Wisconsin-Madison Division of Extension. His areas of expertise include downtown development planning based on commercial district market position and clustering, asset/capital-driven economic development strategies, market-driven transformation strategies, entrepreneurship, and targeted market research. He previously served as the assistant Main Street coordinator with the Wisconsin Main Street Program and as a senior program officer with the National Main Street Center.

Michael Braun, Ph.D. is Director of Employer Partnerships at Accelerate Montana, the University of Montana's workforce and economic development initiative. In this role, Michael manages corporate trainings and workforce solutions for companies, non-profits and government entities throughout Montana. Michael was previously a management professor, teaching strategy, entrepreneurship and the management of family business. His early career was as an investment banker working with family business.

Tessa Conroy, Ph.D., is an associate professor in the Department of Agricultural and Applied Economics and a community economic development specialist at the University of Wisconsin-Madison. Dr. Conroy conducts applied research and provides technical assistance related to economic growth and development, with a particular focus on small business dynamics.

Chris Cooper has a degree in political science from Kent State University (KSU) and directs the Ohio Employee Ownership Center at KSU. He focuses primarily on ownership culture and education and training, working with business owners on succession planning and employee-owned start-ups. He co-authored *Sustainable Jobs, Sustainable Communities: The Union Co-op Model* with Rob Witherell of the United Steel Workers Union and Michael Peck of Mondragon. He also contributed to other business development journals, including the *Economic Development Journal* of the IEDC, and authored *Business Succession Planning: An Owner's Manual*, which covers ownership succession and employee ownership.

Caroline Corona is a graduate research assistant at the Division of Extension and is a master's degree candidate in public affairs at the La Follette School of Public Affairs, University of Wisconsin-Madison.

Jarvis Tyrell Curry, Ph.D., is an accomplished researcher, educator, and audit professional with expertise in strategic management and corporate governance. As audit chief for the State of California, he brings extensive experience in leadership and program development. He is an adjunct professor of business at the University of the Cumberlands with publications on topics ranging from succession planning to business ethics, and is a member of the American Institute of Certified Public Accountants and the Institute of Internal Auditors.

Steven Deller, Ph.D., is a Vilas Distinguished Achievement Professor and extension specialist in the Department of Agricultural and Applied Economics, and community economic development specialist, at the University of Wisconsin-Madison. Dr. Deller's applied research and technical assistance program focuses on modeling community and small regional economies to better understand the changing dynamics of the economy, assess the impact of those changes, and identify local economic strengths, weaknesses, opportunities, and threats.

Ben Doyle, M.A., is president of the Preservation Trust of Vermont, a nonprofit whose mission is to build community through the preservation of Vermont's historic buildings, villages, and downtowns. His professional experience reflects an interest in using community development practices, the arts, and education to build connections within and between communities, government, and the private sector.

Mark C. Hand, Ph.D., is an Assistant Professor of Political Science at the University of Texas at Arlington. His research explores the growth of employee ownership, the development of workplace democracy, and the intersection of politics and entrepreneurship. He serves on the board of the Purpose Trust Ownership Network, which promotes purpose trust ownership in the U.S., and the board of the Texas Center for Employee Ownership, which promotes all forms of broad-based employee ownership in Texas.

Kiah Hochstetler is a third-generation Montanan with expertise and background in technology and the management of global software teams across continents. He started two companies, one an IT consultancy that developed and released software for the U.S. freight logistics industry that managed more than 50,000 semi-truck loads in its first year. The second company, which merged at the end of 2019, provides portfolio management software for the alternative investment industry, boasting more than $150 million in assets under management. Its customers include a publicly traded bank, top tier funds, and family offices.

Dawn McGee, J.D., has worked with a broad base of diversified portfolio companies since 1995. She helped raise and deploy three funds prior to her time at Goodworks Ventures, including Global Partners formed in 1995, Underdog Ventures founded in 2000, and Unitus Equity Fund founded in 2006. She has mentored portfolio companies, structured exits, and leveraged her network to build value and raise capital to grow and build healthy sustainable businesses. Her focus at GWE is acquiring and building robust and healthy portfolio companies, defining long-term strategy, and asking a lot of questions. Dawn is also a faculty member in the RSF Integrated Capital Fellowship program.

Christopher D. Merrett, Ph.D., is dean for Innovation and Economic Development, director of the Illinois Institute for Rural Affairs, and program chair for the Master of Arts in Community and Economic Development at Western Illinois University. His research focus is on regional development, social justice, and cooperatives as they relate to community development. He has co-edited (with Norman Walzer) two books on this topic, and they recently co-edited *Rural Areas in Transition* published by Routledge.

Stacy Mullinex, M.B.A., CExP, is senior project manager for the Iowa Center for Employee Ownership operated by Advance Iowa at the University of Northern Iowa. Her career has included owning a company and consultation with various trades ranging from small family shops to multi-million-dollar operations. At Advance Iowa, she helps companies identify value drivers for business growth, provide strategic/financial valuation assessments, and offer customized succession planning with a specialization in employee ownership models.

Graeme Nuttall, OBE, has a career-long involvement in employee ownership policymaking and research. Former U.K. Government independent adviser on employee ownership, he is a visiting fellow at Kellogg College, University of Oxford, an executive fellow at Rutger's Institute for the Study of Employee Ownership and Profit Sharing, and international ambassador for the UK Employee Ownership Association.

Michael Palmieri, Ph.D., is the program director at the Ohio Employee Ownership Center at Kent State University (KSU), where he coordinates the Center's education and training programs and leads its research efforts. His research focuses on the economic and political impacts of alternative ownership structures within private enterprises. He is a fellow at the Rutgers Institute for the Study of Employee Ownership and Profit Sharing and a contributing author at the Shares Laboratory research team at Rutgers University. He is also a part-time faculty member at KSU's Political Science Department.

Corey Rosen, Ph.D., is the founder and an active staff member of the National Center for Employee Ownership (NCEO), a private, nonprofit membership, information, and research organization in Oakland, CA. He co-founded the NCEO in 1981 after working as a professional staff member in the U.S. Senate, where he helped draft legislation on employee ownership plans. He is the author or co-author of more than 100 articles and numerous books on employee ownership, and co-author of *Equity: Why Employee Ownership is Good for Business* (2005).

Zoe Schlag is co-founder and managing partner of Common Trust, an employee ownership buyout platform. She has been an entrepreneur and investor with expertise that includes implementing employee ownership buyouts, purpose trusts, and shared ownership investing. She is a co-author of Assets in Common, a new strategy for the U.S. economy to scale shared ownership; an executive fellow at the Institute for the Study of Employee Ownership and Profit Sharing at the Rutgers School of Management and Labor Relations; and she also serves on the board of JUST, a leading U.S.-based microfinance organization, and MDaaS, the fastest-growing medical diagnostic care provider in Nigeria.

Tiffany Vargas is a research assistant at the Research Cluster on Employee Ownership and Workplace Democracy (EO+WD), and a political science major at the University of Texas at Arlington.

Norman Walzer, Ph.D., is professor and founding director emeritus, Illinois Institute for Rural Affairs, housed at Western Illinois University. He publishes extensively on local public finance, economic development, and collective impact topics with 28 co-authored or co-edited books on various community development issues. He is past-president of the Community Development Society (CDS) and the Regional Science Association-Midwest Region, and has held leadership positions in other professional organizations. Currently, he is founding co-editor of *Local Development & Society*, an international journal, and is on the editorial board of *Community Development*, both of which are co-published by CDS with Routledge: Taylor and Francis Group.

Errin Welty, M.S. (CEcD, EDFP), is the senior downtown development director at the Wisconsin Economic Development Corporation (WEDC). She works primarily with Main Street and Connect Communities, which comprise more than 130 passionate places around the state. She works with businesses, property owners, and community groups around the state to make local projects a reality.

Charles Zumbrunnen is a research assistant at the Division of Extension. He is studying economics and mathematics at the University of Wisconsin-Madison.

PREFACE

Changing demographics will bring the retirement of many small business owners, some of whom will have difficulty selling their businesses in customary ways. This means they, and local development practitioners, will need to consider alternative ownership models to preserve the businesses in their communities.

This book explores succession planning and alternative ways of transitioning businesses to the next owners. Employee ownership, an increasingly prevalent option, includes models such as employee ownership stock plans, employee ownership trusts, and purpose trusts. The attraction of each approach is examined in some detail in the following chapters.

While employee ownership makes sense for some, in other cases, the most viable option is for residents to pool funds, purchase the business, rehab the structure, and then find a manager to operate the enterprise. These community-supported enterprises have succeeded, especially in rural areas. Still other examples include a nonprofit group purchasing the business, revitalizing it, and then operating or selling it to another agency.

While not intended as a manual, this book offers discussions that will help entrepreneurs and local development groups find ways to work with business owners considering retirement and/or selling the business so that the services remain in the community. Success in these efforts will help maintain quality of life, especially important for small towns or neighborhoods trying to retain and attract residents.

ACKNOWLEDGMENTS

Rural areas are in a state of transition because of many contributing economic and demographic factors, not the least of which is population aging. The U.S. Census Bureau projects that by 2035 the population older than 65 years will outnumber those 18 years and younger. These trends will affect metro and nonmetro areas, but could seriously impact some rural communities in several ways.

Fortunately, advances in communications technology have lessened some of the barriers associated with distance. Residents in rural areas, even those not close to large cities, can participate in remote meetings, market services using the internet, access health services, and work several days a week from their homes. These and other changes make small places with suitable housing, recreational facilities, and a safe environment with good schools more attractive places to live.

The natural aging process has resulted in population declines in many small towns that now must find ways to attract new residents, especially younger age groups, or retain current residents, especially those starting families. Unfortunately, many of these communities do not have suitable housing for younger age cohorts.

In addition, surveys indicate that many business owners are 60 years or older and plan to retire in the relatively near future. These decisions mean that in many small towns or places, especially those in rural areas, long-term essential services like grocery stores will be threatened unless they can be transitioned to new owners.

Some areas have already addressed this issue by taking innovative steps to retain threatened local services, but many others have yet to respond. Thus, it is important to help local developers and community leaders understand options available for transitioning a business to a new owner(or owners) when the current owners want to retire but can't find a suitable buyer.

Discussions in this book are intended to acquaint community and economic development leaders with alternative models or approaches to transitioning ownership of a business when selling through a broker in the usual way does not work. The discussions build on the succession planning literature to explore employee ownership models such as employee stock ownership plans, employee ownership trusts, purposeful trusts, and other approaches.

Basic community development principles and practices are an integral part of these discussions. For the transition process to work, a community must be a suitable place to live with a high quality of life, which usually relies on sound community development practices. Examples include building or strengthening the social, human, financial, built, natural, and cultural capitals; considering options such as community-supported enterprises; and relying on technical assistance and/or support from nonprofits.

This book has benefitted from discussions with both business owners and service providers working with the business succession and transition process. Steve Storkan, of the National Employee Ownership Expansion Network (EOX), suggested various concepts along with introductions to practitioners. Past successes by many practitioners such as the late Paul Bruhn in Vermont, a pioneer who for many years showed how a nonprofit can work with community groups to transition businesses, stimulated our interest in this topic.

Finally, our work in past years with Illinois Institute for Rural Affairs conferences and projects brought many contacts with scholars, practitioners, and best practices. The time and efforts by contributing authors and Professor Amy Patrick Mossman at WIU, who copyedited and prepared the manuscript for publication, are greatly appreciated. As usual, we accept responsibility for any errors and/or misrepresentations in the materials presented.

Norman Walzer and Christopher D. Merrett

1

RETAINING AND TRANSITIONING BUSINESSES

Overview of Issues

Norman Walzer and Christopher D. Merrett

Over the past several decades, many rural places across the U.S. experienced either slow population growth or long-term population decline, which, in some cases, possibly threatens their continued viability as attractive places to live. The 2010s was the first decade in which the aggregate rural population declined (Johnson, 2022). Demographics suggest that these trends could continue in the future.

On the more positive side, pandemic and census figures indicate that some nonmetropolitan areas had substantial population increases because of people leaving large metro areas during the COVID-19 period (Frey, 2022). There is also evidence that during the pandemic, residents shopped closer to home, which helped local businesses, although declines in tourism and hospitality industries reduced economic activity and threatened many small enterprises (Thau, 2021).

At the same time, many small-town residents now commute to larger employment centers, which reduces their purchases in stores in the communities where they live. While federal and state programs helped many small businesses during the pandemic, some business owners approaching retirement age decided to close their enterprises rather than ride out an unknown recovery. Even though the pandemic was relatively short-lived, in some regions of the U.S. rural areas did not respond as well economically as their urban counterparts (Deller & Conroy, 2023). These communities may have more difficulties trying to retain current residents and attract more people in the future.

At the same time, however, advances in telecommunications, such as Zoom and a growing interest by workers in avoiding long daily commutes, increased remote working opportunities that, combined with high housing costs in urban

DOI: 10.4324/9781003497462-1

areas, make rural areas in the region more attractive. Businesses, especially those in tight labor markets, accommodated this working preference, at least part-time, although the future of remote working is not completely clear (Lund et al., 2020).

In this new environment, smaller communities in rural areas need to effectively market their favorable living conditions and social engagement opportunities to potential new residents. To succeed, the communities must have a stable business sector and/or employment and investment opportunities, some of which seriously declined during the past several decades.

High-speed broadband is an essential part of doing business in the current economic climate. Many states realize the importance of affordable access and now work with local agencies to create opportunities for residents and businesses to market over the internet. Telehealth, internet shopping, and other features expanded opportunities for rural areas to increase quality of life, educational opportunities, and access to recreation, which makes them more competitive when suitable housing is available. As an example, older residents who in the past migrated to larger centers for easier access to better health facilities and more convenient shopping may now reconsider their living options, which could help stabilize rural populations.

A recent Gallup Poll (2021) reported that nearly half (48%) of respondents preferred living in a town (17%) or rural area (31%) if given a choice. Perhaps even more importantly, this preference, when expressed by respondents between the ages of 35 and 54 years, increased from 46% to 51% between 2018 and 2021 (Saad, 2021). While some responses can be partly attributed to the COVID-19 pandemic conditions, the shift in expressed attitudes is positive for smaller communities in more rural settings with affordable housing, amenities, natural recreation facilities, and high-quality educational opportunities.

A survey conducted between November 2022 and January 2023 by SaveYour. Town and SmallBizSurvival.com (sample size of 295 across the U.S.) reported that rural residents were "twice as likely to say they were optimistic about their communities' future as negative" (McCray, 2023). Lack of housing, inactive downtowns, and population decline persisted as among the five most important issues faced. Unlike many metro areas, crime, poverty, and drug abuse were listed among the least concerning rural challenges.

The potentially brighter future for many rural areas emphasizes the importance of finding innovative and successful ways to retain important businesses that risk closure when the current owner or owners decide to retire. Much work is currently available on business succession planning with no shortage of programs and technical assistance available to interested owners (Darger, 2022; SCORE, 2024; Symonds, 2024).

Nevertheless, these programs are often less successful in the case of family businesses with few employees or where the owner or owners are near retirement age and/or may have retired from a previous occupation and now work part-time in the business. Young family members expected to continue the enterprise often have pursued higher education and then found more lucrative occupations or professions elsewhere with little, if any, economic incentive to take over the business.

Purpose of the Book

The discussions in this volume explore a variety of alternative approaches to transitioning small businesses to new owners using a different ownership model. A common theme running through these approaches is that employees and/or members of the community are engaged in working with or possibly owning the business in some cases. These residents are concerned about the future of the business and are prone to support its operations in some way.

Selling a small business in a rural community can be difficult. Subsequent chapters describe several approaches to transition the businesses along with examples of where and how they have overcome barriers and succeeded. The discussions are not prescriptive, recommending specific models or strategies. Instead, they provide insights into viable alternatives and suggest additional resource materials.

This book is intended for academics, policymakers, and practitioners alike because they deal with business succession and transition issues. The chapters can be used as supplemental reading materials in a classroom or training venue or as a resource for policymakers and practitioners exploring new approaches. Adopting these strategies, in some instances, would require modifications to local legislation or rules.

Practitioners, including economic developers, regularly encounter situations where a pending retirement may close a long-serving and important business, either with no obvious person to continue the operation or with the possibility that it will be converted into a venture that no longer meets local needs. Neither of these events is usually favored by a prospective business owner who is retiring, so the business may stay open longer than initially planned, causing the business to be even less marketable.

Even more significantly, if a private sale is unlikely or impossible, sometimes the only remaining option is for residents to organize and pool funds to purchase the business or property and then find an experienced manager to operate it (Walzer, 2021). Discussions in later chapters explore examples of this approach along with references to guide groups in their future pursuits.

Overview of Discussions

Documented socio-demographic trends show a large growth in numbers of business owners approaching retirement age because of the aging of the baby boomer population. Some had managed their enterprises for many years and expected the sale of the business to be their retirement income, so they continued to invest in the business venture rather than other venues. However, upon retirement, they see that finding a suitable buyer is difficult or impossible for several reasons.

Local population demographics have changed along with the markets served by these businesses since most started long ago and certainly before the internet. New residents, including remote workers, prefer different types of goods and services and now shop more from internet stores. Thus, markets served for many years have changed and, for the business to continue successfully, serious investments in inventory and/or the buildings may be needed. Existing owners nearing retirement may be reluctant to make these investments, which makes the business less profitable and less attractive to potential buyers.

The retail landscape also changed, with more competition from discount stores, dollar stores, and internet providers offering free shipping with overnight delivery. Likewise, convenience stores sell motor fuels along with snacks, beverages, and a few essential household items, eroding local markets for long-term grocery stores. All these factors can shrink the market for a store that was started many years ago, built a strong clientele and personal relationships, but now is difficult to sell.

The result is that previous business models or approaches may be less suitable, forcing community leaders in small towns to consider alternative, more diversified business establishments, such as the general store approach common in Vermont. These businesses sell locally produced and procured healthy fresh foods, refreshments, meats, cheese, staples, crafts, to-go items, and other services that can effectively compete with other stores. The increased links with local providers and investor-owners provide a more stable and reliable customer base, especially with alternative business ownership approaches such as cooperatives or locally owned, community-supported enterprises discussed more in later chapters.

Fortunately, younger generations who are expressing more interest in living in more rural areas also seem interested in engaging in entrepreneurship opportunities. Thus, these newcomers may participate in a business transition effort as an owner, manager, or investor in rural communities with high quality of life, reasonable housing, access to natural recreation opportunities, and, most importantly, affordable, high-quality internet access.

However, many in this group are also debt-laden from higher education expenses and/or other activities, which can limit their financial involvement. Younger generations may be more attracted to business ventures using the internet rather than operating a retail business such as a grocery store or restaurant that might be for sale, even when profitable and important to the local quality of life. In these cases, an alternative business ownership model may be more appropriate, especially one without high initial investment or startup costs.

Thus, local development leaders are challenged to make their communities attractive to people interested in a more relaxed lifestyle not only with affordable, high-quality internet access, but also with financing opportunities and/or ownership models that can transition businesses providing essential local services. Furthermore, they must be able to market these features to multiple groups in various age ranges who vary in motives, priorities, and communication approaches.

Fortunately, other options for business ownership have sprung up in rural areas, as Palmieri and Cooper discuss in Chapter 4. Employee ownership approaches are gaining popularity as ways to engage more residents in directly managing a business. While worker-owned cooperatives have existed for many years, as Hand et al. discuss in Chapter 6, more recent forms of employee ownership include employee stock ownership plans (ESOPs) and employee-owned trusts (EOTs) which started in the U.K. but are now gaining popularity in the U.S. Many, if not most, local volunteers in rural areas may be unfamiliar with these options, let alone be able to guide business owners seeking to sell their businesses. Successful transitions require that owners are prepared to sell, and that potential buyers understand options available with access to the financing needed.

Changing Demographics

Changing demographics, especially the aging baby boomer generation, must be well understood in discussions of business transitions. In Chapter 2, Conroy et al. describe the wide diversity of populations, especially in rural areas, and examine the complexities of working with potential business sellers who may not be prepared to sell and/or transition the business when they decide to retire. A high personal stake or involvement in the business over many years may delay implementation of a planned succession program. Current owners may want to stay engaged in the business in some way to avoid drastic changes in focus or direction. Likewise, they may avoid alerting customers about retirement plans for fear of losing current trade and reducing profitability. While the current owner(s) might like to mentor a new person or sell the business over time, they may need the money gained from the sale for their retirement now.

Equally important is that younger population cohorts differ in demographics and are more diverse, with a larger proportion of females than in the past. People of color and women traditionally have had less access to capital to buy homes or businesses. Women have more often been self-employed or run a business from their homes, partly in response to a need to take care of young children. One of the challenges cited by rural residents was a lack of childcare (McCray, 2023). These factors can limit the number of buyers for long-standing stores even with an established market and are important to the livability of a place.

In general, rural areas are likely to face increasing difficulties in finding a suitable workforce, as was noted in the Survey of Rural Challenges (McCray, 2023). Jobs in rural areas often pay less, which makes them less attractive to job seekers, even though living costs in rural areas are less. The pending retirements of workers in rural areas means they must be replaced by younger groups, most of whom will come from surrounding, more urban, areas. Lack of suitable housing in many rural communities makes this more difficult.

While an outright sale is preferred, in some cases, either the rate of return is not sufficient or the long-term viability of the business in a shrinking market is not attractive to outside investors. Likewise, the current owner loses control over management and the long-term service to the community could be threatened, even though a shift in focus might help the store serve the community in new and different ways.

Changing the inventory and services may make a business more attractive to incoming and younger residents, meeting preferences not met previously. These changes also could foster a clientele that allows the business to co-exist with internet shopping and growing numbers of residents who work and shop in larger centers. However, long-standing owners may not fully understand or be willing to make these changes.

In Chapter 11, Barman and Welty report that in a survey of 51,000 privately held businesses in Wisconsin, nearly half are owned by baby boomers and 60% expect to sell in the next decade. However, 50% of respondents have no business plan; 80% have no written business succession or transition plan; and 94% have no personal post-business plan. In these circumstances, local development groups must help potential sellers decide on a succession plan for when they retire. This process can be a learning experience for both the sellers and volunteer local development groups.

In other cases, small independent businesses may be bought by large corporations with a regional or national network of establishments that provide similar services such as pharmacies or dollar stores. Purchasing a local business may be to eliminate the competition, which means possibly closing the store or enterprise and possibly offering the service over the internet. Even though current owners might receive money they can use for retirement, their long-term dedication to serving the community is threatened, so they resist selling.

In these cases, potential sellers might consider a stewardship approach that allows owners who preferred to sell to family members or a resident to continue past operations, in order to dispose of the business knowing it will continue its initial purposes. This approach provides income for retirement and allows continued involvement in management to some degree.

Alternatively, an owner might sell to employees willing to take on ownership or management responsibilities with suitable financing. This approach can be more difficult in small establishments with few employees, many of whom are part time and/or are of an age where they want to continue to work.

Succession Planning

Given the importance of a well-thought-out plan, one might ask why so few business owners have such a plan in place. Many factors described in later chapters come into play, depending on the size of business undergoing transition. Curry describes in Chapter 3 some of the important considerations in succession plans, along with examples of the pitfalls and outcomes encountered. A reoccurring issue is that successors have not been well-groomed for managing the business.

An owner may intend for heirs to continue the establishment but when they are unavailable or disinterested, no other person is ready to assume the management tasks. The current owner may not even have fully discussed plans for transition with intended future owners. A Massachusetts Mutual Life Insurance Company (2022) study documented that only 8 percent of surveyed business owners had a written succession plan in place and only one in four successors who were mentioned in the plans knew they were expected to take over the business. The result is that the intended successor is not positioned to continue the operations and/or make the necessary changes to keep or make the business profitable.

Likewise, especially in small operations, the goals for the business may have been personal to the owner(s) e.g., providing long-term service to the community and being an integral part of a downtown. The business may be sold to an owner(s) with a very different vision and operating goals. Fear of this change in approach, and of loss of input by the retiring owner, may cause potential retirement delays with the hope that a new owner with suitable business goals and interests can be found. It is difficult and discouraging to try to build future attitudes and/or approaches into a succession planning process, so the effort is postponed or delayed.

Succession plans also may overlook the attitudes of other key stockholders. A business, especially in a small town or place, can be an integral part of the overall economy, and other groups in the community, including customers, are important to its success. Thus, these groups must be considered in succession planning. Buyer preferences change, as do shopping patterns, so discussions with stakeholders are important in planning successions and may lead to serious modifications that do not always match with the intentions of the previous owner.

Likewise, technology has changed the ways businesses are conducted, and a long-term owner may not have recognized or incorporated these changes into business operations in ways that the next owner will be forced to do. Again, this could mean that after transition, the business will differ considerably from the previous enterprise. Incorporating these types of changes into a succession plan is difficult.

The upshot of these factors is that succession planning, while important to the future of the business, may be postponed or even avoided. During the pandemic, some business owners faced economic trends that encouraged, or forced, them to shutter their businesses and retire without an active succession strategy. For those that continued, however, the positive news is that a variety of approaches such as employee ownership or trusts are available and increasing in use.

Employee Ownership as an Alternative

Depending on size of business and other characteristics, owners contemplating retirement have several viable options for transitioning a business to new owners. Previous discussions described many issues to consider, including preferences by current owners regarding the future direction of the enterprise and possibly retention of a legacy in the community. Depending on circumstances, these interests can sometimes be met under various types of employee ownership.

Each approach offers advantages and limitations. Some involve complex legal and tax considerations that can discourage (or encourage) their use. In some instances, trusts can be used to protect the interests of the business or previous owners and employees. Each approach is best suited to specific conditions, so no attempt is made to evaluate or recommend one over another. Instead, the intent is to provide readers with an overview of how each functions and the circumstances that affect its effectiveness. Three major forms of employee ownership are highlighted next. The distinctions between approaches can blur in implementation but core components are briefly described. Later chapters contain more detailed discussions along with examples of uses in Canada, the U.K., and the U.S.

These forms of business transition all have advantages for both sellers and buyers. First, the employee owners are familiar with the business operations and have a vested interest (their jobs) in keeping the enterprise successful. They agree with the basic principles and understand the potential of the business. As owners, the employees have an additional incentive to perform well, make the business profitable, and encourage others to patronize the business. Employee owners will receive a share of the profits and/or other monetary incentives according to the specific form used.

Research regarding working conditions in all forms of employee ownership confirms the benefits for employees. For example, a study in several countries in 2017 showed that working conditions, salaries, and other benefits are higher with worker cooperatives than with non-employee-owned companies (Schlachter & Prushinskaya, 2021).

Employee ownership is also attractive to a seller because of the flexibility in how the ownership is transferred. With some forms, a previous owner can continue to participate in the decision-making processes and, to a certain extent, can guide the business into pursuing some of the previous directions or purposes. Thus, the sale can with some models occur over time with the elected board of directors assuming a larger share of the management responsibilities along the way. Palmieri and Cooper (Chapter 4) provide a more detailed overview of the various employee ownership models.

Worker-Owned Cooperative

While not well understood by many local development groups, one approach is to use a worker cooperative model that involves employees buying or receiving a share in the business along with democratic voting rights. The business is 100% worker-owned, managed by a board of directors elected by workers. An annual meeting is held to decide important issues facing the business.

In a cooperative ownership approach, employees participate in management decisions depending on how the cooperative is structured. This can make it more suitable for micro and small businesses. In Chapter 9, Mullinex describes the basic structure of worker cooperatives and dispels several myths regarding why worker cooperatives can't succeed in rural areas. She cites Morning Bell Coffee Roaster as an example and illustrates its path to success as an early worker cooperative in Iowa that has become a major business venture.

Employee Stock Ownership Plan (ESOP)

Creating an employee stock ownership plan (ESOP) is the more common approach used in the U.S. when an owner wants an employee ownership succession solution. There are tax advantages that support the financing of this form of employee buy-out, which can deliver significant financial rewards to employees on retirement. According to the National Center for Employee Ownership (NCEO, 2024), ESOPs have been shown to work in both rural and urban areas. However, as with other employee share ownership arrangements, ESOPs involve many technical requirements and require expertise in starting and operating them. This specialized expertise may not be readily available in some rural areas, which could discourage its consideration.

An ESOP is a qualified retirement plan trust that holds the company's stock for participating employees, offering significant tax breaks. The employer makes all the contributions, but the ESOP can also borrow funds to purchase all or a portion of the company. This aspect is especially important because it enables the owner to sell the company to ESOP member employees at the desired extent and pace. It does not involve employees investing their own money. An ESOP can be used to own any percentage of shares, from minority to majority, or 100% employee ownership. The seller can redeem some desired equity needed for retirement while still maintaining some ownership and control over the direction of operations. It also permits other options for sharing resources with other family members or groups.

ESOPs differ from worker cooperatives in that employees do not obtain full voting rights on operating issues. Instead, ESOPs are a trust with an appointed trustee to manage the retirement plan, which includes voting on the employee-owners' interests. The extent of voting rights possessed by employees can vary with the way the trust is organized.

Perhaps the most challenging aspect of using ESOPs, especially in small towns or places, is that they may be better suited for businesses that are larger than a small store or company. Also, they involve complex legal issues requiring professional expertise, perhaps not readily available in sparsely populated areas. This expertise is specialized and does not readily transfer between employee ownership models.

Nevertheless, ESOPs have worked in rural areas and have helped employees capture wealth; they provide a suitable avenue for potential sellers to exit the business on a desired schedule while preserving the purpose and intent of the company. Rosen discusses ESOPs in more detail in Chapter 5, with examples of how they have been used successfully.

Employee-Ownership Trust (EOT)

The most recent employee-ownership approach in the U.S. is the employee-ownership trust (EOT). It is attracting attention partly due to its flexibility in designing what employee ownership looks like for a company, including financial sharing with employees and governance structure. Also, it is relatively simple to both implement and maintain. An EOT does not have extensive federal regulations like an ESOP, for example.

This approach has a long history in the U.K. where it is a mainstream business succession solution for small and medium-sized enterprises and some larger businesses. The U.K. EOT is supported by tax measures that apply if the EOT has a majority or 100% shareholding. It is designed to provide long-term employee ownership of a company. Nuttall describes the U.K. structure in more detail in Chapter 7 and explains why it is popular. The U.K. model is being successfully replicated in the U.S.

The EOT is attractive to sellers because it can help preserve the mission of a company, which can be important to an owner for reasons mentioned previously. The seller can also have serious input into future directions of the business as well as wide latitude regarding the path used to exit the company. An EOT primarily rewards employees through cash profit sharing but there are other options for rewarding employees.

Essentially, in the U.S., a perpetual purpose trust is created that protects the employee ownership of the business. The owner can also incorporate commitments to social purposes or values in the trust. The trust purchases the stock from the owner using cash flow from operations and/or other sources.

All that said, EOTs are not yet as common in the U.S. as they are in the U.K. This may partly be due to a lack of national (federal) EOT legislation to raise knowledge of the concept (in contrast to the U.K.), the absence of which makes EOTs subject to different state regulations. Also, they do not have the tax reliefs that aid the financing of ESOPs, and technical expertise in setting up an EOT may be difficult to access, especially in remote rural areas where local development groups have had no experience with them. Nevertheless, EOTs offer significant advantages and can be an attractive way to structure a business succession and transition plan.

Roles of Community Development Principles and Practices

Successful business transitions are based on established and widely recognized community development principles and practices. Several chapters are devoted to ways in which these principles can be applied in productive ways. Community leaders and developers can support and facilitate the transition process by nurturing social capital and providing a positive local investment climate. This environment includes providing a high quality of life, cost-effective public services, and available affordable housing, and then marketing these qualities to prospective residents.

Importance of Social Capital

Successful business transitions rely heavily on strong local acceptance in the community with customers and community groups or local agencies helping with the process. Nevertheless, a national Main Street America survey reported that while 87% of local Main Street organizations offer support for small businesses and entrepreneurs, only 14% provide business succession assistance (Powe & Morita, 2024). This is when the Survey of Rural Challenges revealed that 33% of responding businesses indicated that lack of support from government and local organizations was a challenge (McCray, 2023). Thus, there will likely be improvements when local organizations can rally around this issue. The relatively small number of retirements or transitions that happen annually in small towns is likely a contributing factor.

Barman and Welty (Chapter 11) discuss how community capitals, especially the human, financial, built, and social capitals as described by Flora et al. (2010), can be used to understand and organize a succession or transition effort in small towns or places, and describe ways to employ the Main Street Approach principles and practices. Specifically, they show that successful capital transfer includes several key aspects: predecessor preparation and successor preparation plus predecessor success and successor success.

Each component can be addressed and fostered by local agencies, such as Main Street organizations, in collaborative initiatives. These local groups can help build a scenario where business owners and customers or residents collaborate to see a transfer of ownership or management as beneficial to the community and thus worth their support of the process. The initiative can help market a new enterprise as well as assist in raising funds needed for the transition. A larger number of transitions happening in the future will likely cause more involvement by local organizations.

Local Investment Alternatives

In situations when an owner is frustrated in selling a business and other options such as employee ownership or trust are not well suited, residents in the community may have to take the lead in purchasing the property or business, updating it as needed, and then either contracting with a manager or hiring an employee to manage the enterprise. This approach may not be the first choice but has worked out well as discussed in Walzer and Doyle (Chapter 8).

A community-owned enterprise is especially useful when the current owner has disinvested in the building and/or inventory to conserve cash for a pending retirement. The business is operating on a thin margin and the venture represents a large part of the owner's retirement assets. An alternative is to invest the money in financial markets or other places to generate a higher future income. The business may continue to operate but does not reach its sales potential or may even decline in sales and profitability.

When the business is placed on the market, prospective buyers face not only the costs of revitalizing the business but also serious costs to upgrade deteriorated and outdated structures. These costs are in addition to restocking and updating an inventory more suitable for buyers from a previous era. The required investments can deter buyers expecting a higher level of profit. Thus, while a market may exist, the condition of the structure and facilities makes a deal not feasible.

If a local group of residents and/or other interested parties purchase the structure and inventory, they may have access to funding sources not available to a private buyer, or available only with a significant investment of time and effort. Using a local nonprofit to pool funds from private investors contributing even relatively small amounts of money with tax benefits can raise sufficient funds to help restart the business. In many, if not most, cases, the local funds are leveraged by loans or grants. The objective of the public group is to retain access to the goods and services in the community by retaining a profitable business. The Elmore Community Store and the East Calais General Store in Vermont are examples described by Walzer and Doyle in Chapter 8.

Federal or state grants are sometimes available to help with remodeling or other infrastructure improvements. A privately owned business may not qualify for these funds, whereas a local public organization can. If the funds are used to renovate the property and buildings, then a local group can offer the building to a prospective tenant or contractor as a potentially profitable arrangement. This situation explains several of the projects in Vermont.

Common elements are found in the successful community-supported enterprises described. Local leaders with credibility among residents or potential investors typically spearhead the effort and entice others to invest time and/or money in the project. In some cases, but not always, the leaders are elected officials. Local leaders can come from many groups or institutions with broad-based support in the community.

Equally important is that the project is widely recognized as a high priority for the future of the town or place and that this fact is communicated well to the public. Loss of the only local grocery store is a prime example that has often been a motivating factor. The transition initiative, however, may include expanding goods and services beyond those provided by the previous establishment, especially in cases where a previous owner had downsized inventory or services in anticipation of retirement. It is important during the transition process that a serious market analysis of the area to be served is undertaken. New services can broaden the clientele, and goods or services that are no longer needed can be identified in the market analysis.

Retaining a venture using a public organization also can reduce operating costs, especially when residents and local investors are willing to donate time to manage or operate the business (for example, stocking shelves or operating a cash register). Likewise, these businesses often purchase locally on demand, which can lower costs as well as enhance the clientele. The more the business can engage residents, the higher its probability is to succeed.

A commonly cited motivation for residents' involvement in a project is to preserve a local gathering place or other activity that builds social capital. This social engagement is especially important in a small place or neighborhood. While not always recognized for its importance, residents are often willing to rally behind preserving such a location. The Main Street Approach offers opportunities to help local leaders not only build social capital but also plan future directions and make the downtown a more effective entrepreneurial place for smoother successions and transitions.

A unique approach in which an external agency helps transition businesses is Goodworks Ventures (GWV) and Goodworks Evergreen (GWE) in Montana. These agencies identify businesses in rural Montana that can be purchased and then revitalized or rebuilt into larger, more profitable enterprises. McGee et al. (Chapter 10) describe how this approach helps communities retain or expand businesses and services that in some cases might not have continued without external assistance. GWE has purchased several lumber and hardware businesses and, in most instances, was able to make them more profitable. More details about the origins of this initiative and previous accomplishments are provided in McGee et al. (2023).

While not every business purchased by GWE met expectations, the concept and model have been shown to work and provide valuable insights for others interested in pursuing a similar direction. Essentially, a business is purchased and the GWE team has a definite process to find new markets, production processes, or other management and financial techniques to improve its profitability. Of utmost importance is due diligence on the part of the purchasing agency to identify the potential for the business as well as internal difficulties that could affect its future performance.

Likewise, the organization purchasing the business must have in-house capacity to manage the company and set a solid course for its future. While this need applies to virtually any business venture, it is especially important in an agency buying businesses that otherwise might close. The same is true in recognizing the need for access to capital in building the businesses and creating an exit ramp if necessary.

While the GWE model is a special case, it has many useful applications to other places, especially where a business important to the future of a community is profitable, but not attractive to a private or employee-owner venture for some reason or reasons. Along with community-supported enterprises, the GWE model is another example of how rural leaders can find new approaches in transitioning needed businesses during a new era of changing demographics.

Concluding Observations

There is general agreement that, given the demographics, the number of retirements and therefore business successions and transitions will increase during the next decade. The impact of these changes is likely to affect rural areas more than metro areas since the loss of a core main street business means a serious decrease in quality of life in a small town or place. While internet shopping provides access to some goods and services, it does not replace grocery stores, for example, and does not provide convenient meeting places to socialize and build camaraderie.

Unfortunately, while providing an essential service, the business may not attract external investment capital, and no residents may step forward to provide the needed time or money. Thus, local development agencies and community leaders must find ways to retain businesses and their retiring owners in the community.

The good news is that the options described in these chapters have been shown to work in both metro neighborhoods and rural areas. Some options are complex in organizational structure while others are relatively simple.

In most cases, however, pursuing one of these approaches requires guidance from someone with technical expertise regarding the specific model under consideration.

Looking ahead, it will be important for local business and community leaders to design strategies for how their places will accommodate the continuing demographic trends. Expansions in telecommunications, acceptance of remote work, telehealth, and other opportunities have reduced the disadvantages of distance and opened new opportunities for small and more remote towns or cities as viable places to live. A key to making this happen, though, is that the location is a high-quality place to live with access to essential goods and services. Therefore, retaining key businesses when long-standing owners decide to retire will be crucial to the success of many such communities. The discussions in this book should help with that effort.

Acknowledgment

The authors thank Graeme Nuttall for comments on a previous draft.

References

Darger, M. (2022). *Introduction to business retention and expansion*. University of Minnesota Extension. https://extension.umn.edu/retaining-community-businesses/introduction-business-retention-and-expansion-bre

Deller, S. C., & Conroy, T. (2023). Regional economic trends across the rural-urban divide. In N. Walzer & C. D. Merrett (Eds.), *Rural areas in transition: Meeting challenges & making opportunities* (pp. 19–44). Routledge. 10.4324/9781003280620

Flora, C. B., Emery, M., Fey, S., & Bregendahl, C. (2010 May 7). *Community capitals: A tool for evaluating strategic interventions and projects*. North Central Region Center for Rural Development. http://winnemuccafutures.com/blog1/wp-content/uploads/2010/05/7-capitalshandout.pdf

Frey, W. H. (2022, April 14). *New census data show a huge spike of movement out of big metro areas during the pandemic*. Brookings Institution. https://www.brookings.edu/articles/new-census-data-shows-a-huge-spike-in-movement-out-of-big-metro-areas-during-the-pandemic/

Johnson, K. (2022, Winter). *Rural America lost population over the past decade for the first time in history* (National issue brief 160). Carsey School of Public Policy, University of New Hampshire. https://scholars.unh.edu/cgi/viewcontent.cgi?article=1446&context=carsey

Lund, S., Madgavkar, A., Manyika, J., & Smit, S. (2020, November). *What's next for remote working? An analysis of 2,000 tasks, 800 jobs and nine countries*. McKinsey Global Institute. https://www.mckinsey.com/featured-insights/future-of-work/whats-next-for-remote-work-an-analysis-of-2000-tasks-800-jobs-and-nine-countries

Massachusetts Mutual Life Insurance Company. (2022). *2022 business owner perspectives study*. https://www.massmutual.com/global/media/shared/doc/sb1020_2022.pdf

McCray, B. (2023). *Survey of rural challenges*. SaveYour.Town & SmallBizSurvival.com. https://saveyour.town/wp-content/uploads/2023/06/Survey-of-Rural-Challenges-Report-2023.1.pdf

McGee, D., Hochstetler, K. & Braun, M. (2023). Acquiring, building, and investing in private businesses: A new approach. In N. Walzer & C. D. Merrett (Eds.), *Rural areas in transition: Meeting challenges & making opportunities* (pp. 236–254). Routledge. 10.4324/9781003280620

National Center for Employee Ownership. (2024). *Employee ownership by the numbers.* https://www.nceo.org/articles/employee-ownership-by-the-numbers

Powe, M., & Morita, E. (2024, April 2). *Main spotlight: Insights from the 2024 trends survey*. Main Street America. https://mainstreet.org/the-latest/news/main-spotlight-insights-from-the-2024-trends-survey

Saad, L. (2021, January 5). *Country living enjoys renewed appeal in U.S.* Gallup. https://news.gallup.com/poll/328268/country-living-enjoys-renewed-appeal.aspx

Schlachter, L. H., & Prushinskaya, O. (2021). *How economic democracy impacts workers, firms, and communities*. Democracy at Work Institute. https://democracy.institute.coop/how-economic-democracy.impacts-workers-firms-and-communities#:~:text=Our%20key%20findings%20include%3A,civic%20fabric%20of%20their%20communities

SCORE. (2024, August 24). *The small business owner's guide to succession planning.* https://www.score.org/resource/eguide/small-business-owner%E2%80%99s-guide-succession-planning

Symonds, C. (2024, February 20). *Business succession planning: A step-by-step guide.* Factorial. https://factorialhr.com/blog/business-succession-planning

Thau, B. (2021, June 1). *Hyper-local commerce and smaller brands benefit from post-pandemic consumer trends*. United States Chamber of Commerce. https://www.uschamber.com/co/good-company/launch-pad/post-pandemic-consumers-demand-smaller-brands

Walzer, N. (Ed.). (2021). *Community owned businesses: International entrepreneurship, finance, and economic development*. Routledge.

2

ON THE BRINK OF BUSINESS TRANSITION IN THE U.S.

Trends, Challenges, and Opportunities

Tessa Conroy, Caroline Corona, Charles Zumbrunnen, and Steven Deller

Changing Generations

The aging and corresponding retirement of the baby boomer generation has created significant impacts on the economy. Baby boomers are leaving behind a workforce shortage that is generating headlines and leading to bottlenecks in economic growth processes. One dimension of this fundamental generational shift that has received insufficient attention is their role as business owners. The average age of business owners in the U.S. is increasing, and many retirement-aged business owners are not adequately planning for the eventual transition of their business. This situation could lead to a wave of business closures, corporate acquisitions, and suboptimal transfers. "Main street" consumer-facing businesses, which serve as the economic and cultural lifeblood of communities across the country, may be especially vulnerable to disappearing as we know them.

The baby boomer generation has made up a large portion of the population throughout their lives. In the most recent 2010–2020 decade—when the first half of baby boomers turned 65—the senior population grew 38.6%, the highest decade-long rate of 65-and-older growth since the 1880s (Frey, 2023). The median age in the U.S. has steadily climbed over the past decade due to the aging of baby boomers, rising to 39 in 2022 (see Figure 2.1).[1]

Simultaneously, the prime age share of the population is declining (see Figure 2.2), which means that business owners of retirement age are not only grappling with succession but also facing the more immediate challenge of a labor shortage. In response, small business owners are increasingly handling day-to-day functions such as stocking shelves, serving food, or running cash registers—activities that become more difficult with age and divert time from planning a seemingly distant succession plan.

DOI: 10.4324/9781003497462-2

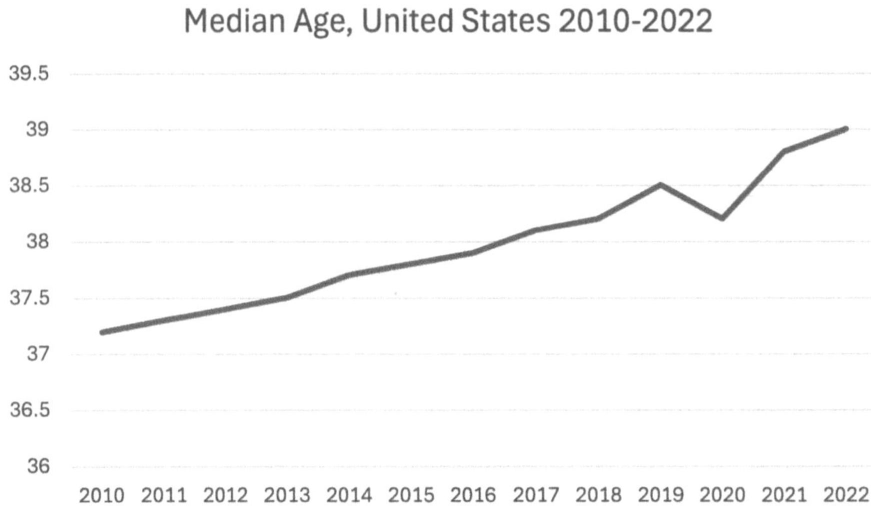

FIGURE 2.1 Median Age, United States 2010–2022.

Source: Authors' analysis of U.S. Census Bureau American Community Survey, 1-year estimates, 2010–2022. 1-year ACS estimates for 2020 not available; 5-year estimate shown instead for 2020 only.

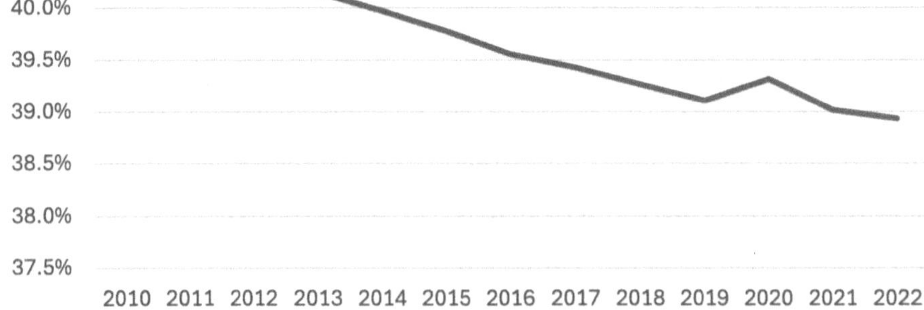

FIGURE 2.2 Prime Age Share of the Population (Ages 25–54).

Source: Authors' analysis of U.S. Census Bureau American Community Survey, 1-year estimates, 2010–2022. 1-year ACS estimates for 2020 not available; 5-year estimate shown instead for 2020 only.

While these trends exist across the country, the older share of the population is larger in some states than others. Maine has the largest share of state population (22.6%) over age 65, and nine states in total have senior populations that represent more than 20% of their total population.[2] While some of these patterns are explained by retirement migration (e.g., Arizona and Maine), other states are experiencing significant aging in place (e.g., Iowa).

The size of the aging population also varies across the rural–urban continuum. Rural counties are older than suburban and urban counties and have lost population since 2000, making them especially vulnerable to the workforce and business transition risks associated with an aging population (Parker et al., 2018).

Other important dynamics are also at play for the younger generations who may be positioned to purchase or takeover for aging business owners. One of the biggest differences between rising generations and baby boomers is that younger generations are more racially and ethnically diverse, especially in urban and suburban areas (Frey, 2023). This "racial generation gap" has important implications for the large-scale transition of businesses during the next decade. The aging population is significantly more white than younger age cohorts, and the gap is growing. Overall, the white population share decreases with younger cohorts. Fewer than half (approximately 47%) of the 0–4 and 5–17 age cohorts are white compared with more than 70% of the over-65 population (Frey, 2023). According to the 2020 census, the white share of the senior population was 27.5 percentage points higher than the white share of the youth population (Frey, 2023). While the share of each non-white racial identity generally increases across younger cohorts, the Latino or Hispanic population had the largest gains and the second largest share of the young population (Frey, 2023).

In rural counties, the white population share is 79% compared with 44% in urban and 68% in suburban counties. While rural areas are still diversifying in alignment with nationwide shifts, it is happening at a slower rate in rural counties than in urban and suburban counties (Parker et al., 2018). Overall, rural counties are aging faster and diversifying more slowly, and most are grappling with continuous population declines at the same time, which can make local businesses more susceptible to the threats of corporate ownership or closure. These forces place rural communities in an especially precarious position for meeting the workforce and business transition needs of the next few decades.

The increased diversity of younger age cohorts nationwide means that potential buyers and future entrepreneurs will likely be of a different racial identity than the current cohort of business owners. Indeed, 49% of 18–29 year-old business buyers identify as a person of color, compared with 9% of buyers age 50 or older (BizBuySell, 2016). This is important to consider when designing resources for future buyers and entrepreneurs because people of color have historically faced barriers to owning and growing a business (McDermott et al., 2023).

Younger generations also differ from their predecessors financially and often hold different views about the roles and responsibilities of owning a business, which will further impact their behavior as buyers and business owners. They are more likely to experience poverty, housing, and food insecurity, and have taken on significantly more debt than older generations did at their age.

Student loans have an outsize impact on today's youth. In the late 1980s and 1990s, fewer than half of college students borrowed money to pay for school, and most high school graduates did not enroll in college at all. Today, nearly two-thirds of high school graduates enroll in college, and a majority take out student loans to do so (CFR.org Editors, 2024). As of early 2024, total outstanding student loan debt in the U.S. was $1.6 trillion (Center for Microeconomic Data, n.d.). This has significantly impacted younger cohorts' ability to buy a home or start a business, which creates barriers to building wealth. One study found that 62% of baby boomers owned homes at age 35, while only 49% of millennials did. Millennials were also more likely to have negative net worth than boomers (University of Cambridge, 2023). This combination of higher debt and lower wealth will affect upcoming generations' ability to purchase or invest in a business.

In many cases, young entrepreneurs also exhibit different views about the role of business: 67% of young entrepreneurs (ages 18–34) emphasized a focus on environmental sustainability, and 58% noted a high likelihood they would take actions that maximize social impact (Global Entrepreneurship Monitor, 2022). On the consumer side, surveys of Gen Z show that they are more likely to consider a company's ethical behavior when making purchasing decisions and believe that companies have a responsibility to address environmental and social issues (McKinsey & Company, 2024). These attitudes are important to consider in succession planning because younger generations may approach buying and running a business differently than their predecessors.

Aging Business Owners

Entrepreneurship is a foundational piece of the American economy and is one of the key pathways to building wealth and driving economic growth. There are more than 16.5 million self-employed individuals in the U.S. (Williamson, 2023) and 32.5 million small businesses (defined as those with fewer than 500 employees). While 81% of those have no employees, small businesses represent 99.9% of all firms and created 12.7 million net new jobs from 1995 to 2020 (Office of Advocacy, 2021). A study by the U.S. Small Business Association found that people who are self-employed are more financially literate, which also could translate to greater retirement savings (Office of Advocacy, 2021).

While there are many benefits, entrepreneurship is also difficult—approximately 30% of new businesses exit within two years, and almost 50% exit in the first five years (J. P. Morgan Chase & Co., n.d.). Many business owners report long hours and low returns, especially in the early stages, because starting a business requires significant financial and social capital, business savvy, and time. When a local business closes, the community loses access to important services and amenities as well as jobs and income, and it can take a long time for another business to take its place.

In line with broader demographic trends, business owners are aging, putting many businesses in the U.S. at risk of closure or corporate acquisition. In the past 20 years the number of retirement-age self-employed people nearly doubled, such that almost 15% of all self-employed people, which includes farmers, were of retirement age in 2022 (see Figures 2.3 and 2.4). Without any large-scale transitions to younger owners, this share is expected to grow even larger as the baby boomer generation continues to age. The seeming lack of retirement is concerning as it may signal that business owners are delaying or failing to plan for an eventual transition, leaving them vulnerable to closure or suboptimal sales, which can have broader impacts on local communities and the U.S. economy.

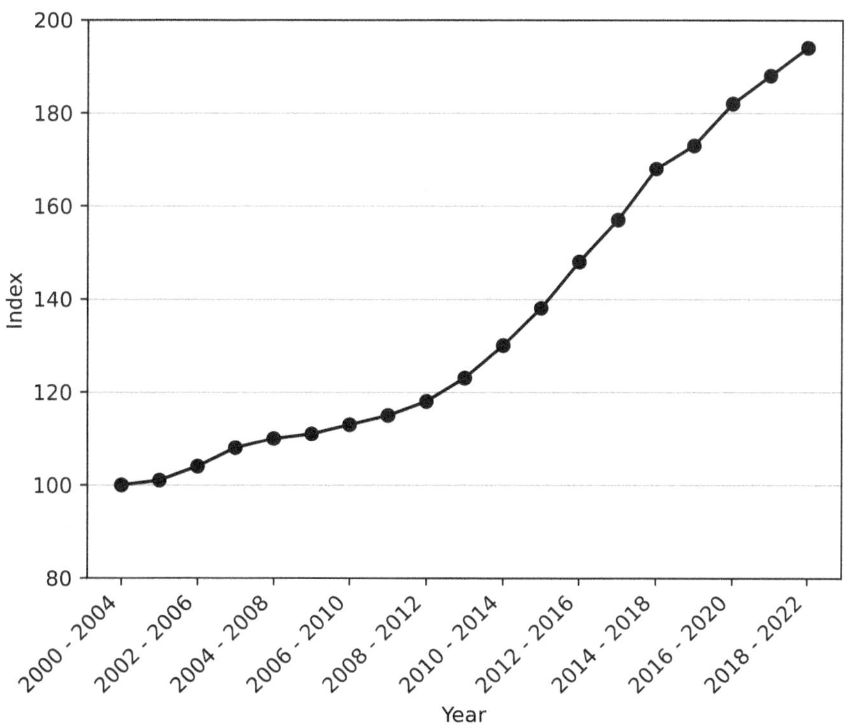

FIGURE 2.3 Growth of Self-Employed Age 67+ (Index = 2000–2004).

Source: Authors' analysis of Ruggles et al. (2024).

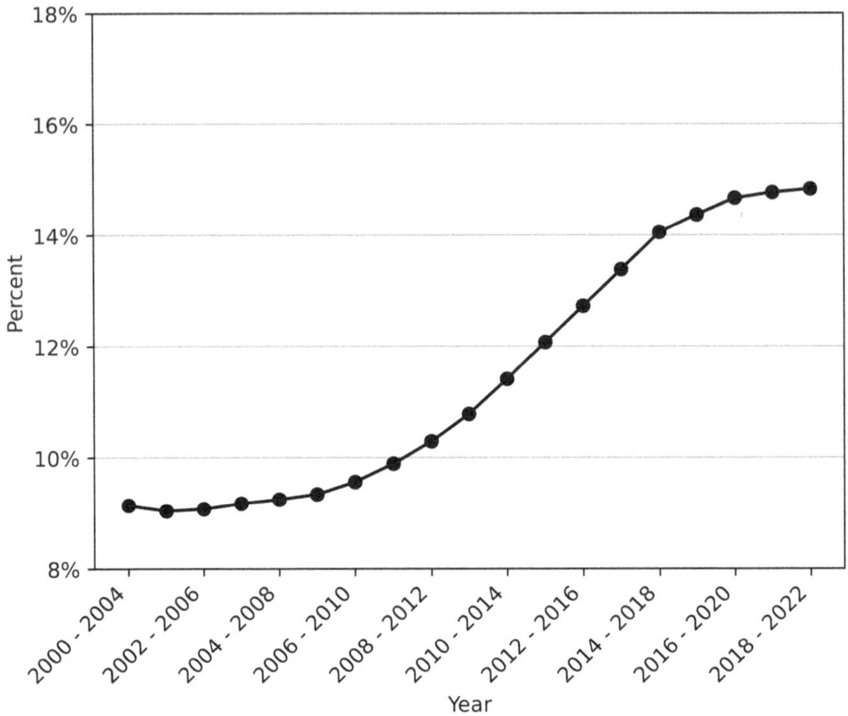

FIGURE 2.4 Share of Self-Employed Age 67+.

Source: Authors' analysis of Ruggles et al. (2024).

While this trend of aging business owners is true across the U.S., rural areas across the U.S. have a larger share of retirement-aged and self-employed business owners: 18%, compared to 14% in urban areas (see Figure 2.5). The share of older self-employed individuals is also growing faster in rural areas, increasing nearly seven percentage points since 2005. This places rural communities at an even larger disadvantage given many rural areas' declining population and low in-migration rates. With fewer young people to succeed aging business owners, rural areas will likely face more business closures, corporate acquisitions, and suboptimal sales—the effects of which are amplified in smaller communities. The loss of a key business, such as a grocery store or pharmacy, can have cascading effects on quality of life as residents must travel farther to obtain vital goods and services (Ayres et al., 1992). Reduced sales, job cuts, and decreased economic activity can also affect local government revenues, which impacts municipalities' ability to deliver key public services.

This aging of business owners is particularly evident among U.S. farmers. While there have been a handful of years (e.g., 1978 and 1982) when the average farmer age ticked downward, the overall trend mirrors the larger demographic trends. Analyzing Census of Agriculture data by Zulauf (2024) shows

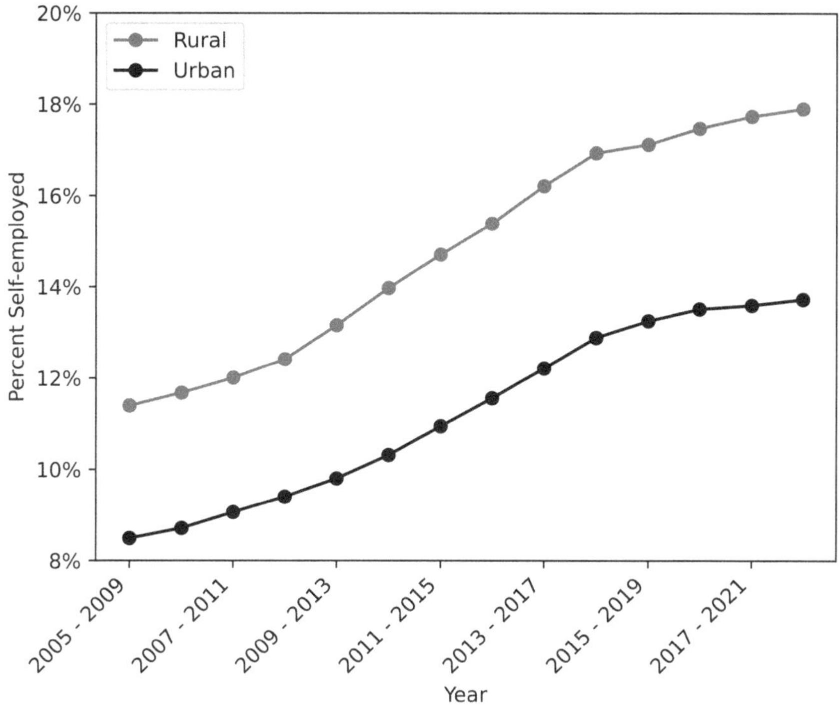

FIGURE 2.5 Share of Self-Employed Age 67+, Rural and Urban.

Source: Authors' analysis of Ruggles et al. (2024).

that since the end of WWII the average age of farmers has consistently increased from a low of 48.7 in 1945 to 58.1 in 2022. The prevalence of farming in rural areas may partly explain the older population of self-employed individuals compared to urban areas shown in Figure 2.6.

Furthermore, during the past six decades the average age of farmers has been consistently higher than the median age of the larger population. For example, in 1959/60 the average age of farmers was 50.5 but the median age of the U.S. population was only 29.6. In 2022, the average age of farmers increased to 58.1 but the median age of the larger population increased to 38.9. So, while the average age of farmers is increasing, the age gap compared with the U.S. population has decreased. Since 1960, the average age of U.S. farmers has increased 7.6 years while the median age of the U.S. population has increased 8.8 years.

The challenge within farming is that the historical generational transfer of the farm from parents to children has become less likely than in the past. Increasingly, younger generations are unlikely to take over operations of the farm from older generations. The continuing decline in the number of farms across the U.S. is partially driven by younger generations who prefer a profession

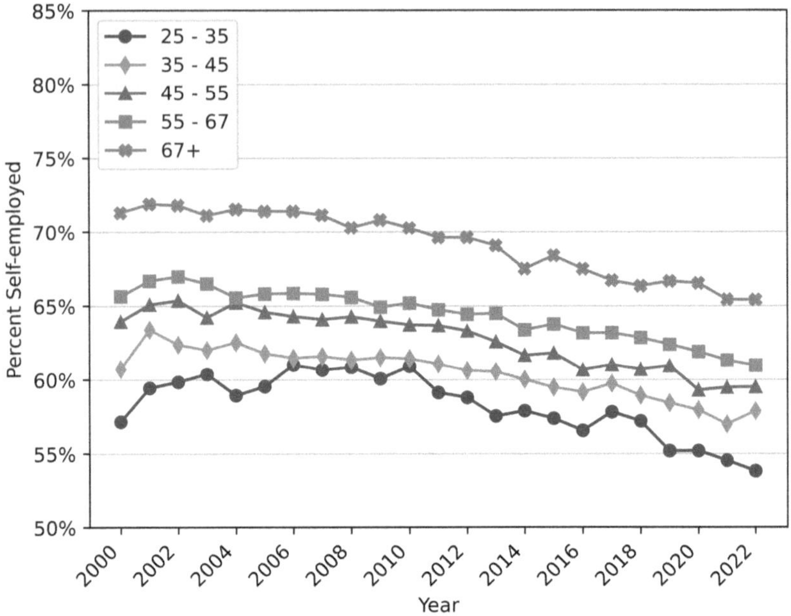

FIGURE 2.6 Male Share of Self-Employed by Age Group.

Source: Authors' analysis of Ruggles et al. (2024).

outside of farming, ruling out family succession. Young people outside farming families who would like to get started may find that the capital requirements necessary to purchase increasingly expensive land and equipment are insurmountable. As a result, many farms have ceased operation or been acquired by another larger farming entity and the farms that remain are operated by an increasingly older population of farmers.

A New and Different Generation of Business Owners

When examining potential strategies for supporting business transition planning, it is also important to consider how the cohorts of younger entrepreneurs differ from current business owners. First, the gender composition of business owners is changing. Self-employed people over the age of 67 are disproportionately male compared with younger cohorts (see Figure 2.6). Among the oldest cohort (age 67 and older), more than 65% are men, whereas among the youngest cohorts it is closer to 55%. Schmidt et al. (2021) similarly find an increase in gender diversity in farming as the number of woman-operated farms has grown over time.

Indeed, women start businesses more frequently now than in the past, which reflects changing norms and a shift in economic conditions. The Affordable

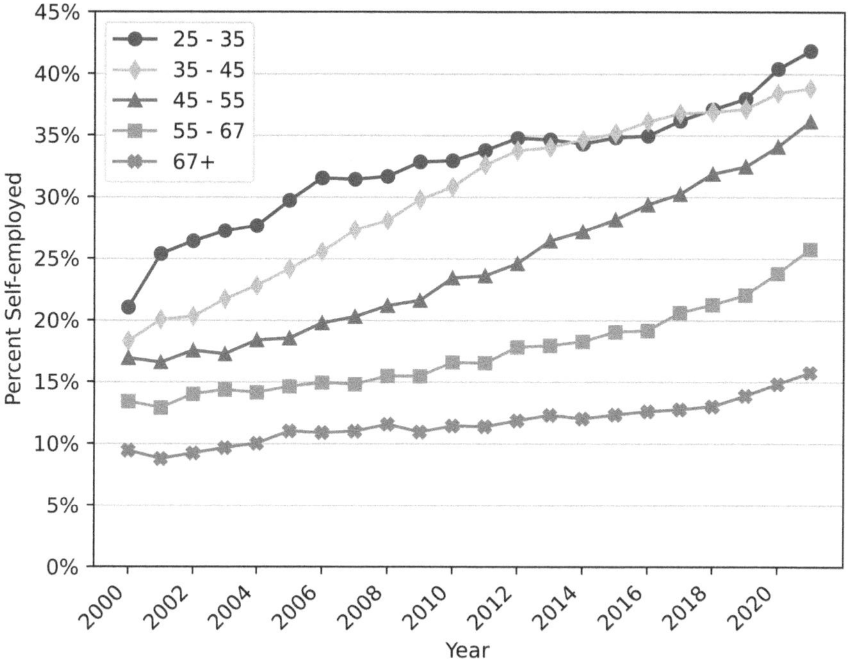

FIGURE 2.7 Minority Share of Self-Employed by Age Group.

Source: Authors' analysis of Ruggles et al. (2024).

Care Act, for example, made it easier for many women to buy health insurance on their own rather than through an employer (Williamson, 2023). This allows women with children to more easily take the leap toward starting a business, rather than trying to balance the responsibilities of entrepreneurship with another job and childcare. Likewise, self-employment offers greater flexibility, and women are more likely than men to pursue entrepreneurship for a better work–life balance, especially given that childcare pressures often fall disproportionately on mothers (Conroy, 2019; Luque & Jones, 2019). However, women also face many barriers to starting and growing a business. In 2023, only 2.1% of venture capital funding went to businesses founded solely by women (PitchBook, n.d.), and 90% of women-owned businesses have no employees—ten percentage points higher than for businesses owned by men (Williamson, 2023).

Younger cohorts of business owners are also more racially diverse, opening the door for stronger representation in entrepreneurship. In parallel with changing population demographics, minority entrepreneurship is on the rise. Twenty percent of the nation's businesses with paid employees are owned by people of color, reflecting an increase over the past decade (Lee, 2023). Figure 2.7 shows the share of self-employed that identify as a racial or ethnic minority, namely Black or African American, Asian, American Indian or Native Alaskan, and Hispanic, by age group.[3] The minority share is slightly over 15% among the oldest cohort and grows increasingly larger with each younger cohort. In the youngest age group, more than 40% identify as a racial or ethnic minority. An analysis of survey data by Zulauf et al. (2021) found that even within farming, the ethnic diversity among first-generation and younger farmers is much higher than established farmers.

Despite growth, non-white entrepreneurs face barriers to starting and scaling their business. Discriminatory lending practices and the continuing impacts of systemic racism have led many business owners of color to report a lack of access to networks, funding, and talent compared to their white peers. Black business owners are three times more likely to be rejected for bank funding (Goldman Sachs, 2020), and firms owned by people of color reported larger revenue losses and were more likely to close during the pandemic than white-owned firms (12 Reserve Banks of the Federal Reserve System, 2021).

As older, predominantly white male business owners consider retirement, they will most likely look to sell to someone very different from themselves in terms of race and gender, but also in terms of education, mission, and financial resources. These demographic and business dynamics at play for current and future business owners are important to consider when designing resources for succession planning. The looming wave of business transitions presents significant wealth-building opportunities for historically underrepresented groups, but reducing current barriers is necessary to sustain any gains and ensure business continuity.

Increasing Business Transitions

The increasing number of business owners at or near retirement age has led many to anticipate a wave of business transitions as these owners pass their companies to new ownership. With more than 11 million business owners over the age of 55, millions of businesses could transition to new ownership in the next 10 to 15 years (Headd, 2021). The large-scale transition of businesses, however, has been slow to materialize, as shown by the aging population of self-employed people (see Figure 2.3). If businesses were transitioning to younger owners, one would expect to see a decrease or at least a stable share of older business owners. Instead, self-employed individuals are holding onto their businesses and the population of business owners continues to grow older.

Indeed, transition to new ownership does not occur for most businesses. The federal government does not keep records of businesses sold, but estimates of business sales are available from surveys by industry and trade groups, as well as consulting agencies using relatively small samples. For example, Teamshares reports more than 200,000 small businesses listed for sale annually, of which only 30% are sold successfully (Baker, 2023).

A 2010 survey by *Business Week* reported that 40% of family-owned businesses transition to the second generation, 13% to the third generation, and 3% to the fourth generation (Conway Center for Family Business, n.d.). In an analysis of farmer survey data, Zulauf et al. (2021) report that 36% of farmers were first-generation, 25% were second-generation, and 39% classified as third-generation or higher-generation farms.

As an alternative to succession, business owners are exiting via other routes. DeTienne et al. (2015) offer a typology of entrepreneurial exit strategies that include stewardship, financial harvest, and voluntary cessation. Stewardship strategies, the focus of our discussion of transition, include those that are pro-social and pro-organizational and allow the founders to influence the future of the business. For example, with farmers the goal of keeping the land in production agriculture can be a major objective in seeking a buyer. Family-business succession, employee buy-out, and independent sale are all included as stewardship strategies. Financial harvest strategies, including both Initial Public Offerings (IPOs) and acquisitions, typically result in significant value accrued to the exiting business owner.

Finally, voluntary cessation strategies include liquidation and discontinuance, where the venture disbands when the main function of the business ends or changes, or the purpose for which the business was formed is fulfilled. One can imagine scenarios where a sale, liquidation, or discontinuance is the preferred option of the business owner as well as where these routes are taken when the business or business owner is in distress and has no better option.

Research based in Sweden suggests that family-owned businesses in distress are more likely to consider a merger first, followed by dissolution, and finally a sale to new ownership; whereas, non-family firm owners in distress are likely to seek a sale first, followed by dissolution, and, lastly, a merger (Chirico et al., 2020). Mergers are generally less financially satisfactory and more logistically complicated, yet they can allow an owner to retain some control over the business. Since family-owned firms often have stronger emotional ties to the business, they may try to preserve some control through a merger, or dissolve it entirely rather than passing it to an outside owner. Non-family-owned firms are more likely to base their decisions purely on financial returns, pushing them to favor an outside sale over dissolution or a merger. This is important to consider when developing tools and strategies to support exit planning, as family business owners may be more apprehensive to sell to a new owner and would likely prefer that a new owner shares a similar passion and connection to the business.

Stewardship strategies that transition the business to new owners via a sale to a family member, individual, or employees may be the best-suited option to benefit both the business owners and the communities affected. More than two-thirds of business owners indicate that this is their preferred path for transition (Exit Planning Institute, 2023). For many business owners, their financial security in retirement depends mainly on selling their business. Typically, a business represents 80% of the owner's net worth and is the largest asset in their personal financial portfolio (Exit Planning Institute, 2023). Rather than save money in other ways, many owners reinvest in their business, intending for its future sale to generate retirement income. These transitions may also have the added benefit of satisfying the business owner's preference for autonomy as well as their mission. Importantly, the sale of a business also sustains employment, income, and services for the community. In rural areas, this may mean that residents are able to work, shop, and meet their needs locally instead of commuting to work or to make purchases.

Financial harvest strategies are likely to benefit the owner, but this form of exit is generally less likely for a typical small business. IPOs are especially rare, but corporate acquisition is becoming increasingly relevant in a time of consolidation. When businesses change hands in this way, there may be negative community-level impacts as wages and profits that were once held locally may leave the community. Revenues may now accrue to distant owners, workers may be displaced, or the business itself may relocate as part of an acquisition.

Local businesses provide many benefits to the local economy, and if they are shuttered or transferred to corporate ownership those benefits can erode. In Portland, Maine, one study found that every $100 spent at a local business generates $58.03 in additional local economic impact, compared to $33.43 for a national retail chain (Patel & Martin, 2011). This represents a 76% greater return to the local economy for local businesses compared to national corporate chains. Local businesses are more likely to purchase goods and services from other locally-owned businesses, while firms with a national presence are usually procuring goods from other national brands or businesses based elsewhere, causing dollars to leave the community. Additionally, a larger number of locally owned small firms is linked to higher per capita income growth, while larger firms are linked to negative effects, especially when they are not owned by local residents (Fleming & Goetz, 2011).

As rural pharmacies, grocery stores, and veterinary clinics are acquired by larger corporations, this challenge becomes reality in many communities. For example, a recently hired new pharmacist looking to take over (purchase) an independent pharmacy is fundamentally different from a larger chain pharmacy considering the same independent pharmacy for access to patient lists. For the former, the independent pharmacy is likely to remain in operation, but for the latter, the pharmacy is likely to be closed and patients transferred to another location. Here, the owner of the pharmacy could gain significantly more financial reward by selling to the chain pharmacy at the detriment to the community. While this form of transition can be lucrative for a business owner, it can also be personally dissatisfying as it may mean a fundamental shift in the mission and priorities of the business. Whereas a local business owner may prioritize service to their clients, a larger corporation may prioritize profits and more conventional business performance metrics.

Cessation strategies, whether liquidation or discontinuance, can be less lucrative and satisfying for the owner compared to a sale (Wennberg et al., 2010). While there may be instances where this is the preferred strategy, it is more common that this strategy results from distress. As many as half of business exits in the U.S. are due to unplanned events that include divorce, death, disability, distress, and disagreement (Exit Planning Institute, 2023). These are all events that can lead to an inopportune sale of a business and these events become more likely as one gets older. A simple failure to plan may also mean that a business owner is more likely to sell in suboptimal circumstances or struggle to sell their business at all, costing financial gain for the owner or beneficiaries. Furthermore, cessation strategies are less desirable from a community development perspective as they mean a local business closes and with it, the community potentially loses a valuable good or service as well as the employment and income that the business provided.

Given the benefits of a stewardship strategy, the lack of such transitions is concerning but presents a significant opportunity for change if more businesses could successfully secure a sale. In a study of 37 rural communities in Indiana, Iowa, and North Dakota that had stronger retail markets than expected, Ayres et al. (1992) report one strategy that these successful communities pursued involved working with businesses owners who were transitioning into retirement. They found that for many small business owners who dominate most communities, especially smaller and more rural communities, the transition to retirement meant closing their business. In helping these retiring business owners find potential buyers, local leaders helped preserve viable businesses within the community. With only 20–30% of small businesses successfully selling, there is likely a large pool of businesses that either liquidate or discontinue (Exit Planning Institute, 2023). Among those business owners that liquidate or close entirely, it is plausible that many would prefer a sale to an individual, a family member, or employees, but they need support and preparation.

What Drives Business Transition?

To support business transitions, it is important to understand factors that drive the decision to sell a business. Business owners are most likely to sell when they are ready to retire, but full retirement age as defined by the Social Security Administration at 67 does not often align with the retirement plans of baby boomer business owners, who often plan to work well into their 70s or beyond. With age being less relevant, exit from business ownership is less understood. There is limited research about the factors that ensure successful business transition. That said, the existing research on the choice of exit strategy can be grouped into characteristics of the entrepreneur, the business, or the environment (Morris et al., 2018).

DeTienne et al. (2015) try to characterize business owners who choose a transition via sale to an individual, family member, or employees as their exit strategy. Perhaps most fundamental to this choice of succession is a strong sense of mission for the business. The authors theorize that business owners who have a strong stewardship perspective of their business are most likely to pursue transition in the form of a sale. Choosing the future owner, whether an individual, family member or employees, allows them to influence the future of their business.

DeTienne et al. (2015) also report that business owners who transition are less likely to prioritize financial or extrinsic rewards. Instead, these business owners more likely prioritize autonomy. Characteristics of the business owner translate to characteristics of the business. A preference for autonomy tends to correspond to tightly held ownership. Few or only one owner enables them to decide who will buy and lead the business in the future. In addition, these business owners are likely to have greater concern for employees, and the more people they employ, the more these business owners feel a responsibility to secure the future of the business. Consequently, businesses with more employees are also more likely to sell to a chosen successor.

The work of DeTienne et al. (2015) highlights, to some extent, what is known anecdotally: for small business owners, their livelihood, identity, and passion are invested in the business and the decision to sell is a deeply personal experience. Many business owners indeed have a strong emotional attachment to their business (Gomez-Mejía et al., 2007) that grows stronger over time (Zellweger et al., 2012). For them, the most important factor in the decision to sell the business is the loss of socioemotional wealth, which refers to aspects of identity, the ability to exercise authority, and the opportunity to be altruistic to others (Gomez-Mejía et al., 2007).

Personal Identity and Readiness

In some cases, the current owner of the business may have such a strong sense of personal identity with the business that the prospect of a new owner taking the business in a different direction is unacceptable. For many family-owned businesses, including farms or independent pharmacies or grocery stores, the issue of socioemotional wealth is also related to the challenging element of legacy, which can hamper a transition. Bruce and Picard (2006) state that these "soft issues," rather than technical issues, are often the reasons business successions fail.

Echoing this point, "personal readiness," which summarizes a business owner's emotional state regarding the business, is often identified as a key component in a successful transition (Exit Planning Institute, 2023). Darger (2024) reports businesses owners who consulted with their spouse, had family discussions, and obtained a formal business valuation had higher personal readiness. He also found that having plans for the owner's life, specifically continuing to work after the ownership transition, is associated with greater readiness. Yet nearly one-third of business owners surveyed indicate that they do not have a good post-transition plan and more than 40% indicate that they plan for a full retirement (Exit Planning Institute, 2023).

A Failure to Succession Plan

A lack of personal readiness can be one reason that business owners avoid preparing for succession (Bruce & Picard, 2006). Many business owners simply act as though they will always be working and neglect to develop a succession plan at all. This avoidance is problematic as a lack of a business succession plan is also often recognized as a main determinant of failure to transition (Bruce & Picard, 2006). Estimates suggest that between one- and two-thirds of business owners have a succession plan, depending on the survey (Edward Jones, 2024; Baker, 2023), meaning many business owners have no plan at all (Curry, in press).

A more recent 2021 report estimates that only 34% of the 32 million family businesses in the U.S. have a succession plan (PwC, 2023). Yet, there is some evidence that the next generation of entrepreneurs is being more intentional about succession planning, with 68% of millennial business owners and 61% of Gen X entrepreneurs reporting having a business succession plan (Edward Jones, 2024). Even with this shift, the lack of business succession planning is apparent.

When surveyed about reasons for not having a plan, business owners' responses point to a focus on more immediate concerns. Edward Jones (2024) report that 38% of small business owners surveyed did not have a succession plan because it was not a priority. Business owners faced with the pressing demands of day-to-day operations have little time to think about a seemingly distant process. Some feel they are simply not yet at a stage where succession is a focal concern.

In one study among business owners without a plan, 60% said that it was too soon to plan (Bruce & Picard, 2006). Instead, they focus on sustaining or growing their business. Yet this can be problematic as professional advisors recommend that it is never too soon to plan, and the process can take longer than business owners think. Many small business transitions require a significant period for new owners to "buy into" the business. Evidence from farm transition programs suggests that the timing of the process, from entering into transition discussion to completion, can take years (Valliant et al., 2019).

Performance Threshold

The choice to focus on performance rather than succession may be explained by performance threshold theory, which states that a business owner will dissolve the business when the level of performance is below their personal performance threshold (Gimeno et al., 1997). A business owner's threshold of performance is shaped by their characteristics, such as education, experience, industry, and age (Gimeno et al., 1997).

In other words, the decision to continue or close the business is based not only on profitability. It also matters how the actual performance of the business compares to the owner's performance threshold. DeTienne and Cardon (2012) relate this concept of a performance threshold to transition and different types of exit strategies. In their conceptualization, a performance threshold can influence a business owner's chosen exit strategy. Many business owners have in mind performance goals for their business that they feel must be attained before the business is ready to sell, and they might delay transition preparations until those goals are met.

For those whose retirement income is tied to the sale, the link between the role of economic performance and personal threshold is clearly relevant. They may choose to wait for better economic conditions that will improve the value of the business before selling. For example, the COVID-19 pandemic, high inflation, and increasing interest rates are all reasons explaining why owners may have chosen to delay the sale of their business in recent years. By waiting for changes in these economic conditions, the performance of their business may increase, bringing it above the threshold where they are ready to sell.

Business Readiness

In addition to personal readiness, there are other reasons business owners fail to transition successfully that have to do with "business readiness" or "financial readiness" (Exit Planning Institute, 2023; Darger, 2024). Business readiness includes completing tasks such as organizing financial records and legal documents. An owner may also need a business valuation, which can inform the strategy for selling as well as help an owner make appropriate retirement plans. Readiness can also include contacting relevant professionals such as an accountant and lawyer to ensure the necessary procedures and documentation are in place. In labor-intensive industries, owners may need to inform managers and employees and train individuals for when they step away so that there can be continuity in operations. In capital-intensive industries, owners need to ensure that delayed or deferred maintenance and reinvestment in equipment are addressed. A successful transition will be difficult if an owner delays or ignores these key steps.

Information Asymmetry

Aside from individual and business-related antecedents, certain external factors also shape the transition process. Dehlen et al. (2014) find that information asymmetry is a key factor that determines the form of business transition.

When business owners go to sell their business, they may have relatively little knowledge of a potential buyer's competencies. For owners with strong preferences about the direction of the business, and by extension, the person who takes over, the risk of selling to an ill-equipped external buyer can hamper the transaction. This is especially relevant if the current owner places high value on the notion of stewardship: the desire to see the business continue to thrive over the long term.

It is well known that information asymmetries, where one party has more information than the other, can lead to broader market failure, resulting in transactions that do not occur because of the perceived risk (Akerlof, 1970). Dehlen et al. (2014) argue that information asymmetry is one reason why business owners are more likely to choose succession to a family member as opposed to an external buyer. Business owners are more likely to have accurate knowledge of a family member's abilities and competencies, making them a safer choice for transition. Lee et al. (2003) similarly argue that because small businesses often require idiosyncratic knowledge to operate, family-run businesses tend to sell to family members who already possess this idiosyncratic knowledge.

Social Capital

The nature of social networks, or dimensions of social capital, can also shape exit strategies. Kaciak et al. (2021) examined the social networks of entrepreneurs and considered the effects of strong and weak network ties. In social network theory, "strong ties" are usually those with family members and friends and can be characterized by a large amount of time spent together, strong emotional intensity, intimacy, and reciprocity (Granovetter, 1973).

Conversely, "weak ties" tend to be those with colleagues and acquaintances and feature lower levels of intimacy, emotional connection, and reciprocity, as well as less time spent together. Kaciak et al. find that entrepreneurs whose networks are dominated by strong ties are more likely to choose a stewardship transition strategy, whereas business owners whose networks are dominated by weak ties are more likely to choose a financial harvest or cessation strategy.

They argue that the primary mechanism for this difference in exit choice may be trust. As business owners undergo the emotionally intense process of transition, they may turn to their most trusted relationships for counsel and support. When those relationships are friends and family, a business owner may be inclined to favor a similarly close relationship for succession. When business owners instead turn to "weak ties" for counsel and support, the scope of opportunities discussed may be broader and the role of social and emotional factors may be minimized, leading more naturally to a financial harvest or cessation strategy.

Considerations to Support Business Transition

With so many business owners prime for retirement and transitioning their businesses, especially in rural areas that, on average, are older, there is a need and opportunity to explore assistance services and models of transition that can ensure the continuity of business assets for the next generation. Clearly, there is an opportunity for economic development professionals and business development organizations to encourage business owners to plan for the sale, succession, or closure of their business.

The first step may involve helping owners address aspects of personal readiness. The personal and emotional aspects of selling are fundamental to the subsequent process of preparing and selling the business. Assisting with personal readiness may include helping business owners gain clarity on how they view the goals for their business and their plan for retirement, especially the extent to which they would still like to be involved after it transitions to new ownership.

A second critical component of support is educating business owners on the value of taking steps to prepare that optimize their position and meet their goals, whether personal or financial, when they do decide to sell. A better understanding of the time it can take to sell and the changes that may be necessary will be valuable. For example, a business owner may need to gather necessary records and modernize their record-keeping procedures as well as consult with an accountant and lawyer, all of which can take time.

Educational and technical assistance programs to assist in this process may require a sensitivity to the very personal nature of many small businesses. Business owners may feel strongly about the continuity of goods and services provided and that may lead to a resistance to change. Valliant et al. (2019) note that in assessing farm transition programs, as new owners move to have greater influence in the operation of the farm, conflict with the original owner can become a stumbling block.

Preparing for a sale should also include a consideration of how race and gender might affect the process. Compared to males, female sellers feel significantly more equipped to sell their business (BizBuySell, 2016). Justo et al. (2015) also state that women are more likely to transition from their businesses *voluntarily* for personal reasons. In other words, women may have higher levels of personal readiness.

In terms of motivation, white sellers are also much more likely to sell so that they can retire compared with African American, Hispanic, and Asian/Pacific Islander business owners, who are more likely to pursue another form of business ownership or return to the workforce, which can also contribute to higher levels of personal readiness (BizBuySell, 2016). These findings suggest that education and training to support business transitions should recognize how race and gender play a role in the extent of personal readiness, different motivations owners have for selling their businesses, and their goals post-transition.

Beyond educating owners of businesses on the process of transition and necessary business preparation, there is also a role for educating owners about potential buyers. Choosing a successor is an important component of a successful transition. The socioeconomic and demographic differences between current business owners and the next generation of potential buyers may mean it will take additional support to help business owners identify and align with potential buyers. This transaction may require a high level of trust and a shared vision for the future of the business. To the extent that current and future business owners belong to different social networks and have different values and challenges, there are opportunities to help buyers understand the pool of sellers, build relationships, and find common ground, which can serve as the foundation for transition.

For example, younger generations may place a greater emphasis on sustainable business practices. Aligning a current owner with a successor may require certain updates or investments in sustainability to make the business more attractive to potential buyers. Future business owners may also prioritize work–life balance and seek a business that is flexible enough to support those goals. For example, partnership or co-ownership may be conducive to a shared workload that suits their needs, but a business owner would have to be open to selling to partners rather than an individual and allow the ownership model to change. Creating opportunities for discussion, prioritization, and convergence where such differences arise could help.

A key aspect of helping sellers learn about buyers is understanding their skill sets. Given the importance many business owners place on choosing the right successor, processes that increase sellers' knowledge of buyer candidates can help facilitate successful transitions because it reduces risk and uncertainty (Dehlen et al., 2014). Opportunities to reveal their abilities by sharing their education, work experience, and accomplishments, also known as "signaling," are one way for sellers to learn about their potential buyers.

Sellers may also actively engage in "screening" candidates by searching for information from past employers, past employees, and past or current customers through online searches or industry-based research. Dehlen et al. find that both signaling and screening mechanisms can mitigate information asymmetries and result in a more likely transfer of the business. An analysis of the effectiveness of farmer transition programs by Valliant et al. (2019) found that facilitated networking amongst exiting and new farmers and business service providers (e.g., agricultural lenders) as well as individual counseling is particularly useful, perhaps because such programs facilitate important information exchanges.

Effective signaling and screening are especially important in the context of business transfer partly because of the permanence of the transaction (Dehlen et al., 2014). Unlike hiring an employee, the opportunity to undo a contract to purchase a business is quite limited. Effective signaling and screening is also important because a business owner is likely to engage in this type of transaction very few times or maybe only a single time. The opportunities to assess and adjust what kind of information they need to make a good decision are very limited. Last, the stronger the emotional attachment (e.g., stewardship) to the business, the less effective these mitigation strategies tend to be, making the personal readiness component even more important (Dehlen et al., 2014).

As far as the buyers are concerned, a range of considerations may be necessary. On the positive side, there is evidence to suggest that younger generations are more likely to engage in entrepreneurial activity (Primrose, 2023). Yet, they are also more likely to experience difficulties in securing adequate financing due to a range of factors from unproven financial histories (i.e., limited credit ratings) to higher levels of student debt. Business owners may benefit from thinking creatively about how to overcome financial challenges. For example, business owners may consider providing financial assistance for formal training, if feasible, to someone who is likely to take over the business. A work-to-own model where an employee accrues an ownership stake over time may also help in overcoming financial challenges.

Many future business owners are first-generation college students, women, or people of color who often have fewer key connections and opportunities for mentorship that can be so important for business owners. While trends show signs of increasing diversity among business owners, it is important to continue investing in entrepreneurship among underrepresented populations as a means to both reducing inequities and supporting the large-scale transition of businesses owned by aging entrepreneurs. Helping to facilitate connections between business owners and interested individuals, especially those outside of established networks, could help. It may also be as simple as helping business owners know where to look, whether connecting with a business broker or local business association. In this vein, one of the primary policy recommendations from a study of rural communities by Ayres et al. (1992) is building out networks among current and potential business owners.

Economic development and business leaders can continue to address disparities in education, access to capital, business ownership, and performance, as many businesses will likely transition from white owners to owners of color. Many national, state, and local programs have sought to close racial entrepreneurship gaps, such as the Minority Business Development Agency through the U.S. Department of Commerce and the Small Business Administration's 8(a) federal contracting assistance program for disadvantaged entrepreneurs. Recent court cases on affirmative action and business support programs for people of color have challenged the ability of policymakers and business development practitioners to directly support historically disadvantaged groups.[4,5] While the policy initiatives may be challenged, there are still opportunities for local and one-on-one efforts to address barriers.

Finally, buyers also face a problem of asymmetric information in that the sellers know far more about the financial soundness of the business (Dehlen et al., 2014). They may also be uncertain about the current business owner's future plans—whether they plan to open a competing business or act as an unwelcome advisor to their successor. Without full information about the performance of the business and an accurate sense of its trajectory, potential business owners may opt out of a promising sale just because of the risk associated with incomplete information. Helping business owners to access and assess the necessary information could also be a useful form of assistance.

In sum, the large and growing population of aging business owners presents both a challenge and an opportunity. With the potential for millions of businesses to change hands in the next decade, the low rate of successful transition and the consequences for business owners as well as communities that may lose an important service as well as employment and income is concerning. There is a clear need for supporting transitions to help business owners meet their personal and financial goals and to ensure a continuity of services in the community.

The survey data from business owners is encouraging since many indicate a sale is their most preferred path for exiting the business. This intention can be leveraged to match business owners with appropriate support. Importantly, transition programs may need to be creative in addressing generational differences between current business owners and interested buyers. Future business owners are more likely to be people of color and women, and they are more likely to face significant financial barriers, prefer a different work–life balance, and embrace an idea of success that encompasses sustainability. These differences are likely to require relationship building, new network connections, information sharing, and compromise to align buyers with their future successors.

Notes

1 Based on the U.S. Census Bureau, American Community Survey 1-Year Estimates (2010–2022), https://data.census.gov/table/ACSST5Y2020.S0101.
2 Based on the U.S. Census Bureau, "ACS Demographic and Housing Estimates," American Community Survey 1-Year Estimates Data Profiles, Table DP05, 2022, https://data.census.gov/table/ACSDP1Y2022.DP05?g=010XX00US$0400000.
3 The graph uses the RACESING variable from the IPUMS USA data set. The variable assigns a single race to multiple-race individuals as follows: White, Black/African American, Asian/Pacific Islander, American Indian/Alaskan Native, or unspecified. For this graph we say that minority is an individual who is not White and is not listed as unspecified.
4 Nuziard v. Minority Bus. Dev. Agency, No. 4:23-cv-1234, slip op. (N.D. Tex. Feb. 1, 2024).
5 Edward Blum v. Fearless Fund Management, LLC, No. 23-3424 (11th Cir. 2024).

References

12 Reserve Banks of the Federal Reserve System. (2021, April 15). *2021 report on firms owned by people of color: Based on the 2020 small business credit survey*. Fed Small Business. 10.55350/sbcs-20210415

Akerlof, G. A. (1970). The market for "lemons": Quality uncertainty and the market mechanism. *Quarterly Journal of Economics*, *84*(3), 488–500. 10.2307/1879431

Ayres, J., Leistritz, L., & Stone, K. (1992). Rural retail business survival: Implications for community developers. *Journal of the Community Development Society*, *23*(2), 11–21. 10.1080/15575339209489927

Baker, J. (2023, December 22). *Succession planning statistics in 2024: Preserving a legacy*. Teamshares. https://www.teamshares.com/resources/succession-planning-statistics/

BizBuySell. (2016, May). *The demographics of U.S. small business buyers & sellers*. https://www.bizbuysell.com/shared/BizBuySell_DemographicSurvey_WhitePaper_2016.pdf

Bruce, D., & Picard, D. (2006). Making succession a success: Perspectives from Canadian small and medium-sized enterprises. *Journal of Small Business Management*, *44*(2), 306–309. 10.1111/j.1540-627X.2006.00171.x

Center for Microeconomic Data. (n.d.). *Student debt*. Federal Reserve Bank of New York. https://www.newyorkfed.org/microeconomics/topics/student-debt

CFR.org Editors. (2024, April 16). *Is rising student debt harming the U.S. economy?* Council on Foreign Relations. https://www.cfr.org/backgrounder/us-student-loan-debt-trends-economic-impact

Chirico, F., Gómez-Mejia, L. R., Hellerstedt, K., Withers, M., & Nordqvist, M. (2020). To merge, sell or liquidate? Socioemotional wealth, family control, and the choice of business exit. *Journal of Management*, *46*(8), 1342–1379. 10.1177/0149206318818723

Conroy, T. (2019). The kids are alright: Working women, schedule flexibility and childcare. *Regional Studies*, *53*(2), 261–271. 10.1080/00343404.2018.1462478

Conway Center for Family Business. (n.d.). *Family business facts*. Retrieved March 2, 2023, from https://www.familybusinesscenter.com/resources/family-business-facts/

Curry, M. (in press). Traditional business succession planning: Effectiveness, limitations, and innovative practices. In N. Walzer (Ed.), *Successfully transitioning small businesses*. Routledge.

Darger, M. (2024, June 25). How well are business owners preparing for succession and transition? *Entrepreneur & Innovation Exchange*. 1–5. 10.32617/1087-667ab73c71942

Dehlen, T., Zellweger, T., Kammerlander, N., & Halter, F. (2014). The role of information asymmetry in the choice of entrepreneurial exit routes. *Journal of Business Venturing*, *29*(2), 193–209. 10.1016/j.jbusvent.2012.10.001

DeTienne, D. R., & Cardon, M. S. (2012). Impact of founder experience on exit intentions. *Small Business Economics*, *38*(4), 351–374. 10.1007/s11187-010-9284-5

DeTienne, D. R., McKelvie, A., & Chandler, G. N. (2015). Making sense of entrepreneurial exit strategies: A typology and test. *Journal of Business Venturing*, *30*(2), 255–272. 10.1016/j.jbusvent.2014.07.007

Edward Jones. (2024, June 11). A business succession boom is coming, and one-third of business owners don't view a plan as a priority, Edward Jones research finds [Press release]. https://www.edwardjones.com/us-en/why-edward-jones/news-media/press-releases/research-indicates-business-succession-planning-emotional

Exit Planning Institute. (2023). *2023 national state of owner readiness report*. https://exit-planning-institute.org/hubfs/Member%20Center%20Resources/2023%20National%20State%20of%20Owner%20Readiness%20Report.pdf

Fleming, D. A., & Goetz, S. J. (2011). Does local firm ownership matter? *Economic Development Quarterly*, *25*(3), 277–281. 10.1177/0891242411407312

Frey, W. H. (2023, August 1). *New 2020 census data shows an aging America and wide racial gaps between generations*. The Brookings Institution. https://www.brookings.edu/articles/new-2020-census-data-shows-an-aging-america-and-wide-racial-gaps-between-generations/

Gimeno, J., Folta, T. B., Cooper, A. C., & Woo, C. Y. (1997). Survival of the fittest? Entrepreneurial human capital and the persistence of underperforming firms. *Administrative Science Quarterly*, *42*(4), 750–783. 10.2307/2393656

Global Entrepreneurship Monitor. (2022, September 14). *GEM USA report highlights increases in entrepreneurship and startup intentions*. https://gemconsortium.org/news/new-gem-usa-report-highlights-increases-in-entrepreneurship-and-startup-intentions

Goldman Sachs. (2020, October 13). *Running a business while Black: Analyzing the obstacles of Black entrepreneurship*. https://www.goldmansachs.com/community-impact/10000-small-businesses/us/news-and-program-information/infographic-running-a-business-while-black

Gómez-Mejía, L. R., Haynes, K. T., Núñez-Nickel, M., Jacobson, K. J. L., & Moyano-Fuentes, J. (2007). Socioemotional wealth and business risks in family-controlled firms: Evidence from Spanish olive oil mills. *Administrative Science Quarterly*, *52*(1), 106–137. 10.2189/asqu.52.1.106

Granovetter, M. S. (1973). The strength of weak ties. *American Journal of Sociology*, *78*(6), 1360–1380. http://www.jstor.org/stable/277639

Headd, B. (2021, March). *Small business facts: Business ownership demographics*. Office of Advocacy, U.S. Small Business Administration. https://advocacy.sba.gov/wp-content/uploads/2021/03/Business-Ownership-Demographics-Fact-Sheet.pdf

J. P. Morgan Chase & Co. (n.d.). *A large share of small businesses are young businesses*. https://www.jpmorganchase.com/institute/research/small-business/small-business-dashboard/longevity

Justo, R., DeTienne, D. R., & Sieger, P. (2015). Failure or voluntary exit? Reassessing the female underperformance hypothesis. *Journal of Business Venturing*, *30*(6), 775–792. 10.1016/j.jbusvent.2015.04.004

Kaciak, E., Koladkiewicz, I., Thongpapanl, N., & Wojtyra, M. (2021). The role of social networks in shaping entrepreneurial exit strategies. *International Entrepreneurship and Management Journal*, *17*(4), 1619–1655. 10.1007/s11365-020-00668-9

Lee, K. S., Lim, G. H., & Lim, W. S. (2003). Family business succession: Appropriation risk and choice of successor. *Academy of Management Review 28*(4), 657–666. 10.5465/amr.2003.10899446

Lee, L. (2023, January 4). *Minority business ownership differs by sector*. U.S. Census Bureau. https://www.census.gov/library/stories/2023/01/who-owns-americas-businesses.html#:~:text=January%2004%2C%202023,which%20declined%20during%20the%20decade

Luque, A. & Jones, M. R. (2019, September). *Gender differences in self-employment duration: The case of opportunity and necessity entrepreneurs*. Center for Economic Studies, U.S. Census Bureau. https://www2.census.gov/ces/wp/2019/CES-WP-19-24.pdf

McDermott, M., Conroy, T., & Kures, M. (2023, December). *Business owners of color in Wisconsin: Strategies to strengthen businesses and the economy* (The Wisconsin Economy: Study Series No. 9). Extension, University of Wisconsin-Madison. https://economicdevelopment.extension.wisc.edu/files/2024/01/1.26.24_EDAUC_StudySeries_PolicyBrief_TWE.pdf

McKinsey & Company (2024, August). *What is Gen Z?* https://www.mckinsey.com/~/media/mckinsey/featured%20insights/mckinsey%20explainers/what%20is%20gen%20z/what-is-gen-z.pdf?shouldIndex=false

Morris, M. H., Santos, S. C., Pryor, C., & Neumeyer, X. (2018). The nature of entrepreneurial exit. In R. Blackburn, D. De Clercq, & J. Heinonen (Eds.), *The SAGE handbook of small business and entrepreneurship* (pp. 242–258). Sage Publications. 10.4135/9781473984080.n13

Office of Advocacy. (2021, December). *Frequently asked questions.* U.S. Small Business Association. https://advocacy.sba.gov/wp-content/uploads/2021/12/Small-Business-FAQ-Revised-December-2021.pdf

Parker, K., Horowitz, J. M., Brown, A., Fry, R., Cohn, D., & Igielnik, R. (2018, May 22). *Demographic and economic trends in urban, suburban and rural communities.* Pew Research Center. https://www.pewresearch.org/social-trends/2018/05/22/demographic-and-economic-trends-in-urban-suburban-and-rural-communities/

Patel, A., & Martin, G. (2011, December). *Going local: Quantifying the economic impacts of buying from locally owned businesses in Portland, Maine.* Maine Center for Economic Policy. https://www.mecep.org/wp-content/uploads/2011/12/MECEP_Report_-_Buying_Local-12-5-2011.pdf

PitchBook. (n.d.). *US VC female founders dashboard.* Retrieved June 4, 2024, from https://pitchbook.com/news/articles/the-vc-female-founders-dashboard

Primrose, E. (2023, August 12). Shaping a new generation of entrepreneurs: How can we make entrepreneurship more diverse? *Cognito.* https://oecdcogito.blog/2023/08/12/shaping-a-new-generation-of-entrepreneurs-how-can-we-make-entrepreneurship-more-diverse/#:~:text=They%20are%20also%20more%20racially,full%2Dtime%20work%20with%20school

PwC. (2023, May 16). *2023 U.S. family business survey.* https://www.pwc.com/us/en/services/audit-assurance/private-company-services/library/family-business-survey.html

Ruggles, S., Flood, S., Sobek, M., Backman, D., Chen, A., Cooper, G., Richards, S., Rogers, R., & Schouweiler, M. (2024). *U.S. census data for social, economic, and health research* (IPUMS USA; Version 15.0) [dataset]. IPUMS USA. 10.18128/D010.v15.0.

Schmidt, C., Goetz, S. J., & Tian, Z. (2021). Female farmers in the United States: Research needs and policy questions. *Food Policy, 101*, Article 102039. 10.1016/j.foodpol.2021.102039

University of Cambridge. (2023, November 16). *Boom and bust? Millennials aren't all worse off than Baby Boomers, but the rich-poor gap is widening* [News release]. https://www.cam.ac.uk/research/news/boom-and-bust-millennials-arent-all-worse-off-than-baby-boomers-but-the-rich-poor-gap-is-widening

Valliant, J. C. D., Ruhf, K. Z., Gibson, K. D., Brooks, J. R., & Farmer, J. R. (2019). Fostering farm transfers from farm owners to unrelated, new farmers: A qualitative assessment of farm link services. *Land Use Policy, 86*, 438–447. 10.1016/j.landusepol.2019.05.004

Wennberg, K., Wiklund, J., DeTienne, D. R., & Cardon, M. S. (2010). Reconceptualizing entrepreneurial exit: Divergent exit routes and their drivers. *Journal of Business Venturing, 25*(4), 361–375. 10.1016/j.jbusvent.2009.01.001

Williamson, M. W. (2023, September 21). *Understanding the self-employed in the United States.* Center for American Progress. https://www.americanprogress.org/article/understanding-the-self-employed-in-the-united-states/

Zellweger, T. M., Kellermanns, F. W., Chrisman, J. J., & Chua, J. H. (2012). Family control and family firm valuation by family CEOs: The importance of intentions for transgenerational control. *Organization Science, 23*(3), 851–868. 10.1287/orsc.1110.0665

Zulauf, C. (2024, May 8). Age of US farmers: Not a problem [Gardner policy series]. *farmdoc daily 14*: 88. Department of Agricultural and Consumer Economics, University of Illinois at Urbana-Champaign. https://farmdocdaily.illinois.edu/2024/05/age-of-us-farmers-not-a-problem.html

Zulauf, C., Schnitkey, G., Swanson, K., & Paulson, N. (2021, November 3). New and beginning farmers [Gardner policy series]. *farmdoc daily 11*: 151. Department of Agricultural and Consumer Economics, University of Illinois at Urbana-Champaign. https://farmdocdaily.illinois.edu/2021/11/new-and-beginning-farmers.html

3

TRADITIONAL BUSINESS SUCCESSION PLANNING

Effectiveness, Limitations, and Innovative Practices

Jarvis Tyrell Curry

Introduction

Succession planning is an integral part of business strategy and is vital for ensuring organizational continuity and stability. It is essential for small and/or family-owned businesses where the enterprise's legacy and sustainability hinge on effective power transitions (Campopiano et al., 2020). Traditional succession planning methods have long been employed to ensure capable leaders are prepared to take the helm when needed. This chapter explores the evolution of these traditional practices along with their effectiveness, and limitations, supplemented with statistical analyses, case studies, and innovative approaches that enhance traditional frameworks (Atwood, 2020).

Recent studies emphasize the unique challenges faced by small family-owned businesses in succession planning, especially in regions such as Nigeria and Indonesia. Musa and Dissanayake (2014) highlight that many small family businesses in Nigeria struggle with leadership transitions due to a lack of formal succession planning and the founders' reluctance to relinquish control. This reluctance often stems from a deeply personal connection to the business, leading to the founders' over-reliance on their leadership and a failure to adequately prepare successors. The situation is exacerbated in environments where there is a cultural or familial expectation for the business to remain within the family, even when successors may not be adequately prepared or interested in taking over (Musa & Dissanayake, 2014).

In Indonesia, Tirdasari and Dhewanto (2020) observe that while many family businesses lack formal succession plans, they often manage successful

DOI: 10.4324/9781003497462-3

transitions through a gradual involvement of successors in the business. The study highlights the importance of timing in the succession process, noting that earlier involvement of potential successors in business operations often leads to smoother transitions. This gradual integration allows successors to develop the necessary skills and knowledge while still benefiting from the guidance of incumbent leaders. The Indonesian case studies underscore that while formal succession plans are beneficial, the success of small family businesses often depends on the ongoing interaction between the current and future leaders and their ability to adapt to the business's evolving needs (Tirdasari & Dhewanto, 2020).

The necessity of succession planning must be balanced. Businesses that fail to plan for leadership transitions risk facing disruptions that can lead to operational inefficiencies, financial losses, and even business failure (Ahmad et al., 2021). This chapter provides a comprehensive understanding of traditional succession planning, its evolution over time, metrics for evaluating its success, and its challenges. In addition, it describes best practices and innovative approaches that can be integrated into traditional frameworks to improve outcomes. Through case studies and statistical analysis, later discussions will illustrate the critical role of succession planning in achieving business continuity and long-term success.

Historical Context and Evolution

Succession planning has long been a cornerstone of business continuity, especially within family-owned enterprises. The historical roots of succession planning can be traced to medieval guilds, where the transfer of craft and trade knowledge was meticulously managed within families to preserve wealth and control. This hereditary system ensured that businesses remained within families, maintaining stability across generations. However, the emphasis on bloodline succession often led to challenges, such as inadequate leadership preparation and resistance to external expertise (Chirapanda, 2020).

The Industrial Revolution brought profound changes, necessitating more formalized and structured succession strategies. As businesses expanded, the complexities of management increased, prompting a shift from purely familial succession to incorporating professional management. This era brought the introduction of systematic approaches to ensure that leadership transitions did not disrupt operations. Traditional succession plans during this era typically involved designating a successor from among the family or close associates, often overlooking the need for merit-based selection. This practice sometimes leads to appointing underprepared or unsuitable leaders, ultimately jeopardizing business continuity (Rondi et al., 2022).

Despite the structured nature of traditional succession plans, they have faced significant criticisms and limitations. For instance, a common issue involves inadequate grooming of successors. Many traditional plans focus on seniority or familial ties rather than assessing candidates' leadership potential and readiness. As a result, successors often need more skills and experience, leading to business challenges post-transition. Research shows that only about 30% of family businesses successfully transition to the second generation, with a mere 12% making it to the third generation (Ahmad et al., 2021). Furthermore, approximately 60% of businesses fail within five years following a leadership transition due to insufficient planning and preparation (Al Suwaidi et al., 2020).

Traditional succession planning has also been criticized for its need to align with broader business objectives. Often, these plans should have considered evolving market conditions or the strategic direction of the business. This misalignment has led to leadership that needs to be equipped to handle new challenges, innovation, and adaptability. Moreover, excluding key stakeholders, such as non-family executives and employees, from the planning process has sometimes resulted in resistance and lack of support for new leaders (Campopiano et al., 2020). Box 3.1 shows a sample checklist organizations may use to plan succession.

The long-term effects of traditional succession plans have been mixed. While some businesses have managed to sustain themselves, many have needed help with the rigidity and outdated practices inherent in these plans. The historical focus on maintaining family control often came at the expense of operational efficiency and competitive edge. For example, reluctance to bring in external expertise limited the ability of businesses to innovate and respond to market changes effectively (Rondi et al., 2022).

Despite these challenges, traditional succession plans provide valuable lessons regarding the importance of continuity and planning. They underscore the need for a more holistic approach, including thorough preparation of successors, alignment with strategic goals, and broader stakeholder involvement. As the business landscape continues to evolve, there is a growing recognition of the need to integrate modern practices, such as talent management and digital tools, to enhance the effectiveness of succession planning (Jackson & Dunn-Jensen, 2021).

While traditional succession planning has been pivotal in preserving family businesses' legacies, its limitations highlight a need for more dynamic and inclusive approaches. The evolution of these practices reflects a broader trend toward professionalization and meritocracy, designed to balance tradition with the demands of a rapidly changing business environment. The success rates of these transitions and their impact on business longevity remain critical areas of study to provide insights into best practices for future leadership transitions (Mahusain & Raman Nair, 2022; Matias & Franco, 2021).

BOX 3.1 SUCCESSION PLANNING CHECKLIST. SOURCE: COMPILED BY AUTHOR.

- **Early and Ongoing Planning**
  - Initiate succession planning early to allow ample time for development.
  - Ensure ongoing updates to the succession plan based on changing business needs and market conditions.
- **Comprehensive Talent Assessments**
  - Conduct thorough assessments to identify skills, competencies, and potential at various organizational levels.
  - Use tools like performance appraisals, 360-degree feedback, and leadership assessments.
- **Alignment with Strategic Objectives**
  - Integrate succession planning with the organization's strategic planning process.
  - Regularly review and align succession plans with changing business objectives and market conditions.
- **Stakeholder Involvement**
  - Involve key stakeholders in the planning process, including senior management and potential successors.
  - Foster transparency and buy-in to reduce resistance and facilitate smoother transitions.
- **Mentorship and Development Programs**
  - Implement mentorship programs to provide guidance and support for potential successors.
  - Design leadership development programs focusing on essential skills and strategic thinking.
- **Regular Reviews and Updates**
  - Conduct regular reviews of the succession plan to ensure its relevance and effectiveness.
  - Update the plan based on feedback, changing business needs, and market conditions.

Effectiveness of Traditional Succession Plans

Evaluating the effectiveness of traditional succession plans involves analyzing several key metrics, including business survival rates, leadership stability, and financial performance. These metrics provide insights into how well businesses transition leadership and maintain continuity. Traditional succession plans, often rooted in family values and heritage, have shown varied success depending on their structure and execution.

Studies show that businesses with well-defined and executed succession plans have higher survival rates. For example, Ahmad et al. (2021) report that family firms with formalized succession strategies are more likely to survive beyond the third generation, with approximately 30% achieving this milestone. However, without proper planning, the likelihood of failure within five years of a leadership transition significantly increases, highlighting the critical importance of thorough preparation (Al Suwaidi et al., 2020). Moreover, traditional plans with strong family involvement and a focus on innovation are better positioned for long-term sustainability, as these elements foster resilience and adaptability in a competitive market (Ahmad et al., 2021). Table 3.1 provides metrics to use in evaluating the effectiveness of a succession plan.

Leadership stability is another essential indicator of the success of traditional succession plans. Stable leadership transitions ensure continuity in business operations, which is crucial for maintaining employee morale and customer trust. Matias and Franco (2021) emphasize that businesses with clear and structured succession protocols have fewer disruptions during leadership changes, contributing to a seamless transition process. This stability is often

TABLE 3.1 Key Metrics for Evaluating Succession Plan Effectiveness

Metric	*Description*
Business Survival Rate	Percentage of businesses that continue to operate after leadership transition
Leadership Stability	Measurement of continuity and stability in leadership roles
Financial Performance	Assessment of financial health and performance post-transition
Innovation Capability	Evaluation of the business's ability to innovate and adapt to market changes
Stakeholder Satisfaction	Measurement of satisfaction among stakeholders, including employees and customers

Note: Compiled by author based on information from Chirapanda (2020); Jackson and Dunn-Jensen (2021); Mahusain and Raman Nair (2022); Marques and da Silva (2020); and Soares et al. (2021).

achieved through rigorous grooming and mentorship of successors, ensuring they are well prepared to assume leadership roles.

However, traditional plans sometimes are revised by emphasizing family ties over merit, leading to the appointment of underqualified leaders. This prioritization can result in leadership lacking the necessary skills to manage the business effectively, threatening the company's stability and growth. The consequences of such inadequacies can result in internal conflicts, loss of strategic direction, and, ultimately, a decline in business performance.

Financial performance post-transition is a critical measure of the effectiveness of succession planning. Successful leadership transitions typically correlate with stable or improved financial health, as consistent leadership allows the continuous implementation of strategic plans. Campopiano et al. (2020) found that family businesses with structured succession plans exhibit better financial outcomes, mainly due to the seamless integration of new leadership and their ability to maintain the company's core values and mission. This financial stability is especially crucial in family-owned enterprises, where the business's financial well-being is closely tied to the family's legacy. However, succession plans failing to align with broader business goals can hinder the company's financial performance. He and Ortiz (2021) highlight the necessity for businesses to evolve their succession strategies, incorporating modern practices such as digital tools and data analytics, to remain competitive in an increasingly dynamic market.

Traditional succession plans have limitations, especially regarding adaptability and stakeholder involvement. A significant criticism of these plans is their tendency to focus on maintaining the status quo, often at the expense of innovation and strategic flexibility. This focus can stifle the business's ability to adapt to new challenges and seize emerging opportunities.

Moreover, traditional succession planning often excludes critical stakeholders, such as non-family executives and employees, from the decision-making process. This exclusion can lead to a need for more buy-in and support for the new leadership, as these stakeholders may feel sidelined. Involving a broader range of perspectives is crucial to ensure the succession plan is comprehensive and aligns with the company's strategic vision. Ge and Campopiano (2022) argue that including diverse voices in the succession planning process enhances the quality of decisions and fosters a culture of inclusivity and transparency.

Limitations and Challenges

While offering a structured approach to leadership transitions, traditional succession planning faces numerous challenges that can undermine its effectiveness. A significant issue is the inadequate preparation and grooming of successors. Often, businesses fail to invest the necessary time and resources into developing potential leaders, resulting in a leadership void during transitions. This lack of preparation is evident in approximately 60% of family businesses that only survive within the second generation, primarily due to insufficient grooming of successors (Al Suwaidi et al., 2020). Successors who need more skills and experience can lead to operational disruptions and reduced organizational performance, exacerbating the challenges of leadership transitions (Campopiano et al., 2020).

Organizational culture and resistance to change also present significant barriers in traditional succession planning. Entrenched cultural norms can create an environment resistant to new leadership, especially when the transition is perceived as imposed rather than earned. This resistance is often rooted in a rigid attachment to established ways of doing things, making it difficult for new leaders to implement necessary changes. Mahusain and Raman Nair (2022) highlight that such resistance can foster a hostile work environment, undermining the authority and effectiveness of new leaders. This issue is especially pronounced in family businesses where familial loyalty can overshadow objective assessments of leadership capabilities, leading to internal conflicts and a lack of support for new leadership (Ahmad et al., 2021).

Another critical area for improvement is the misalignment between business goals and succession planning strategies. Traditional plans often focus on maintaining continuity and stability, sometimes at the expense of innovation and growth. This focus can lead to the selection of more conservative successors less inclined to pursue new opportunities, which can stifle the organization's adaptability and responsiveness to market changes (Porfírio et al., 2020). For example, businesses prioritizing family succession over merit-based selection may overlook better-qualified external candidates, potentially compromising the company's ability to compete in a dynamic market environment. This misalignment can be detrimental in industries that require rapid innovation and adaptation, as seen in the technology sector, where the inability to embrace new ideas can lead to obsolescence (Matias & Franco, 2021).

Inadequate communication and involvement of critical stakeholders further complicate traditional succession planning. Effective succession planning requires the engagement of various stakeholders, including employees, shareholders, and external advisors. However, traditional plans often exclude these groups, leading to a need for more transparency and buy-in during the transition process. This exclusion can result in conflicts and uncertainty, as stakeholders may feel disconnected from the decision-making process. Al Aina and Atan (2020) emphasize that the presence of stakeholder involvement can lead to trust and improved morale, positively impacting the overall success of the succession plan. Furthermore, the absence of clear communication can create ambiguity regarding the organization's future direction, affecting employee engagement and retention. Table 3.2 lists the most common challenges to the effectiveness of traditional succession planning.

TABLE 3.2 Common Challenges in Traditional Succession Planning

Challenge	*Description*
Inadequate Successor Grooming	Failure to adequately prepare and develop potential leaders (Mahusain & Raman Nair, 2022)
Organizational Resistance	Resistance to change and acceptance of new leadership (Rondi et al., 2022)
Misaligned Objectives	Lack of alignment between succession planning strategies and overall business goals (Jackson & Dunn-Jensen, 2021)
Stakeholder Involvement	Insufficient involvement of key stakeholders in the succession planning process (Matias & Franco, 2021)

Source: Compiled by author.

Long-Term Outcomes

The long-term outcomes of traditional succession planning can vary significantly, influenced by market conditions, industry dynamics, and robustness of the plans. Traditional succession plans often involve a straightforward, hereditary transfer of leadership, especially within family-owned businesses. These plans, however, can be fraught with challenges, such as inadequate grooming of successors and resistance to professional management, which can adversely affect the business's sustainability (Ge & Campopiano, 2022). Despite these challenges, businesses with well-structured traditional succession plans often demonstrate higher sustainability and resilience. Research shows that such businesses tend to perform better financially, maintain their market positions more effectively, and have a greater capacity to weather economic downturns than those without such plans (Rondi et al., 2022).

Long-term studies indicate diminishing trends in survival rates for traditional succession plans. These statistics highlight the inherent difficulties in maintaining business continuity through traditional means. The key issues often include a need for more alignment between the incoming leadership's vision and the current business strategy, leading to strategic missteps and loss of market share. Moreover, traditional plans that do not incorporate continuous leadership development or align with the company's long-term strategic goals often fail to adapt to changing market conditions, making them less effective in the long run (Al Aina & Atan, 2020).

The rigidity of traditional succession plans can also stifle innovation and limit a company's ability to capitalize on new opportunities. For example, businesses in fast-evolving industries such as technology require adaptive and forward-thinking leadership to navigate rapid changes and technological advancements. Traditional succession planning, which often emphasizes stability over innovation, may not adequately prepare leaders for such dynamic environments. Consequently, companies that rely solely on traditional succession strategies may be at a competitive disadvantage (He & Ortiz, 2021). In heavily regulated industries, traditional succession plans must also account for compliance and regulatory changes, which can impact the selection and training of future leaders (Tucker, 2020).

The traditional succession plans that exclude vital stakeholders, such as non-family executives and external advisors, may need help in implementation since these stakeholders may resist the changes brought about by new leadership. This lack of inclusion can lead to the loss of critical talent and institutional knowledge, further destabilizing the business. Conversely, more inclusive approaches that engage a broader range of stakeholders are more likely to result in smoother transitions and organizational stability (Umans et al., 2021).

Innovative Approaches within Traditional Frameworks

Incorporating innovative practices into traditional succession planning frameworks can significantly enhance their effectiveness and relevance in contemporary business environments. One of the most impactful innovations involves integrating technology and data analytics. These tools provide valuable insights into talent management and succession readiness, allowing companies to identify potential leaders and assess their capabilities systematically.

For instance, data analytics can examine employee performance records, identifying patterns that indicate leadership potential. This information enables organizations to tailor development programs and track progress over time, ensuring that identified successors are adequately prepared for future roles (Martínez-Morán et al., 2021). By leveraging these technologies, companies can address common shortcomings of traditional succession plans, such as inadequate grooming of successors and lack of alignment with strategic goals (Jackson & Dunn-Jensen, 2021).

Traditional succession plans often need to catch up to the pace of contemporary business due to their rigid structures and failure to adapt to rapidly changing market conditions. Adaptive strategies, such as scenario planning, have proven essential for maintaining the relevance and practicality of succession plans. Scenario planning allows businesses to anticipate potential market changes and design strategies to address them, ensuring that succession plans are aligned with current business realities and future-proofed against uncertainties. This approach is especially beneficial in industries characterized by high volatility, such as technology and finance, where market conditions can shift dramatically within short periods (He & Ortiz, 2021). Regularly updating succession plans to reflect these projections can help mitigate the risks associated with unexpected leadership transitions and ensure a smoother handover process (Tucker, 2020).

Moreover, engaging stakeholders through innovative approaches such as succession planning workshops and collaborative platforms fosters a more inclusive and dynamic planning process. For example, companies can organize workshops where employees at various levels discuss succession planning and leadership development. These workshops provide valuable insights from different organizational perspectives and foster a sense of ownership and commitment among employees. Such inclusive practices can help mitigate organizational resistance, a common challenge in traditional succession planning, by ensuring all stakeholders are aligned and support the chosen succession strategy (Ge & Campopiano, 2022). Engaging a broad range of stakeholders, including non-family executives and external advisors, can also bring fresh perspectives and innovative ideas into the succession planning process, enhancing the overall strategy (Umans et al., 2021).

However, while these innovative approaches offer significant benefits, they also have potential challenges and limitations. Traditional succession plans, especially in family-owned businesses, often emphasize maintaining family control, which can conflict with the meritocratic principles underlying modern talent management practices. This focus on family control sometimes leads to selecting less-qualified leaders, undermining the long-term sustainability of the business. Past research shows that approximately 60% of family businesses fail to survive beyond the second generation, often due to inadequate succession planning and leadership development (Anggadwita et al., 2020). Furthermore, integrating digital tools and data analytics requires significant investment and a cultural shift toward data-driven decision-making, which can be challenging for traditionally managed companies (Wassell & Bouchard, 2020).

Case Studies of Innovative Traditional Succession Plans

Examining businesses that successfully integrated innovative practices within traditional succession frameworks provides valuable lessons and insights. For example, companies using data analytics to inform their succession planning reported more accurate and effective leadership transitions. These businesses have successfully navigated common challenges by continuously updating their plans and involving key stakeholders (Martínez-Morán et al., 2021).

Case Study #1: Manufacturing Business

This manufacturing business, established in 1982, specialized in producing household goods, including soap and detergents, which were widely distributed across Gombe State. The business quickly gained a significant market share within the local market, capturing 20% of the regional market by 1990. Despite its success, the founder managed the business with a highly centralized approach, making all critical decisions independently and resisting any delegation of authority.

By the mid-1990s, as the founder approached his late 60s, his health began to decline. Although aware of the need for succession, he hesitated to formalize a plan, fearing a loss of control. No potential successor was identified or trained. When the founder passed in 2001, the business was left in disarray. Family members, unfamiliar with the operational complexities, struggled to manage the business. Market share quickly eroded, and the business was forced to cease operations by 2002. This collapse underscores the importance of early succession planning and the dangers of centralizing authority without preparing for leadership transition (Musa & Dissanayake, 2014).

For manufacturing businesses, succession planning should begin with the identification and grooming of potential successors early in the business's life cycle. A phased delegation of responsibilities, where successors are gradually given more control over critical aspects of the business, can ensure a smoother transition. In addition, implementing management training programs for potential successors can help them understand the intricacies of the business and prepare them for leadership roles.

Case Study #2: Distribution Business

Founded in 1975, this distribution business became a major supplier of consumer goods from multinational corporations to local retailers across Gombe and neighboring states. By the 1990s, the business had secured contracts with several leading brands, accounting for 15% of the distribution market in the region. The founder, however, maintained strict control over all aspects of the business, from negotiating contracts to managing logistics. When approaching his 60s in the early 2000s, he recognized the need for succession but failed to implement a formal plan. His eldest son, who was viewed as the natural successor, had minimal involvement in the business, having pursued a career in engineering. When the founder died unexpectedly in 2005, the business was thrust into chaos. The son, lacking the necessary experience and business acumen, struggled to maintain relationships with key clients and manage operations efficiently. Within two years, the business lost several key contracts, resulting in a sharp decline in revenue and eventual closure in 2007 (Musa & Dissanayake, 2014).

Distribution businesses, where relationships and logistics are critical, must prioritize succession planning. This means early involvement of potential successors in day-to-day operations and the establishment of formal training programs that cover critical aspects of the business, including contract negotiation, supply chain management, and client relations. Mentorship by the founder can also help successors build the necessary skills and confidence to lead.

Case Study #3: Oil Mill Processing Industry

This oil mill processing business, established in 1969, was one of the leading producers of palm oil in the region, with a production capacity of 1,000 liters per day by the late 1980s. The business supplied both local markets and larger processors in neighboring states. Despite its success, the founder managed the business autocratically, refusing to delegate significant responsibilities. Even when approaching his 70s in the late 1990s, the founder resisted efforts to introduce modern management practices or involve family members in the business.

By 2002, the founder's health had severely deteriorated, but no succession plan was in place. After his death in 2003, the business quickly fell apart. Family members, who had not been involved in the business, lacked expertise to manage operations. Disputes over inheritance further complicated the situation, and the business was liquidated by 2005, with its market share absorbed by competitors (Musa & Dissanayake, 2014).

For businesses in the oil processing industry, where operational efficiency and market relationships are key, early succession planning is essential. This includes not only identifying potential successors but also involving them in the early stages of the business's strategic planning and operational management efforts. Establishing a formal succession plan that includes clear guidelines for inheritance and leadership transition can help avoid disputes and ensure the business remains operational after the founder's departure.

Case Study #4: BG (19 Years in Business, West Java)

Founded in 2001, BG operates in the bakery sector, producing traditional Indonesian baked goods for local markets. By 2010, the business had established a strong presence in West Java, with a market share of 15% in the regional bakery market. Recognizing the importance of succession, the founder began involving his son in the business at a young age. The son started working in the business part time while still in school, gradually taking on more responsibilities.

By 2012, the son was managing key aspects of the business, including production and sales. The founder continued to provide guidance but allowed his son to make critical decisions. In 2015, the founder formally handed over leadership to his son, having spent the previous three years mentoring him and ensuring he was prepared to take over. The transition was smooth, and under the son's leadership, the business expanded its market share to 20% by 2020, further solidifying its position in the regional market (Tirdasari & Dhewanto, 2020).

In the bakery and food production sector, early involvement and gradual delegation of responsibilities are crucial for successful succession. Founders should identify potential successors early and involve them in both strategic and operational aspects of the business. Formalizing the mentorship process and setting clear milestones for the transition can help ensure the successor is well prepared to take over. Table 3.3 shows business succession success rates across industries.

TABLE 3.3 Business Succession Success Rates in Different Contexts and Industries

	Digital Transformation Economy (%)	*Corporate Entrepreneurship Education (%)*	*Sustainability in Family Businesses (%)*
Year 1	78	76	77
Year 2	80	79	80
Year 3	83	81	82
Year 4	85	84	85

Source: Compiled by author.

Note: Table 3.3 provides an overview of succession rates for businesses experiencing leadership change in the four years following the transition in different contexts and industries, as reported by various studies (Jackson & Dunn-Jensen, 2021; Soares et al., 2021; Chirapanda, 2020).

Future Directions and Recommendations

As businesses face increasing complexity and rapid technological changes, succession planning is no longer confined to traditional methods. To remain competitive, organizations must evolve their approach to leadership transitions by embracing modern tools and practices. This shift involves not only identifying and preparing future leaders but also ensuring that succession planning aligns with broader strategic goals, such as digital transformation, stakeholder engagement, and continuous learning. The following sections outline important directions and recommendations for enhancing succession planning in today's dynamic business environment, especially by leveraging cutting-edge technologies and fostering an adaptable, learning-focused organizational culture.

Embracing Digital Transformation

The modern business landscape is undergoing a significant shift toward digitalization, a transformation that profoundly impacts all facets of an organization, including succession planning. Digital transformation involves integrating advanced technologies into business processes, enhancing efficiency, and providing valuable insights. In succession planning, digital tools can streamline the process, from identifying potential leaders to ensuring a seamless transition. Performance management software can track employee performance metrics such as key performance indicators (KPIs), goal attainment, and leadership competencies. This data-driven approach enables a more objective evaluation of employees, helping identify high-potential individuals who could be groomed for leadership roles (Martínez-Morán et al., 2021).

Predictive analytics is another powerful tool in digital succession planning. By analyzing historical data, predictive models can forecast future leadership needs, identify potential skill gaps, and suggest training programs to address them. For example, IBM uses predictive analytics to manage its global workforce, predicting turnover and planning for talent gaps well in advance. This foresight allows companies to proactively develop their talent pipeline, ensuring they know of sudden leadership vacancies (Jackson & Dunn-Jensen, 2021). Digital learning platforms are revolutionizing employee development.

These platforms provide access to a wealth of resources, from online courses to webinars, allowing employees to update their skills continually. Companies such as LinkedIn Learning and Coursera offer a broad range of courses that cater to various professional development needs, making it easier for organizations to tailor learning experiences to individual career paths. For instance, Accenture, a leading global consulting firm, encourages employees to complete online certifications and participate in virtual training programs. This initiative enhances their skills and prepares them for future leadership roles within the company (Wassell & Bouchard, 2020).

Furthermore, integrating artificial intelligence (AI) and machine learning (ML) in succession planning processes can significantly improve decision-making. AI-powered platforms can analyze large volumes of data to identify patterns and trends that may not be immediately apparent to human analysts. As an example, AI can help identify soft skills and leadership qualities critical for specific roles but challenging to quantify. These insights enable more accurate matching of candidates to potential leadership positions, enhancing the overall effectiveness of the succession planning process (He & Ortiz, 2021).

The benefits of embracing digital transformation in succession planning are manifold. It enhances the accuracy of talent assessments, improves the efficiency of training and development programs, and provides a more transparent and data-driven approach to leadership transitions. However, companies must also be mindful of the challenges associated with digital transformation. These include ensuring data privacy and security, managing the change process, and addressing the potential resistance from employees who may be uncomfortable with new technologies. Therefore, organizations must invest in training programs to familiarize employees with digital tools and foster a culture of innovation and adaptability (Martínez-Morán et al., 2021).

Fostering a Culture of Continuous Learning

A culture of continuous learning is essential for organizational resilience and growth because it encourages employees to pursue ongoing education and professional development that enables them to adapt to new challenges and opportunities. This culture is especially critical in succession planning, ensuring potential leaders continually enhance their skills and knowledge. To cultivate a culture of continuous learning, organizations must provide ample opportunities for employees to engage in professional development. This process can be achieved through various means, such as offering in-house training programs, sponsoring external courses, and providing access to online learning platforms. Deloitte employees, for example, can access a comprehensive range of learning opportunities, including on-the-job training, formal coursework, and e-learning modules. These programs help employees build the skills needed to excel in their current roles and prepare for future leadership positions (Rondi et al., 2022).

Moreover, organizations should encourage employees to take ownership of their learning and development. This process can be facilitated by creating personalized development plans that align with individual career goals and organizational needs. At Google, for example, employees are encouraged to allocate 20% of their time to projects outside their core job responsibilities, a policy known as the "20% time" rule (Jackson & Dunn-Jensen, 2021). This initiative fosters innovation and continuous learning, as employees can explore new areas of interest and develop new skills

Another critical aspect of fostering a culture of continuous learning is promoting a growth mindset within the organization. This is based on the belief that abilities and intelligence can be developed through dedication and hard work. Organizations can promote this mindset by recognizing and rewarding learning and development efforts. For instance, Microsoft shifted its corporate culture toward a growth mindset by emphasizing learning from failures, encouraging experimentation, and celebrating curiosity and open-mindedness (Wassell & Bouchard, 2020).

Likewise, companies should leverage technology to facilitate continuous learning. Digital learning platforms and learning management systems (LMS) make it easier for employees to access training materials and track their progress. These platforms can also be used to deliver customized learning experiences tailored to the specific needs of each employee group. SAP uses an advanced LMS to deliver personalized learning content to employees, ensuring they have the skills to succeed in their roles and advance in their careers (He & Ortiz, 2021).

Creating a culture of continuous learning also involves leadership commitment. Leaders play a crucial role in setting the tone for learning and development within an organization. They must model lifelong learning behavior, encourage team members to pursue new knowledge, and provide the necessary resources and support. Amazon founder Jeff Bezos has consistently emphasized the importance of learning and experimentation, encouraging employees to "fail fast and learn quickly." This philosophy has been instrumental in fostering a culture of innovation and continuous improvement in the firm (Rondi et al., 2022).

Enhancing Stakeholder Engagement

Effective succession planning requires stakeholders' active involvement and commitment, including senior management, employees, shareholders, and external advisors. Stakeholder engagement is crucial to ensuring alignment with the organization's strategic goals and values and gaining buy-in and support for succession initiatives. To enhance stakeholder engagement, companies must establish transparent communication channels, foster collaboration, and create mechanisms for regular feedback. Table 3.4 illustrates key approaches to enhance stakeholder engagement.

TABLE 3.4 Key Approaches for Enhancing Stakeholder Engagement in Succession Planning

Approach	*Description*	*Example*	*Reference*
Creating Advisory Boards	Advisory boards are typically composed of experienced professionals and industry experts who offer guidance on critical issues, including succession planning. They provide valuable perspectives on leadership development and mediating complex transitions.	At family-owned businesses like Cargill, advisory boards mediate family dynamics and provide impartial advice during the succession planning process.	Matias & Franco, 2021
Regular Stakeholder Meetings	Regular meetings with stakeholders, including senior executives and board members, to review the succession plan help ensure alignment with the organization's vision and objectives and encourage collaboration on leadership transitions.	Procter & Gamble holds regular meetings to review talent pipelines and discuss leadership transitions with senior executives, ensuring that decisions are aligned with organizational needs.	Jackson & Dunn-Jensen, 2021

(Continued)

Table 3.4 (Continued)

Approach	*Description*	*Example*	*Reference*
Conducting Surveys and Feedback	Surveys can gather input from a broader range of stakeholders, including employees and middle management. This feedback helps identify areas for improvement and gauge the organization's readiness for leadership transitions.	IBM conducts employee surveys to gather feedback on leadership development programs and succession planning initiatives, refining strategies based on this input.	Wassell & Bouchard, 2020
Transparency in Communication	Transparent communication about the succession planning process helps build trust and confidence among stakeholders. It involves clearly explaining the criteria for leadership selection and decisions about the succession process.	At PepsiCo, transparent communication about leadership development paths and succession plans fosters a sense of fairness and helps manage stakeholder expectations.	He & Ortiz, 2021
Involving External Advisors	External advisors, such as consultants and executive search firms, provide objective perspectives and expertise in areas where the organization may need more experience. They can mediate conflicts and ensure smooth leadership transitions.	External advisors helped Ford Motor Company navigate leadership transitions and manage family involvement, ensuring the transition aligned with corporate governance standards.	Matias & Franco, 2021

Source: Compiled by author.

Note: Table 3.4 outlines critical strategies for enhancing stakeholder engagement in succession planning, focusing on advisory boards, regular stakeholder meetings, surveys, transparent communication, and the involvement of external advisors.

Developing a Robust Leadership Pipeline

Building a robust leadership pipeline is another fundamental aspect of effective succession planning. A strong pipeline ensures an organization has a pool of qualified and prepared candidates ready to step into leadership roles when needed. This involves identifying high-potential employees early, providing them with development opportunities, and preparing them for future leadership positions.

A first step in developing a robust leadership pipeline is identifying high-potential employees, often called "high-potentials" or "HiPos." These individuals typically exhibit exceptional performance, leadership potential, and a strong alignment with the company's values and culture. Companies can identify high-potential employees through performance evaluations, leadership assessments, and feedback from managers and peers. For example, Johnson and Johnson uses a rigorous assessment process to identify these individuals, including behavioral interviews, assessment centers, and psychometric tests (Atwood, 2020).

Once identified, high-potential employees should be provided targeted development opportunities to enhance their skills and prepare them for leadership roles. This can include rotational assignments, which allow employees to gain experience in different business functions and geographies. For instance, Siemens offers a global leadership development program with international assignments, providing participants with a broad perspective and cross-cultural experience (He & Ortiz, 2021).

Mentorship programs are another useful tool for developing future leaders. By pairing high-potential employees with experienced mentors, companies can facilitate knowledge transfer, provide career guidance, and help mentees navigate the complexities of the business. IBM has a well-established mentorship program that matches senior leaders with emerging talent, fostering a culture of continuous learning and leadership development (Wassell & Bouchard, 2020).

Leadership development courses and executive education programs are also critical components of a robust leadership pipeline. These programs provide high-potential employees with the knowledge and skills to succeed in leadership roles. Harvard Business School offers executive education programs tailored to specific industries and leadership challenges, providing participants with cutting-edge insights and practical tools. Many companies, including Google and Microsoft, partner with top business schools to offer customized leadership development programs for their employees (Jackson & Dunn-Jensen, 2021).

In addition to formal training programs, companies can create opportunities for high-potential employees to take on challenging projects and leadership roles. This hands-on experience is invaluable in developing critical leadership competencies, such as decision-making, strategic thinking, and team management. At Amazon, the company encourages employees to take ownership of key initiatives and projects, providing them with the autonomy and responsibility needed to develop their leadership skills (Rondi et al., 2022).

Companies should focus on building a diverse leadership pipeline reflecting the broader workforce and customer base. This approach involves implementing policies and practices that promote diversity and inclusion, such as diverse hiring practices, unconscious bias training, and inclusive leadership development programs. Intel has set specific diversity goals and regularly reports on progress, ensuring accountability and transparency in building a diverse leadership pipeline (Matias & Franco, 2021).

Addressing Diversity and Inclusion

Diversity and inclusion are increasingly recognized as critical components of effective succession planning. A diverse leadership pipeline reflects the broader workforce and customer base and brings various perspectives and ideas, enhancing decision-making and innovation. Companies that prioritize diversity and inclusion in their succession planning processes are better positioned to navigate the complexities of the global market and respond to the needs of a diverse customer base.

To address diversity and inclusion in succession planning, companies must implement policies and practices promoting equitable employee opportunities. This approach starts with setting clear diversity goals and metrics to measure progress. As an example, Microsoft publicly committed to increasing the representation of women and historically marginalized groups in its workforce and leadership positions. The company regularly reports on its progress, providing transparency and accountability (Wassell & Bouchard, 2020).

Unconscious bias training also helps promote diversity and inclusion in succession planning. Biases, whether conscious or unconscious, can influence hiring and promotion decisions, leading to a need for more diversity in leadership positions. Companies can address this issue by providing training programs that help employees recognize and mitigate their biases. Google offers unconscious bias training to all employees, emphasizing the importance of fair and objective decision-making in the workplace (He & Ortiz, 2021).

In addition to training, companies should implement diverse hiring practices that actively seek out candidates from various backgrounds. This approach can include partnering with diverse professional organizations, attending career fairs targeting historically marginalized groups, and utilizing diverse job boards. Intel has partnered with organizations such as the National Society of Black Engineers and the Society of Women Engineers to attract diverse talent (Matias & Franco, 2021).

Inclusive leadership development programs are also essential for building a diverse leadership pipeline. These programs should address historically marginalized groups' unique challenges and provide them with the skills and support needed to succeed in leadership roles. For instance, Deloitte offers a Women in Leadership program that focuses on developing the skills and confidence of female employees, helping them navigate the challenges of advancing in a predominantly male industry (Jackson & Dunn-Jensen, 2021).

Furthermore, companies should create an inclusive organizational culture that values and respects diversity. This involves promoting open communication, encouraging diverse perspectives, and fostering an environment where all employees feel valued and included. At Salesforce, the company is firmly committed to diversity and inclusion, with initiatives such as the Equality Group, which promotes inclusive practices and policies across the organization (Rondi et al., 2022).

Adapting to Changing Market Conditions

Succession planning must be flexible and adaptable to new challenges and opportunities within an ever-changing business environment. Market conditions can shift rapidly due to technological advancements, economic fluctuations, regulatory changes, and other external factors. To ensure that succession plans remain relevant and practical, companies must regularly review and update them to reflect these changes.

A key strategy for adapting succession planning in changing market conditions is to conduct scenario planning exercises, which involves exploring potential scenarios and assessing their impact on the organization. This process helps companies identify potential risks and opportunities, allowing them to develop contingency plans and strategies to address them. For example, Shell uses scenario planning to explore future energy markets and assess the potential impact on its business. This approach has helped the company prepare for various potential future developments, from shifts in energy demand to changes in environmental regulations (He & Ortiz, 2021).

Another important aspect of adapting succession planning during changing market conditions is maintaining a flexible talent management strategy, which involves being open to hiring external candidates for key leadership positions, especially when specific expertise is needed to navigate new challenges. For instance, when Microsoft faced challenges in transitioning to cloud computing, the company hired a CEO who brought extensive experience in cloud technologies. This strategic decision helped Microsoft successfully navigate the shift to cloud services and regain its position as a technology leader (Matias & Franco, 2021).

In addition to external hiring, companies can focus on developing internal talent to ensure they have the skills and knowledge needed to address new challenges. This approach can involve offering specialized training programs, providing opportunities for cross-functional experience, and encouraging employees to stay current with industry trends and developments. For example, IBM has a comprehensive leadership development program that includes training on emerging technologies, such as artificial intelligence and blockchain, ensuring its leaders are prepared to navigate the rapidly evolving technology landscape (Wassell & Bouchard, 2020).

Succession planning must also consider the potential impact of mergers and acquisitions (M&A) on leadership transitions. M&A activities can significantly alter the organizational structure, creating new leadership roles or eliminating existing ones. Companies must be prepared to manage these changes and ensure the succession plan aligns with the new organizational reality. For instance, after the acquisition of Time Warner, AT&T had to integrate new leadership teams and align them with its strategic goals. The company successfully navigated this transition by developing a comprehensive succession plan that addressed the unique challenges of the merger (Rondi et al., 2022).

Companies must also consider the impact of regulatory changes on succession planning. Regulatory environments vary significantly across regions and industries, affecting leadership requirements and qualifications. For example, in the financial services industry, regulatory changes often impact the qualifications and responsibilities of key executives, such as chief compliance officers and risk officers. Companies must be current with regulatory developments and ensure that their succession plans comply with relevant laws and regulations (Jackson & Dunn-Jensen, 2021).

Conclusion

Succession planning is critical to organizational strategy and ensures continuity and stability during leadership transitions. While traditional succession planning methods have proven effective in many cases, they also face several challenges and limitations. By incorporating best practices and innovative approaches, companies can enhance the effectiveness of their succession plans and ensure long-term success. Integrating digital tools, continuous learning, stakeholder engagement, strategic alignment, leadership pipeline development, diversity and inclusion, and adaptability to market conditions are key factors that can improve succession planning outcomes. As the business landscape continues to evolve, companies must remain proactive and forward-thinking in their approach to succession planning. By doing so, they can ensure they are well-prepared for future leadership transitions and maintain their competitive advantage in a rapidly changing environment.

Traditional succession planning remains vital for business continuity, especially in family-owned enterprises. While proven effective in many cases, the planning processes also have had challenges and limitations. By incorporating best practices and innovative approaches, businesses can enhance the effectiveness of their succession plans and ensure long-term success (Tucker, 2020).

Continued changes in the business climate will make integrating technology, adaptive strategies, and stakeholder engagement crucial in preparing for the future of succession planning, which is an ongoing process requiring continuous attention and adaptation. Businesses must remain vigilant and proactive in identifying potential leaders and preparing them for future roles. By doing so, they can ensure that leadership transitions occur smoothly, and that the organization remains resilient and competitive in the face of change. The case studies and research presented in this chapter clearly demonstrate that effective succession planning is critical to business continuity and long-term success.

References

Ahmad, S., Omar, R., & Quoquab, F. (2021). Family firms' sustainable longevity: The role of family involvement in business and innovation capability. *Journal of Family Business Management*, *11*(1), 86–106. 10.1108/JFBM-12-2019-0081

Al Aina, R., & Atan, T. (2020). The impact of implementing talent management practices on sustainable organizational performance. *Sustainability*, *12*(20), 8372. 10.3390/su12208372

Al Suwaidi, M., Jabeen, F., Stachowicz-Stanusch, A., & Webb, M. (2020). Determinants linked to executive succession planning in public sector organizations. *Vision*, *24*(3), 284–299. 10.1177/0972262920932405

Anggadwita, G., Profityo, W. B., Alamanda, D. T., & Permatasari, A. (2020). Cultural values and their implications to family business succession: A case study of small Chinese-owned family businesses in Bandung, Indonesia. *Journal of Family Business Management*, *10*(4), 281–292. 10.1108/JFBM-03-2019-0017

Atwood, C. G. (2020). *Succession planning basics* (2nd ed.). Association for Talent Development.

Campopiano, G., Calabrò, A., & Basco, R. (2020). The "most wanted": The role of family strategic resources and family involvement in CEO succession intention. *Family Business Review*, *33*(3), 284–309. 10.1177/0894486520927289

Chirapanda, S. (2020). Identification of success factors for sustainability in family businesses: Case study method and exploratory research in Japan. *Journal of Family Business Management*, *10*(1), 58–75. 10.1108/JFBM-05-2019-0030

Ge, B., & Campopiano, G. (2022). Knowledge management in family business succession: Current trends and future directions. *Journal of Knowledge Management*, *26*(2), 326–349. 10.1108/JKM-09-2020-0701

He, J., & Ortiz, J. (2021). Sustainable business modeling: The need for innovative design thinking. *Journal of Cleaner Production*, *298*, 126751. 10.1016/j.jclepro.2021.126751

Jackson, N. C., & Dunn-Jensen, L. M. (2021). Leadership succession planning for today's digital transformation economy: Key factors to build for competency and innovation. *Business Horizons*, *64*(2), 273–284. 10.1016/j.bushor.2020.11.008

Mahusain, M. A., & Raman Nair, S. (2022). Individual differences in succession planning and leadership qualities: A conceptual paper. *Asia-Pacific Journal of Innovation in Hospitality and Tourism*, *11*(1), 293–307.

Marques, A. P., & da Silva, L. A. (2020). Portuguese and Brazilian family business: In between urgency and delay perceptions in the succession process. *European Journal of Social Sciences*, *3*(2), 34–42. 10.26417/940lth96j

Martínez-Morán, P. C., Urgoiti, J. M. F.-R., Díez, F., & Solabarrieta, J. (2021). The digital transformation of the talent management process: A Spanish business case. *Sustainability*, *13*(4), 2264. 10.3390/su13042264

Matias, C., & Franco, M. (2021). The role of the family council and protocol in planning the succession process in family firms. *Journal of Family Business Management*, *11*(4), 440–461. 10.1108/JFBM-01-2020-0004

Musa, B. M., & Dissanayake, S. (2014). Leadership succession problem: An examination of small family businesses. *European Journal of Business and Management*, *6*(34), 301–306. 10.13140/RG.2.2.16036.45443

Porfírio, J. A., Felício, J. A., & Carrilho, T. (2020). Family business succession: Analysis of the drivers of success based on entrepreneurship theory. *Journal of Business Research*, *115*, 250–257. 10.1016/j.jbusres.2019.11.054

Rondi, E., Überbacher, R., von Schlenk-Barnsdorf, L., De Massis, A., & Hülsbeck, M. (2022). One for all, all for one: A mutual gains perspective on HRM and innovation management practices in family firms. *Journal of Family Business Strategy*, *13*(2), 100394. 10.1016/j.jfbs.2020.100394

Soares, G. G., da Silva Braga, V. L., da Encarnação Marques, C. S., & Ratten, V. (2021). Corporate entrepreneurship education's impact on family business sustainability: A case study in Brazil. *The International Journal of Management Education*, *19*(1), 100424. 10.1016/j.ijme.2020.100424

Tirdasari, N. L., & Dhewanto, W. (2020). When is the right time for succession? Multiple cases of family businesses in Indonesia. *Journal of Family Business Management*, *10*(4), 349–359. 10.1108/JFBM-10-2019-0064

Tucker, C. A. (2020). Succession planning for academic nursing. *Journal of Professional Nursing*, *36*(5), 334–342. 10.1016/j.profnurs.2020.02.002

Umans, I., Lybaert, N., Steijvers, T., & Voordeckers, W. (2021). The influence of transgenerational succession intentions on the succession planning process: The moderating role of high-quality relationships. *Journal of Family Business Strategy*, *12*(2), 100269. 10.1016/j.jfbs.2018.12.002

Wassell, S., & Bouchard, M. (2020). Rebooting strategic human resource management: Integrating technology to drive talent management. *International Journal of Human Resources Development and Management*, *20*(2), 93–113. 10.1504/IJHRDM.2020.106275

4

EMPLOYEE OWNERSHIP IN SUCCESSION PLANNING

Michael Palmieri and Chris Cooper

Introduction

Business owners can spend a lifetime building their business. Typically, the business represents a large (or the largest) financial investment and a major personal and emotional investment. The business plays a central role in the owner's life, a way of making a living, a sense of purpose, and a type of legacy. However, a lack of a succession plan, or one done poorly, can destroy all these things quickly.

In the next 5–10 years, the number of baby boomer business owners (and many Gen Xers) needing to transition out of their business will result in one of our most significant intergenerational wealth transfers. Currently, approximately half of all small businesses are owned by individuals who are 55 years old or older. How this transition happens will be a significant issue not only for the business owners and their families but also for employees, economic developers, policymakers and politicians, and the communities across the country where these companies are located. In small towns and rural areas across the United States, the loss of a single business can be keenly felt. Perhaps one of the area's biggest employers has shut down, or an important provider of a needed service is no longer available. It is not hard to see how such an event can have a cascading impact on secondary businesses and communities.

This chapter reviews what the current and ongoing wave of small business transitions will mean for rural areas and small towns and provides a context for business owners' challenges and issues as they begin and develop their succession plans. It then discusses three forms of broad-based employee ownership and how they can address business owners' succession needs. Finally, it addresses common misconceptions about employee ownership that deter business owners and their advisors from considering a sale to employees.

DOI: 10.4324/9781003497462-4

Baby Boomer and Gen X Business Owner Retirements

The U.S. is in the middle of a significant economic development challenge that will affect nearly 20% of the nation's labor force: baby boomer retirements. Baby boomers, defined as individuals between 60–78 years old, are retiring at a staggering rate of 10,000 a day. In most localities, this group owns half of all privately held businesses. However, this number is even higher in rural areas where baby boomers comprise a larger population (Federal Reserve Banks, 2024). Today, baby boomer business owners own 2.9 million firms, employing 32 million people and representing over $6.5 trillion in revenue. Cities and states nationwide that rely on these businesses staying open to provide good-paying jobs and the needed tax base to keep communities thriving must be serious and proactive in response to what is often termed the "silver tsunami."

The need is profound. According to a 2022 survey, 80% of business owners do not have a written succession plan in place, meaning there is no plan for what to do after the current owner retires, becomes incapacitated, or dies "on the job" (Business Enterprise Institute, 2023). For many of these businesses, the owner's retirement can result in the business being packaged for a quick sale, a quiet liquidation, or another catastrophic event that can leave the owner's family, the employees, and the broader community suffering.

In addition, small businesses actively planning a succession strategy find it more challenging to sell their businesses (Biery, 2017). Fewer family-owned businesses pass to the next generation, and finding a buyer outside the family is difficult. The numbers are even starker for companies operating over 25 years with 20–100 employees in key service sectors, including grocery stores, food manufacturing, home care agencies, residential care facilities, and childcare centers. Businesses with these characteristics have a 9 to 1 ratio of business closures to business sales (ICA Group, 2018).

Without a timely and forward-thinking approach to succession planning, business owners struggle to catch up when circumstances require quick action. This often results in options that range from suboptimal to catastrophic for the business, the business owner, the employees, and the community. Still, it is essential to remember that there are reasons why so few business owners have a formal succession plan. The process is multi-step and requires technical, complicated, emotional, and challenging considerations to work through.

The Succession Process

Nearly all business owners intuitively understand the need to plan for what happens when they leave their company, yet so many choose not to create a formal plan. There are many reasons for this, and they all impact the success of this last test of entrepreneurship. One of the main impediments to successful ownership succession is the business owner. A typical owner (assuming there is such a person) spends much more time working in the business than on the business. An owner's entire life and sense of self-worth can be so closely tied to the business that it can be hard to step back. The difference between the expectations and the reality of business value can induce delay based on the hope that next year will bring a windfall. Alternatively, it may be as simple as owners not wanting to quit what they love doing.

Despite all these factors, every business owner will eventually exit their company—one way or another. Some options allow a business owner to begin cashing out of the business while staying involved. Creating a plan that provides value for the business owner while addressing the business's goals and objectives and the owner's life after succession is possible.

Essential Items in a Succession Plan:

1 **Goals and Objectives**—It is important for business owners to consider what they want and need for themselves and their families, for the business going forward, for their employees, and for the community.
2 **Assessment of Business Worth**—Do they have realistic expectations of the business's value, and will that be enough to finance their retirement?
3 **Exploration of Transfer Options**—Many methods and strategies exist for transferring a business, but a business rarely has all those options. A realistic exploration of likely transfer options must be part of the planning.
4 **Plan Development and Implementation**—Many business owners spend time and money preparing a succession plan, only to let it collect dust on the shelf.
5 **Personal Planning**—Figuring out the next stage of life can be difficult for a business owner. While this includes financial and estate planning, it also includes identifying how they will spend their time and energy.

In each of these steps, business owners will face difficult, sometimes existential, questions that must be addressed. These can include dealing with a change in purpose, understanding the expectations of family members (whether they work in the business or not), and even highly emotional considerations of personal mortality or legacy.

At one point, it was not uncommon to see a business be in its third or fourth generation of family ownership; it was an important part of the family legacy and the expectations for a family business. However, second- and third-generation business ownership is less common today. Today, a typical business owner has likely been successful enough to send their children to college, permitting them to find their own path and perhaps a profession. Witnessing the amount of effort and time away from the family that parents spent to build the business or finding a preferred profession of their own disincentivizes children to choose the same path.

Selling to an outsider is an appealing option for business owners and the goal of most for several reasons. Absent a distressed or liquidation situation, an outside sale can provide the selling owner with the best price for the business. The potential downside is that after the transaction is complete, owners have no control over the changes implemented in (and on) the company, including name changes, layoffs, dismantling of the business, and so on. Moreover, a viable external buyer is not always easy to find. Buyers have choices in where they invest their money, and no matter how financially successful it is, a specific business is not always of interest to buyers or investors.

What should a business owner do if neither a financial investor nor children are prepared to purchase and run the business? There is an alternative option for the business owner: selling to most or all employees. A sale to employees can meet several goals for the selling owner. All employee ownership options provide a fair sale price for the business. They also have enough flexibility that the seller can stay active in the business if desired. When the legacy of the business is important, selling to employees who helped build the business can be the next best thing to transfer the business to heirs.

For successful businesses having trouble locating an outside buyer, employee ownership models allow owners to create the buyer of their business. Furthermore, employee ownership is a good alternative for those who do not find a sale to private equity appealing.

In the U.S., three major employee-owned business models are used for succession planning: employee stock ownership plans (ESOPs), worker-owned cooperatives, and employee ownership trusts (EOTs). One characteristic these models share is their broad-based structures that include most, if not all, employees in the ownership structure. This differentiates them from management or key-person buyouts, where a select minority of employees purchase the business.

What Is Employee Ownership?

On its face, employee ownership seems straightforward—an arrangement where employees have a financial stake in the company (National Center for Employee Ownership [NCEO], n.d.-d). However, the concept is not so simple. A literature review discloses numerous examples that, in practice, seem very different. Worker cooperatives, employee stock ownership plans, employee share purchase plans, employee stock option plans, employee-owned trusts, profit sharing, and gainsharing plans—all of these (and more) are examples where employees have a financial stake in the firm.

So, how does one make sense of employee ownership models? To answer this question, it is helpful to unpack essential elements in ownership. The concept

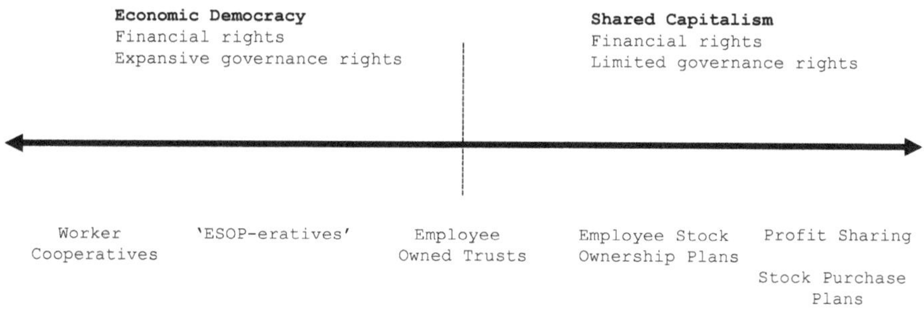

FIGURE 4.1 Framework for Understanding Shared Ownership.

Source: Compiled by authors.

of ownership generally confers two dimensions of rights: the right to control use and the right to control the enjoyment of its returns (Ben-Ner & Jones, 1995). Applying this to businesses, "control of use" refers to determining the objectives of the business, what positions exist within it, and how they are filled and carried out—what can be termed governance rights. Control over the "enjoyment of its returns" refers to any financial and physical payoffs the business produces—what can be termed financial rights. Despite their differences, what employee-owned firms of all kinds have in common is that they give employees rights over the company's returns, use, or some combination of both. The kinds of rights employees hold, the extent of those rights, and the mechanisms those rights are exercised through differentiate employee ownership models. Using the allocation of financial and governance rights amongst employees as a distinguishing feature, one can place the vast array of existing models onto a continuum with two poles: economic democracy and shared capitalism (see Figure 4.1).

Economic Democracy

Firms practicing economic democracy give employees expansive governance and financial rights over the business (Ellerman, 1990). The most ubiquitous model is the worker cooperative, where individuals become members by purchasing a membership share. Once members, workers have the right to participate in the firm's financial success through "patronage." This takes the form of workers receiving allocations of a portion of the business's profits at the end of the year based on their labor contribution. Members of a worker cooperative also have meaningful governance rights. This includes voting for and having representation on the board of directors (Democracy at Work Institute [DAWI], n.d.). Importantly, votes are based on the principle of one worker, one vote, hence economic democracy (Dahl, 1985).

Shared Capitalism

Firms practicing models of shared capitalism typically provide fewer governance rights and adhere to a corporate structure familiar to outside observers. These models differ from conventional businesses because they offer employees a range of financial rights, allowing them to participate in the firm's financial success (Kruse et al., 2010). For example, in ESOPs, employees are granted shares of company stock and cash each year, which are credited to individual employee accounts. When employees leave or retire, the company must repurchase shares and provide the employee-owner with the monetary value of their accounts in cash.

Other models provide financial ownership using shares, but unlike ESOPs, shares in the company are usually purchased by employees. Such plans include employee share purchase plans, which allow for the purchase of company stock at a discount, and employee stock option plans, which allow employees to purchase stock at a set purchase price for 10 years, allowing employees to benefit from the stock's future gains.

The shared capitalism category can also include models providing employees financial rights without individual stock ownership. For example, EOTs hold company shares in a single trust on behalf of all employees, who receive portions of the company's yearly profits (Michael, 2017). Profit sharing and gainsharing programs also provide employees with a portion of the profits generated by the company each year but do so without using a trust. In profit-sharing schemes, the monetary value of these bonuses is tied to overall company profitability, while gainsharing ties bonuses to specified benchmarks such as productivity or waste reduction (Jones et al., 1994).

While the two poles of economic democracy and shared capitalism help make sense of the diversity of models, there is still a significant variation within and between models that lean towards either pole. For example, in worker cooperatives, governance rights, at minimum, include electing the board of directors, but these rights can extend to managing day-to-day operations. Likewise, ESOPs and other employee trusts can own anywhere from 1% to 100% of company stock, which can impact the financial rights workers enjoy. Some employee ownership models combine features of shared capitalism with governance rights associated with economic democracy. For example, the United Kingdom's (U.K.) John Lewis Partnership, one of the largest and oldest EOTs in the world, shares profits with workers and has a democratically elected council system that provides input on decision-making and company management (Cathcart, 2013). Similarly, some companies with ESOPs provide expanded governance rights, similar to worker cooperatives, in what is colloquially termed an "ESOP-erative" (Staubus, 2017). Finally, it is common for companies to layer different programs on top of one another. For example, companies with an ESOP can include additional profit-sharing programs. All employee ownership models are complemented by various human resource and management practices that stymie or encourage the development of an ownership culture (Kruse et al., 2004).

All the forms outlined above seek to broaden ownership of productive assets but do so in various ways not captured by a prototypical example. As one pre-eminent field scholar stated, "Employee ownership is not a simple, unidimensional concept that permits an easy classification of a firm as 'employee-owned' or of an employee as an 'employee-owner'" (Kruse, 2002, p. 66). As such, "generalizations about employee share ownership have to be made cautiously" (Park et al., 2004, p.3). The continuum presented here is no different. Key differences are found between models of shared capitalism and economic democracy, but no hard lines exist between the two poles. Instead, economic democracy and shared capitalism overlap in the real world of employee ownership, and they can be adapted to fit the needs and goals of a given business.

Three Models of Broad-Based Employee Ownership

When focusing on models of broad-based employee ownership most often used as succession planning tools, our focus narrows to three models: employee stock ownership plans (ESOPs), worker cooperatives, and employee-owned trusts (EOTs). All three models are used successfully in the U.S. to transition the ownership of a business from the selling owner to employees. Each model has professional service providers, specialists, and support organizations who can assist with implementing the transition process. Table 4.1 provides some basic information about the prevalence of each model in the U.S.

A sale to employees has many appealing aspects, including the ability to ensure the legacy of the business, reward the people who helped build it, and continue operations in the community it is located. This might be a viable option for the business owner who does not have an heir waiting or an outside buyer willing to make a bona fide offer. In some respects, these three options allow an owner to create a buyer for the business where one did not previously exist.

TABLE 4.1 Broad-Based Employee Ownership in the U.S.

Business Model	*Number of Firms*	*Number of Employees*	*History*
Worker Cooperative	750	10,000	1880s
Employee Stock Ownership Plan	6,500	10.3 million	1974
Employee-Owned Trust	40	400	2010s

Note: ESOP estimates obtained from (NCEO, n.d.-c).
Cooperative estimates obtained from (DAWI, 2024).
Employee-owned trust estimates obtained from (Broughton et al., 2022).

In addition, depending on the model, the resulting sale price will be a middle-range fair market value standard, and the sale can be combined with substantial tax breaks for the seller and the business. Table 4.2 provides details on each of the three models as they relate to succession planning.

TABLE 4.2 Broad-Based Employee Ownership and Succession Planning

	Employee Stock Ownership Plans	*Worker Cooperatives*	*Employee-Owned Trusts*
What Kinds of Companies?	• Established companies with owners seeking ownership transition. • Companies must be C corporations or S corporations, or LLCs taxed as a C or S corporation.	• Typically, smaller companies with a philosophical commitment to democratic corporate governance. • Companies looking for a lower-cost way to set up an employee ownership plan.	• Companies who want to give legal protection for preserving legacy, community, social, and environmental goals, or that do not want to comply with rules and costs of an ESOP and are willing to trade the tax benefits to do so.
Primary Uses	• Transferring ownership to employees in closely held companies. • Providing incentives and rewards broadly to the workforce.	• Starting up a new company. • Transferring ownership to employees in closely held companies.	• Preserving culture, protecting workforce, or maintaining values-based decision-making processes. • Transferring ownership to employees in closely held companies.
Owner Tax Benefits	• Sellers can defer capital gains taxes on a sale if the sale meets certain requirements. • Purchase of shares by the ESOP can be funded with pretax dollars out of future profits.	• Sellers can defer capital gains taxes on a sale if the sale meets certain requirements.	None.

(*Continued*)

Table 4.2 (Continued)

	Employee Stock Ownership Plans	*Worker Cooperatives*	*Employee-Owned Trusts*
Company Tax benefits	• Contributions are tax-deductible, including principal and interest payments on ESOP loan. • Profits attributable to the ESOP trust in an S corporation ESOP are not taxable.	• Patronage (dividends paid out to members of the worker cooperative) are tax-deductible to the company.	• Profit sharing paid to employees is a deductible expense.
Set-up & Ongoing Costs	Set-up: Between $100K to $300K, depends on company size/ complexity. Ongoing: Between $20K and $30K, depending on size.	Set-up: Between $10,000 to $30,000. Ongoing: not significant.	Set-up: Between $20K and $50K. Ongoing: not significant.
Governance	The ESOP Trust is the legal shareholder. The trustee is appointed by the board. The trustee votes the shares. Employees have limited voting rights unless the company chooses to provide greater rights.	Workers decide if they want to become a member (not mandatory). Each worker-member has one vote, and members elect the board of directors. The board typically includes worker-members.	Companies can choose the control rights the trust exercises and whether employees have a say. The seller generally determines the purpose toward which the trust must operate and what role the employees have in governing the trust.
Complexity	Subject to detailed federal rules. More complicated than other employee ownership plans, but less complicated than sale to another company.	Minimal complexity, relatively straightforward.	Less complicated than ESOPs, more flexible than worker cooperatives.

Source: Compiled by authors.

Employee Stock Ownership Plans

Employee stock ownership plans (ESOPs) are the most common form of broad-based employee ownership in the U.S. An estimated 6,533 companies have an ESOP that owns at least a portion of the company (NCEO n.d.-c). This overall number includes publicly traded companies with ESOPs, but privately held companies make up most of these plans (5,973). ESOPs cover over 10 million active workers and hold $2.1 trillion in assets. They exist in all major industries but are most common in manufacturing. Geographically, most ESOPs are in urban areas but have a measurable footprint in rural areas, too. According to one analysis, 28% of ESOPs are in rural areas and employ roughly 300,000 individuals who hold an average of $155,329 in their accounts, demonstrating that this employee ownership model can succeed in the rural context (Kruse et al., 2024).

ESOPs were the idea of Louis Kelso, an investment banker in San Francisco who, in the 1950s and 60s, started what came to be called "Kelso Plans." In establishing these plans, he proved a retirement plan that invested in the sponsoring company's stock helped workers generate long-term wealth. Kelso built political support for federal legislation that would lead to the creation and development of ESOPs (Menke, 2011). Through his efforts, the federal government formally recognized the structure under the Employment Retirement Income Security Act (ERISA) of 1974. Importantly, the legislation included significant tax breaks to encourage the adoption of ESOPs.

An ESOP is a qualified retirement plan trust that holds the sponsoring company's stock for participating employees. ESOPs share aspects with other qualified retirement plans with key differences. First, ESOPs invest primarily in the sponsoring company's stock. Second, all contributions are from the employer. Third, ESOPs can borrow money to partially or fully purchase a company.

Most ESOP companies are created as part of a succession planning event for the business owner, who can sell anywhere from 1% to 100% of the business. The company can remain a minority ESOP forever; it is not required to become 100% employee-owned. Similarly, a sale to an ESOP can be combined with other transfer options, such as a sale to family members or key management.

ESOPs are typically the most expensive of the three options. However, the tax breaks can offset many, if not all, of these costs. Thus, set-up costs for an ESOP are typically on par or lower than the average sale to an outside or strategic buyer. Because of these costs and some technical aspects related to ESOPs, they are most feasible in companies with 30–35 employees or more.

ESOPs are complex. ERISA law, which recognizes and regulates ESOPs, requires knowledge and expertise to ensure the transaction complies with rules and regulations. However, a robust community of service providers exists, including bankers, attorneys, third-party administrators, and trustees, that can help navigate the details of ESOPs and ensure the goals and objectives of the business owner are met. Despite their complexity, ESOPs offer many benefits to the seller, the employees, and the company. They are still the most common choice for business owners seeking to cash out equity from their business or exit the business entirely through a sale to employees.

Worker Cooperatives

Worker cooperatives have a long history in the U.S., with notable examples emerging in the late 19th century (Leikin, 2005). Then, as now, worker cooperatives were used to create workplaces that provided workers with autonomy, employment stability, and decent working conditions. Today, an estimated 751 known worker cooperatives in the U.S. employ approximately 10,000 workers (DAWI, 2024). Worker cooperatives exist in nearly every industry, and are most common in food and beverage, business support services, agriculture, and manufacturing. Since 2009 the number of worker cooperatives has grown rapidly, tripling over the past 15 years (Deller et al., 2009).

Worker cooperatives are part of the broader family of cooperatives, including agricultural cooperatives (Ocean Spray), consumer cooperatives (REI), insurance mutuals (Nationwide), purchasing cooperatives (ACE Hardware), utility cooperatives, and housing cooperatives. A key characteristic is that they are owned and democratically controlled by those who work for them or utilize the services provided. This means, for example, Ocean Spray is owned by the producers who supply the cooperative with cranberries. In a worker cooperative, the business is owned by those working there.

It is worth noting the role of cooperatives in rural development. Historically, cooperatives address economic or social needs that the market fails to provide (Pitman, 2018). In the 1930s, motivated by profit-seeking, power companies ignored the development of electricity in rural areas. Instead, consumer-owned electric cooperatives organized by rural citizens brought electricity to these areas. Agricultural cooperatives are important in rural development, too, enabling farmers to buy necessary supplies and services and distribute, market, and sell their products. Today, 2 million farmers are members of more than 2,100 cooperatives in the U.S. (National Cooperative Business Association CLUSA International, n.d.). Like their cooperative relatives, worker cooperatives are an important tool that benefits its members and communities. Business owners can sell their businesses at a fair price, workers are provided with good jobs and opportunities for wealth building, and the community retains businesses.

A worker cooperative is a formal corporate entity. This fact has important implications. First, the decision to become a worker cooperative is complete—there is no option to become a 20% or 30% cooperative. Sales to a cooperative can take the form of a stepped transaction, but this assumes that the employees will eventually own 100% of the company. Second, strong governance rights for worker members are baked into this model. Any worker who becomes a cooperative member can elect and serve on the board of directors. In addition, worker cooperatives operate on one person, one vote, meaning each worker member has one share and can cast one vote in major corporate decisions. Third, becoming a member is optional. Typically, worker cooperatives set up some probationary period that new employees must complete before being able to apply for membership. Once conditions are satisfied, employees can apply for membership. Finally, worker members participate in the firm's financial success through "patronage." This takes the form of workers receiving allocations of a portion of the business's profits at the end of the year based on their labor contribution to the cooperative (U.S. Federation of Worker Cooperatives, n.d.).

Worker cooperatives are not federally regulated retirement plans, making their set-up and annual costs much lower. Accordingly, smaller companies find the model better suited to their needs. Because no federal law exists, cooperative law operates at the state level. Each state has slightly different statutes that define how the cooperative is set up. Some statutes are more flexible than others, and nothing prevents a company from incorporating under a cooperative statute in a state outside where the business operates.

The number of advisors with expertise in setting up and maintaining a worker cooperative has grown over the last decade, making it relatively easy to find professional support. The democratic voting rights built into the model are sometimes a culture shock to entrepreneurs not already committed to democratic corporate governance. However, on a day-to-day basis, most worker cooperatives operate like any other business with a board, management team, and workers. Because of the broader governance rights inherent in the model, training and educating employees is vital to success. On this front, there is a vibrant community of support organizations that can help develop and deliver the needed education and training, ensuring a smooth transition and continued growth.

Employee-Owned Trusts

A third model of broad-based employee ownership is an Employee-Owned Trust (EOT). Unlike ESOPs and worker cooperatives, the history of EOTs can be traced back to the U.K., where they are the dominant form of employee ownership (Pendleton et al., 2023). EOTs are relatively new within the U.S., with an estimated 40 in operation in 2022 (Broughton et al., 2022). In the U.S., EOTs are usually structured as perpetual purpose trusts. These have historically been used in asset management and estate planning to hold and protect assets for beneficiaries. An EOT is simply a way of designing a perpetual purpose trust to become a succession planning tool capable of implementing employee ownership.

Typically, in an EOT, the company is held in trust, with the primary purpose of the trust defined as upholding the mission, values, and purpose of the company (Everett et al., 2024). One common purpose among EOTs is sharing company success with employees. As in an ESOP, the selling owner will establish a trust, and the selling owner's stock will be redeemed by the trust using a mix of financing from the selling owner and other financial lenders. The selling owner and financers are paid over time through company cash flow. Unlike ESOPs and worker cooperatives, the selling owner has no capital gains tax benefit.

One of the most attractive aspects of EOTs is their flexibility in structuring the governance and financial rights for employees. This flexibility enables EOTs to avoid the complexities and costs associated with ESOPs and the changes to corporate governance associated with worker cooperatives. Because EOTs are not qualified retirement plans, the implementation and ongoing costs are lower than those of ESOPs. Absent federal legislation, EOTs face a similar legal landscape as worker cooperatives, where statutes vary from state to state (Michael, 2017). Unlike worker cooperatives, the EOT structure does not dictate how governance operates. While there will be a trustee in any EOT, the ways workers participate in corporate decision-making processes are adaptable to the needs of the business, varying between the democratic style of a worker cooperative or that found in traditional corporate structures. How employees participate is also flexible. Workers can automatically participate upon being hired, or participation can be restricted to employees meeting specific requirements. Typically, EOTs implement a profit-sharing plan in which current employees receive a percentage of company profits following a custom formula. These payments are usually made at the corporate level and are tax-deductible. One final aspect of EOTs that appeals to business owners is their unique ability to enshrine other values into the business itself. These include practices related to the company's commitment to the environment, community, or other stakeholders; values-driven hiring and sourcing of materials; or protecting the company from a future sale out of employee ownership.

EOTs are the most flexible broad-based employee ownership option, enabling the selling owner to design the governance and financial aspects of employee ownership in ways that reflect the company's mission and operations. This form of broad-based employee ownership is still in its infancy. As the number of EOTs and awareness about them grows, so too does the number of experts who assist in implementing them.

Common Misconceptions

Broad-based models of employee ownership are well-poised to meet the needs of selling owners. A significant obstacle to expanding employee ownership is more awareness among business owners, professional advisors, economic development professionals, policymakers, and business support organizations. Even those familiar with employee ownership may need clarification about what it means, how it operates in practice, its impacts on workers and companies, or how successful implementation can be ensured. This section addresses common misconceptions by drawing on practical experience and research published over the past four decades.

Employees Cannot Afford to Purchase the Business

When first hearing about the option to sell a company to employees, it is common to ask how the sale occurs. Lurking in the background is the observation that, in most companies, workers lack the capital to purchase the business, and even if they did have the funds, they would not be interested in taking on that level of risk. This is one of the most common misunderstandings about how businesses are sold to employees via broad-based employee ownership models. Workers need not raise funds to purchase the business. Instead, financing is organized through a mix of loans and seller financing, paid back through the company profits. This financing model overcomes the fundamental issue of most employees lacking the capital to purchase the company and reduces the risk employees take when the company becomes employee-owned.

Employee Ownership Is a Risky Proposition for Workers

Another common concern is that employee ownership is a risky investment for workers. A truthful response is, yes, employee ownership models involve risk, as does private business ownership. However, risk-based concerns often misunderstand the nature and level of risk associated with different forms of employee ownership and how those risks can be minimized.

The first concern is that employees are granted an ownership stake in their business by making wage or benefit concessions. High-profile cases of this occurring exist. However, the evidence finds that these cases are the exception. A study of 1,000 public firms that adopted models of employee ownership found only 40 reports of wage concessions (Blasi & Kruse, 1992). Another comprehensive study of ESOP adoptions in public companies between 1980 and 2001 reported that employee wages either remained constant or increased (Kim & Ouimet, 2014). Likewise, wages in employee-owned companies are higher or on par with comparable companies in privately held ESOP companies (Kardas et al., 1998; NCEO, 2017), worker cooperatives (Burdin & Dean, 2009; Palmer, 2020), and companies practicing profit sharing (Long & Fang, 2012). Using a National Bureau of Economic Research dataset of 40,000 employees, Buchele et al. (2010) find "no evidence that employees' ownership gains are offset by lower wages or benefits" (p. 374). Overall, the accumulated evidence on this question suggests that the economic returns of employee ownership models "come on top of standard pay and benefits" and that "workers are not sacrificing for risky pay" (Blasi et al., 2018, p. 48). Thus, employee ownership's economic benefits can be considered "gravy on top of other wealth" rather than a substitute for wages or other benefits (Kruse et al., 2019, p. 23).

In ESOPs, contributions to employee accounts are company-financed. Likewise, in EOTs, profit sharing comes at no cost to employees. Worker cooperatives require an initial membership share purchase, which requires using employee income. This membership share is purchased once, and, once purchased, the annual distribution of profits to members comes at no additional cost. Some worker cooperatives allow prospective members to purchase membership shares over time via payroll deductions, making the purchase less onerous. Simply put, what is at risk is often not the individual employees' income; when it is, the amount is much less than assumed.

Another common concern is that employee ownership models concentrate workers' investments in a single asset because they replace other defined benefit plans or are the only retirement plans offered. In the U.S., studies find that ESOP companies are more likely to have a second retirement plan in addition to the ESOP than traditional companies are to offer any plan (Ernst & Young, 2022; Rodgers & Keeling, 2010). Research also shows that ESOP companies provide higher contributions to those plans when compared to traditional companies (Blasi et al., 2013; Kruse, 2002; NCEO, n.d.-a; Rodgers, 2010). Diversification risk is a real concern. However, it can be greatly mitigated by providing an additional retirement plan, and evidence shows that many employee-owned companies do just that. Another way to consider this type of risk is to review the level of defaults on the loans used to transition to employee ownership. A study of leveraged ESOPs between 2009 and 2013 found these loans had an annual default rate of .2% (NCEO, n.d.-b).

The U.S.' general state of retirement savings also places the diversification argument in perspective. According to the Survey of Consumer Finances, more than 50% of U.S. households report zero retirement savings (USAFacts Team, 2023), and nearly 40% lack enough money to cover a $400 emergency expense (Daniel, 2023). For these individuals, wealth-building opportunities of any kind are an improvement from their current situation. An analysis of data from the U.S. General Social Survey reported that employees working at ESOP companies had, on average, $134,000 in wealth from company stock (Flamisch, 2018). A study of low- and moderate-income employee-owners found their wealth was many times higher than the national averages for their respective demographic groups. For example, Black women in the study group held $55,000 in total wealth compared to the national average of $200 (Boguslaw & Schur, 2019). Similarly, studies of worker cooperatives find that the average annual profit distribution is over $8,000 (Palmer, 2020).

Finally, one must consider another risk that, on average, is lower for workers in employee-owned firms: job loss. Unemployment presents risks to workers' financial well-being, family stability, and mental and physical health. Evidence shows that employee-owned companies are less likely to lay off workers in general and during economic crises (Blair et al., 2002; Kurtulus & Kruse, 2017; Park et al., 2004; Rodgers, 2013). Studies conducted during the COVID-19 pandemic found a similar pattern, with employee-owned firms more likely to retain staff through the economic downturn (Employee Ownership Foundation, 2020; Mankling et al., 2020; NCEO, 2022). Relatedly, a dataset spanning 2002–2022 finds that employee-owners are two and a half times less likely to report being laid off and enjoy longer tenure at their companies (Palmieri et al., 2024).

Thus, evidence suggests that risk-based objections to employee ownership are not nearly as applicable as many assume. Risk is associated with an ownership stake, but the level of risk can be significantly mitigated in employee-owned companies. First, risk is minimized when employee ownership models are an additional rather than a substitutional benefit. Second, providing a financial stake to workers that requires no or minimal use of their income or savings lessens potential hazards. Third, diversification issues can be addressed by offering employee ownership models alongside diversified retirement plans. Finally, workers' most significant risk, unemployment, is far less likely when working at an employee-owned firm.

Employee Ownership Will Harm Company Performance

It is common for those new to the idea to assume that employee ownership models hurt company performance. This may be through the added costs of the models themselves, by introducing inefficiencies in the decision-making process, or by creating a set of incentives that result in workers being rewarded for "free riding" off the hard work of others. Such assumptions are reasonable and predicted by academics in economics and management. However, empirical research demonstrates that employee-owned firms, on average, perform as well or better than similar conventional companies on various metrics.

Space constraints limit our review of company performance studies conducted on employee-owned firms. Instead, our focus will be on two types of studies. The first kind is called a meta-analysis, a research technique that reviews results from multiple studies on a similar topic to identify a general trend or understanding that accumulates over time. The second type of study reviewed here compares conventionally owned companies to employee-owned companies with similar characteristics or compares the performance of the same company before and after employee ownership is adopted. These studies are considered the gold standard since their design allows for disentangling factors that could otherwise influence results.

One of the earliest meta-analyses by Weitzman and Kruse (1990) summarized results from 16 studies measuring the productivity effects of profit sharing. They concluded that "the evidence from all the studies taken together provides a quite strong indication that profit sharing and productivity are positively related" (p. 138). Doucouliagos (1995) synthesized the results of 43 published papers. He found that profit sharing, worker ownership, and worker participation in decision-making were positively associated with productivity, and the relationship was stronger in firms practicing models of economic democracy. Kruse and Blasi (1997) surveyed 27 studies examining productivity and profitability and found that "while several studies indicate better or unchanged performance under employee ownership, almost no studies find worse performance" (p. 26). They estimated that studies from the 1980 and 90s found productivity increased 4–5%, on average, in the year a company adopted an ESOP.

Finally, O'Boyle et al. (2016) reviewed all English language studies of employee ownership published as of 2013. The sample included 102 studies representing over 56,984 firms and measured either efficiency-related outcomes (e.g., productivity, value-added, return on assets) or growth-related outcomes (e.g., sales, assets, profitability). They found that "employee ownership has a small, but positive and statistically significant relation to firm performance" (p. 452) with the relationship holding across geographic location, firm size, type of ownership model, and whether the company was public or private.

We now turn to studies comparing employee-owned and traditional companies. One of the first examples of this approach was adopted by the U.S. General Accounting Office (1987), which tracked newly formed ESOPs over six years, along with a sample of traditional companies. The study found no evidence of a general positive (or negative) effect on company productivity and profitability. Importantly, it found that ESOP companies where "nonmanagerial employees participate in corporate decision making through work groups and committees tended to have had more improvement in the measure of productivity relative to their pre-ESOP period" (p. 3). A study tracking private ESOP companies between 1988 and 1997 reported that they were only half as likely to go bankrupt and three-fifths as likely to disappear for any reason (Blasi et al., 2013). In the same study, the authors compared sales, employment, and productivity growth and found that they increased 2.4%, 2.3%, and 2.3%, respectively. Stretcher et al. (2006), comparing public companies with and without ESOPs between the years of 1998 and 2004, reported that ESOP companies experienced higher return on assets (5.5%), net profit margin (10.3%), and return on equity (5.6%).

Kurtulus and Kruse (2017) tracked the full population of publicly traded companies in the U.S. with and without ESOPs, profit sharing, or any other kind of broad-based stock ownership plan from 1991 to 2011. They found that companies with broad-based employee ownership shed jobs at half the rate over this period and were less likely to go out of business. In an interesting experimental study, Peterson and Luthans (2006) tracked 21 fast-food franchises owned by one firm that randomly introduced profit sharing in some stores and not others. During the 6-month study period, stores with profit sharing witnessed a 30% increase in profits, a 19% decrease in drive-through times, and a 13% decrease in turnover.

Studies conducted in contexts outside of the U.S. arrive at similar results. For example, an extensive survey in the U.K. found that employee-owned firms were, on average, 8–12% more productive and more likely to report expansions to their workforce and increases in profits (Employee Ownership Association, 2023). Similarly, Pérotin (2012), who surveyed the performance of worker cooperatives in the U.K., U.S., France, and Italy, concluded that "solid, consistent evidence across countries, systems, and periods shows that worker cooperatives are at least as productive as conventional firms, and more productive in some areas" (p. 220).

Research on the relationship between employee ownership and company performance is extensive. Existing evidence strongly suggests that employee ownership does not negatively impact company performance. If a relationship does exist, it appears to be positive. Certainly, causation is always difficult to establish, and research continues to explore this topic. However, the perverse outcomes raised by theoreticians and feared by business owners are "overcome more often than not under employee ownership" (Blasi et al., 2017, p.18).

Employee Ownership Alone Automatically Leads to Improved Company Performance

After reading the previous section, the relationship between employee ownership and corporate performance seems straightforward. Adopt a broad-based employee ownership model, and the company will take off! However, this is not the case. Research has revealed that positive effects on company performance result from pairing a given employee ownership model with education, training, and participation in decision-making. Instituting employee ownership is necessary but insufficient to achieve meaningful performance outcomes.

One way to think about how employee ownership is linked to better company performance is through what Akerlof (1982) calls a "gift exchange." Applying this to employee ownership, workers, given the "gift" of employee ownership alongside competitive wages and benefits, respond with a reciprocal "gift" of high effort, lower absenteeism, and more company pride and loyalty. That increased effort and loyalty is then translated into better performance at the individual and firm levels. The specific ways this process occurs are still being studied. However, organizational scholars find identity is key to motivating employees and increasing their commitment and feelings of responsibility to a firm (Akerlof & Kranton, 2005). Cultivating an ownership identity for workers can help develop feelings of responsibility, including "a responsibility to invest time and energy to advance the cause of the organization—to be protective, caring and nurturing" (Pierce et al., 2001, p. 303). Phrased another way, "Formal employee ownership encourages employees to believe that they share financial interests with the organization and act in a manner that promotes these shared financial interests" (Wagner et al., 2003, p. 865).

While employee ownership has the potential to motivate employees, it is not guaranteed. As Kruse and Blasi (1995) note, "employee ownership does not magically and automatically improve employee attitudes and behavior whenever it is implemented" (p. 24). To achieve these outcomes, something more is needed, "something akin to developing a corporate culture that emphasizes company spirit, promotes group cooperation, [and] encourages social enforcement mechanisms" (Weitzman & Kruse, 1990, p. 100). An ownership share means very little if not coupled with opportunities to participate and provide decision-making input or with managerial and human resource practices that entice engagement (Logue & Yates, 1999, 2001). Likewise, giving workers opportunities to participate in decision-making without providing education and training will not suffice. Asking workers to "think like owners" without building the skills required for informed participation can have negative consequences and can result in workers viewing the arrangement "as an attempt to shift financial risk onto the workers rather than empower them" (Whitfield et al., 2017, p. 1292).

Research generally shows that improvements to company performance are achieved via a multi-pronged approach, presented in Figure 4.2. A successful approach typically combines a financial stake, which motivates employees; education and training, which provides employees with needed skills; and opportunities to participate in company decisions, which allows them to apply the skills they learn (Summers & Chillas, 2019). Without such policies and practices, employee ownership can send a mixed message along the lines of,

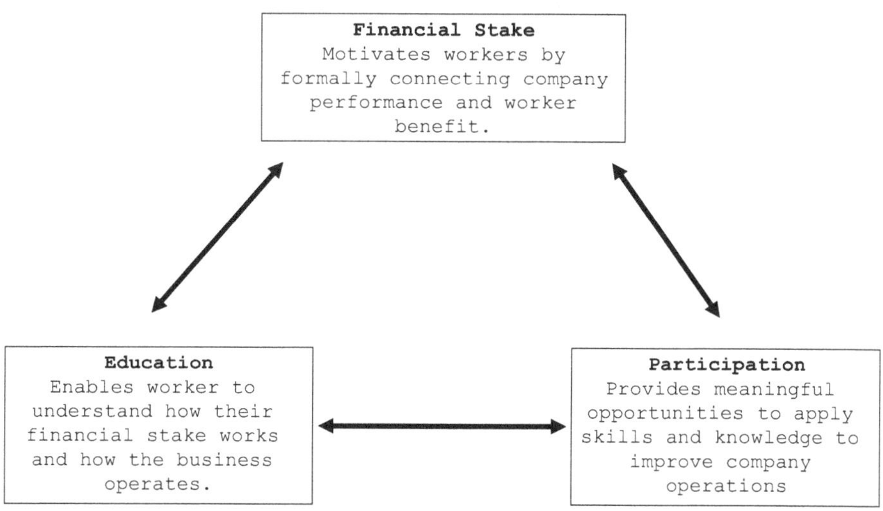

FIGURE 4.2 Employee Ownership and Company Performance.

Source: Compiled by authors.

"We want you to be more productive as employee-owners, but we are not going to give you the tools to be more productive" (Kruse, 2022, p. 8).

Coupling employee ownership with education, training, and participation is a best practice. Not every employee-owned company will implement these practices or do so similarly. However, when such policies and programs are instituted, the results are positive. An analysis of 40,000 workers across 14 firms reported that workers with company stock and other financial incentives were more likely to intervene when they saw co-workers not working. When asked why they would take this action, workers reported, "Poor performance will cost other employees and me in bonus or stock value." The same study also found that employee-owners had lower turnover and absenteeism and were more likely to make suggestions about improving company performance (Freeman et al., 2010).

In another study, Blasi et al. (2016) analyzed records of more than 700 companies that applied to Fortune's "100 Best Companies to Work For" between 2005 and 2007. They found that employees working in companies with broad-based employee ownership were more likely to "extensively participate in more decisions, have greater information sharing, trust in supervisors, and report a more positive workplace culture than in other companies," which in turn "reduces voluntary turnover, increases employee intent to stay, and raises return on equity" (p. 55). Combining the financial benefit of broad-based employee ownership with meaningful participation is not a simple process and takes years to implement. However, research shows that when systems are put in place, they provide tangible and measurable returns—for the company and employees.

Employees Are Not Prepared to Run the Business

A significant concern of selling owners is that employees are unprepared to run the business. A good part of this belief is wrapped up with the idea that adopting employee ownership will come with drastic changes to company operations. Contrary to these ideas, it is typical for roles and management hierarchies to remain after a business becomes employee-owned. The board of directors continues setting a company's strategic priorities; management continues overseeing day-to-day operations; and shop floor employee-owners continue carrying out tasks performed before the transition. Companies can change the existing management hierarchy as part of their transition to employee ownership, but the law does not require it.

In many cases, the question of readiness also stems from a truthful analysis of workers' skill sets at the time of a transition to employee ownership. Workers may not be fully prepared to think and act like owners on day one. Over time, skill sets can be developed within the company by delivering education and training alongside opportunities for participation. In most cases, early education will focus on how a specific employee ownership model works and how employees benefit from it. Other forms of education include basic financial training that enables workers to understand how the company makes (or loses) money. With those building blocks in place, the company can provide more detailed training focusing on specific skill sets, such as training those serving as a board member.

Conclusions

Baby boomer business owner retirements will have impacts that reverberate across the country, in communities big and small. However, the effects will be profound for rural communities, where businesses often act as the backbone and center of economic and social activity. While demographic trends pose a real challenge to the business landscape in these communities, employee ownership is an underutilized tool that can reliably meet the goals and objectives of business owners and other important stakeholders. Business owners transfer the business to the next generation for fair market value, workers build wealth and participate in the companies where they work, and the community keeps businesses locally rooted.

The needs and tastes of selling owners vary greatly, and employee ownership is not a good fit for every business owner considering retirement. The three models of employee ownership examined here provide a new set of options typically not discussed with or known by business owners. All three models have proven track records of success and a network of professionals who assist with the technical and educational needs required for a successful transition. As such, we strongly encourage business owners, policymakers, and professional service providers to take employee ownership seriously and actively engage with it as a proven succession planning tool.

References

Akerlof, G. A. (1982). Labor contracts as partial gift exchange. *The Quarterly Journal of Economics*, *97*(4), 543–569. 10.2307/1885099

Akerlof, G. A., & Kranton, R. E. (2005). Identity and the economics of organizations. *Journal of Economic Perspectives*, *19*(1), 9–32.

Ben-Ner, A., & Jones, D. C. (1995). Employee participation, ownership, and productivity: A theoretical framework. *Industrial Relations: A Journal of Economy and Society*, *34*(4), 532–554. 10.1111/j.1468-232X.1995.tb00387.x

Biery, M. E. (2017, February 6). *Study shows why many business owners can't sell when they want to.* Forbes. https://www.forbes.com/sites/sageworks/2017/02/05/these-8-stats-show-why-many-business-owners-cant-sell-when-they-want-to/

Blair, M. M., Kruse, D., & Blasi, J. (2002). Employee ownership: An unstable form or a stabilizing force? In M. M. Blair & T. A. Kochan (Eds.), *The new relationship: Human capital in the American corporation* (pp. 241–289). Brookings Institution Press.

Blasi, J., Freeman, R., & Kruse, D. (2016). Do broad-based employee ownership, profit sharing and stock options help the best firms do even better? *British Journal of Industrial Relations*, *54*(1), 55–82. 10.1111/bjir.12135

Blasi, J., Kruse, D., & Freeman, R. (2017, February 1). *Having a stake: Evidence and implications for broad-based employee stock ownership and profit sharing*. Third Way. https://thirdway.imgix.net/pdfs/having-a-stake-evidence-and-implications-for-broad-based-employee-stock-ownership-and-profit-sharing.pdf

Blasi, J., Kruse, D., & Freeman, R. B. (2018). Broad-based employee stock ownership and profit sharing: History, evidence, and policy implications. *Journal of Participation and Employee Ownership*, *1*(1), 38–60. 10.1108/JPEO-02-2018-0001

Blasi J., Kruse, D., & Weltmann, D. (2013). Firm survival and performance in privately held ESOP companies. In D. Kruse (Ed.), *Sharing ownership, profits, and decision-making in the 21st century* (pp. 109–124). Emerald Group Publishing. 10.1108/S0885-3339(2013)0000014006

Blasi, J. R., & Kruse, D. L. (1992). *The new owners: The mass emergence of employee ownership in public companies and what it means to American business*. Harper Business.

Boguslaw, J., & Schur, L. (2019, March). *Building the assets of low and moderate income workers and their families: The role of employee ownership*. Institute for the Study of Employee Ownership and Profit Sharing. https://smlr.rutgers.edu/sites/default/files/Documents/Centers/Institute_Employee_Ownership/rutgerskelloggreport_april2019.pdf

Broughton, A. C., Blasi, J., Schlag, Z., Razo, D., Hand, M. (2022). *Employee ownership trusts and perpetual purpose trusts in the United States* (Version 5) [Data set]. Harvard Dataverse. 10.7910/DVN/EYGHCW

Buchele, R., Kruse, D. L., Rodgers, L., & Scharf, A. (2010). Show me the money: Does shared capitalism share the wealth? In D. L. Kruse, R. B. Freeman, & J. R. Blasi (Eds.), *Shared capitalism at work: Employee ownership, profit and gain sharing, and broad-based stock options* (pp. 351–375). University of Chicago Press.

Burdin, G., & Dean, A. (2009). New evidence on wages and employment in worker cooperatives compared with capitalist firms. *Journal of Comparative Economics*, *37*(4), 517–533. 10.1016/j.jce.2009.08.00

Business Enterprise Institute. (2023). *2022 business owner survey report*. https://104201.fs1.hubspotusercontent-na1.net/hubfs/104201/2022%20Business%20Owner%20Survey%20Report.pdf?hsCtaTracking=1a6eccf2-37f1-46c4-9c37-ed733ca47eeb%7C50c6d12e-8a87-4c8c-9c3c-03babf7333cd

Cathcart, A. (2013). Directing democracy: Competing interests and contested terrain in the John Lewis Partnership. *Journal of Industrial Relations*, *55*(4), 601–620. 10.1177/0022185613489424

Dahl, R. A. (1985). *A preface to economic democracy*. University of California Press.

Daniel, W. (2023, May 23). *"Turbulence ahead": Nearly 4 in 10 Americans lack enough money to cover a $400 emergency expense, Fed survey shows*. Fortune. https://fortune.com/2023/05/23/inflation-economy-consumer-finances-americans-cant-cover-emergency-expense-federal-reserve/

Deller, S., Hoyt, A., Hueth, B., & Sundaram-Stukel, R. (2009, June 19). *Research on the economic impact of cooperatives*. University of Wisconsin Center for Cooperatives. https://resources.uwcc.wisc.edu/Research/REIC_FINAL.pdf

Democracy at Work Institute. (2024). 2023 Worker cooperative state of the sector report. State of the Sector Report 2023 by wearedawi - Issuu

Democracy at Work Institute. (n.d.). *What is a worker cooperative?* Retrieved August 12, 2024, from https://institute.coop/what-worker-cooperative

Doucouliagos, C. (1995). Worker participation and productivity in labor-managed and participatory capitalist firms: A meta-analysis. *Industrial and Labor Relations Review*, *49*(1), 58–77. 10.2307/2524912

Ellerman, D. P. (1990). *The democratic worker-owned firm: A new model for East and West*. Unwin Hyman, Inc.

Employee Ownership Association. (2023). *EO knowledge programme 2023: People powered growth*. https://employeeownership.co.uk/Site/content/News-and-Insights/EO-Knowledge-Programme/EO-Knowledge-Programme.aspx

Employee Ownership Foundation. (2020). *Employee-owned firms in the COVID-19 pandemic: How majority owned ESOP & other companies have responded to the COVID-19 health and economic crisis*. https://assets-eof.s3.us-east-2.amazonaws.com/assets/public/2020-10/EOF_CovidResearch_Oct23b.pdf

Ernst and Young. (2022, April). *Contribution of S ESOPs to participants' retirement security and employee-owner benefits: Prepared for the employee-owned S corporations of America*. https://esca.us/wp-content/uploads/2022/04/EY-ESCA-S-ESOP-Analysis-2022.04.2257.pdf

Everett, J., Hand, M., Reitman-White, N. (2024, April 2). Rethinking ownership: Putting purpose at the center. *Social Impact Review*. https://www.sir.advancedleadership.harvard.edu/articles/rethinking-ownership-putting-purpose-at-center

Federal Reserve Banks. (2024, May 31). *2024 Firms in Focus chartbooks on small business data*. Small Business Credit Survey. 10.55350/sbcs-20240531

Flamisch, S. (2018, May 14). *Study: In ESOP companies, the average worker has a $134,000 share* [Press release]. Rutgers School of Management and Labor Relations. https://smlr.rutgers.edu/news-events/news/study-esop-companies-average-worker-has-134000-share

Freeman, R. B., Kruse, D. L., & Blasi, J. R. (2010). Worker responses to shirking under shared capitalism. In D. L. Kruse, R. B. Freeman, & J. R. Blasi (Eds.), *Shared capitalism at work: Employee ownership, profit and gain sharing, and broad-based stock options* (pp. 77–103). University of Chicago Press.

ICA Group. (2018, August). *CO-OP conversions at scale: A market assessment for expanding worker co-op conversions in key regions & sectors*. Capital Impact Partners & Citi Community Development and Inclusive Finance. https://icagroup.org/wp-content/uploads/2019/04/Co-op-Conversions-At-Scale.pdf

Jones, D. C., Kato, T., & Pliskin, J. (1994, September). *Profit sharing and gainsharing: A review of theory, incidence, and effects* (Working Paper No. 125). https://www.researchgate.net/publication/23748218_Profit_Sharing_and_Gainsharing_A_Review_of_Theory_Incidence_and_Effects

Kardas, P., Scharf, A. L., & Keogh, J. (1998). Wealth and income consequences of ESOPs and employee ownership: A comparative study from Washington State. *Journal of Employee Ownership Law and Finance*, *10*(4), 3–52.

Kim, E. H., & Ouimet, P. (2014). Broad-based employee stock ownership: Motives and outcomes. *The Journal of Finance*, *69*(3), 1273–1319. 10.1111/jofi.12150

Kruse, D. (2002). Research evidence on prevalence and effects of employee ownership. *Journal of Employee Ownership Law and Finance*, *14*(4), 65–90.

Kruse, D. (2022, May). *Does employee ownership improve performance?* IZA World of Labor.https://wol.iza.org/uploads/articles/613/pdfs/does-employee-ownership-improve-performance.pdf?v=1

Kruse, D., Blasi, J., & Moriarity, J. (2024, April 8). *ESOPs in rural areas* [Issue brief]. Aspen Institute Economic Opportunities Forum & Institute for the Study of

Employee Ownership and Profit Sharing at Rutgers University. https://www.aspeninstitute.org/publications/esops-in-rural-areas/

Kruse, D., Blasi, J., Weltmann, D., Kang, S., Kim, J. O., & Castellano, W. (2019). *Do employee share owners face too much financial risk?* (Discussion Paper No. 12303). IZA Institute of Labor Economics. https://docs.iza.org/dp12303.pdf

Kruse, D., Freeman, R., Blasi, J., Buchele, R., Scharf, A., Rodgers, L., & Mackin, C. (2004). *Motivating employee-owners in ESOP firms: Human resource policies and company performance*. Emerald Group Publishing Limited.

Kruse, D. L., & Blasi, J. (1995, September). *Employee ownership, employee attitudes, and firm performance* (NBER Working Paper No. w5277). National Bureau of Economic Research. https://papers.ssrn.com/sol3/papers.cfm?abstract_id=225341

Kruse, D. L., & Blasi, J. (1997). Employee ownership, employee attitudes, and firm performance: A review of the evidence. In D. J. B. Mitchell, D. Lewin, & M. Zaidi (Eds.), *Handbook of resource management* (pp. 113–151). JAI Press.

Kruse, D. L., Freeman, R. B., & Blasi, J. R. (Eds.). (2010). *Shared capitalism at work: Employee ownership, profit and gain sharing, and broad-based stock options*. University of Chicago Press.

Kurtulus, F. A., & Kruse, D. L. (2017, January). *How did employee ownership firms weather the past two recessions? Employee ownership, employment stability, and firm survival in the United States: 1999–2011*. W.E. Upjohn Institute for Employment Research. 10.17848/9780880995276

Leikin, S. B. (2005). *The practical utopians: American workers and the cooperative movement in the Gilded Age*. Wayne State University Press.

Logue, J., & Yates, J. (2001). *The real world of employee ownership*. ILR Press.

Logue, J., & Yates, J. S. (1999). Worker ownership American style: Pluralism, participation and performance. *Economic and Industrial Democracy*, *20*(2), 225–252. 10.1177/0143831X99202004

Long, R. J., & Fang, T. (2012). Do employees profit from profit sharing? Evidence from Canadian panel data. *ILR Review*, *65*(4), 899–927.

Mankling, M., Trenholm, Z., & Prushinskaya, O. (2020). *Worker co-ops: Weathering the storm of COVID-19*. Democracy at Work Institute. https://institute.coop/resources/worker-co-ops-weathering-storm-COVID-19

Menke, J. D. (2011, May 12). *The origin and history of the ESOP and its future role as a business succession tool*. Menke ESOP Advisors. https://www.menke.com/esop-archives/the-origin-and-history-of-the-esop-and-its-future-role-as-a-business-succession-tool/

Michael, C. (2017). The employee ownership trust, an ESOP alternative. *Probate & Property*, *31*(1), 42–47. https://smlr.rutgers.edu/sites/default/files/Images/Centers/NJ-NY-CEO/michael._2017._the_employee_ownership_trust%20%282%29.pdf

National Center for Employee Ownership. (2017, May 15). *Employee ownership and economic well-being: Household wealth, job stability, and employment quality among employee-owners age 28 to 34*. https://www.ownershipeconomy.org/wp-content/uploads/2017/05/employee_ownership_and_economic_wellbeing_2017.pdf

National Center for Employee Ownership. (2022). *Employee ownership in the U.S. food system during COVID-19: New evidence on outcomes for firms and workers*. https://www.nceo.org/sites/default/files/2022-05/NCEO%20research%20report%20-%20Employee%20Ownership%20in%20the%20U.S.%20Food%20System%20During%20COVID-19.pdf

National Center for Employee Ownership. (n.d.-a). *Are ESOPs good retirement plans?* https://www.nceo.org/articles/esops-too-risky-be-good-retirement-plans

National Center for Employee Ownership. (n.d.-b). *Default rates on ESOP loans, 2009–2013*. https://www.nceo.org/articles/default-rates-esop-loans-2009-2013

National Center for Employee Ownership. (n.d.-c). *Employee ownership by the numbers*. https://www.nceo.org/articles/employee-ownership-by-the-numbers

National Center for Employee Ownership. (n.d.-d). *What is employee ownership?* https://www.nceo.org/what-is-employee-ownership

National Cooperative Business Association CLUSA International. (n.d.). *Agriculture co-ops*. Retrieved August 12, 2024, from https://ncbaclusa.coop/resources/co-op-sectors/agriculture-co-ops/

O'Boyle, E. H., Patel P. C., and Gonzalez-Mulé, E. (2016). Employee ownership and firm performance: A meta-analysis. *Human Resource Management Journal, 26*(4), 425–448. 10.1111/1748-8583.12115

Palmer, T. (2020). *2019 worker cooperative state of the sector report*. Democracy at Work Institute. https://institute.coop/resources/2019-worker-cooperative-state-sector-report#:~:text=Description%3A,business%20in%20the%20United%20States.&text=The%20report%20draws%20upon%20the,our%20understanding%20of%20the%20sector

Palmieri, M., Han, J. H., Kruse D. L., Castellano, W., Klein F. B., Scharf, A., & Blasi, J. R. (2024). *Job quality of employee share owners in the United States: January 1st 2024 shares lab quarterly report*. Institute for the Study of Employee Ownership and Profit Sharing, Rutgers University. https://uploads-ssl.webflow.com/5cdc97dbfcbd7455a5788315/6632754dd1f8bf96a41e5e57_2024_Q1_SharesLabReport_JobQuality(fn).pdf

Park, R., Kruse, D., & Sesil, J. (2004). Does employee ownership enhance firm survival? In V. Pérotin & A. Robinson (Eds.), *Employee participation, firm performance and survival* (pp. 3–33). Emerald Group Publishing. 10.1016/S0885-3339(04)08001-9

Pendleton, A., Robinson, A., Nuttal, G. (2023). Employee ownership in the UK. *Journal of Participation and Employee Ownership, 6*(3), 194–214. 10.1108/JPEO-11-2022-0030

Pérotin, V. (2012). The performance of workers' cooperatives. In P. Battilani & H. G. Schröter (Eds.), *The cooperative business movement, 1950 to the present* (pp. 195–221). Cambridge University Press.

Peterson, S. J., & Luthans, F. (2006). The impact of financial and nonfinancial incentives on business-unit outcomes over time. *Journal of Applied Psychology, 91*(1), 156–165. 10.1037/0021-9010.91.1.156

Pierce, J. L., Kostova, T., & Dirks, K. T. (2001). Toward a theory of psychological ownership in organizations. *Academy of Management Review, 26*(2), 298–310.

Pitman, L. (2018, December). *History of cooperatives in the United States: An overview*. University of Wisconsin-Madison Center for Cooperatives. https://resources.uwcc.wisc.edu/History_of_Cooperatives.pdf

Rodgers, L. (2010). Are ESOPs good for employees? *Pension & Benefits Daily, 100*, 1–2.

Rodgers, L. (2013, February 1). *Employee ownership and the costs of unemployment*. National Center for Employee Ownership. https://www.nceo.org/blog/employee-ownership-and-costs-unemployment

Rodgers, L., & Keeling, J. M. (2010, September 20). *ESOPs as retirement benefits: An analysis of data from the U.S. Department of Labor*. National Center for Employee Ownership & The Employee Ownership Foundation. https://www.nceo.org/assets/pdf/articles/ESOPs-as-Retirement-Benefits.pdf

Staubus, M. (2017, August 17). A new design: Worker cooperative governance with ESOP tax benefits. *Fifty by Fifty: Employee Ownership News*. https://medium.com/fifty-by-fifty/the-esop-erative-daaa98c1174f

Stretcher, R., Henry, S., & Kavanaugh, J. K. (2006). The ESOP performance puzzle in public companies. *The Journal of Employee Ownership Law and Finance*, *18*(4), 3–18.

Summers, J., & Chillas, S. (2019). Working in employee-owned companies: The role of economic democracy skills. *Economic and Industrial Democracy*, *42*(4) 1029–1051. 10.1177/0143831X19835319

U.S. Federation of Worker Cooperatives. (n.d.). *What is a worker cooperative?* Retrieved August 12, 2024, from https://www.usworker.coop/what-is-a-worker-cooperative/

U.S. General Accounting Office. (1987, October). *Employee stock ownership plans: Little evidence of effects on corporate performance* (GAO/PEMD-88-1). https://www.gao.gov/assets/150/145909.pdf

USAFacts Team. (2023, November 9). *Nearly half of American households have no retirement savings*. USAFacts. https://usafacts.org/data-projects/retirement-savings

Wagner, S. H., Parker, C. P., & Christiansen, N. D. (2003, December). Employees that think and act like owners: Effects of ownership beliefs and behaviors on organizational effectiveness. *Personnel Psychology*, *56*(4), 847–871. 10.1111/j.1744-6570.2003.tb00242.x

Weitzman, M. L., & Kruse, D. L. (1990). Profit sharing and productivity. In A. Blinder (Ed.), *Paying for productivity: A look at the evidence* (pp. 95–140). Brookings Institution.

Whitfield, K., Pendleton, A., Sengupta, S., & Huxley, K. (2017). Employee share ownership and organisational performance: A tentative opening of the black box. *Personnel Review*, *46*(7), 1280–1296. 10.1108/PR-09-2016-0243

5

USING AN EMPLOYEE STOCK OWNERSHIP PLAN FOR BUSINESS TRANSITION*

Corey Rosen

One of the most difficult problems facing owners of closely held businesses is finding a way to turn their equity in a business into cash for retirement or other purposes. The decision to sell is more than an economic one, however. After putting years into a business, an owner develops a strong feeling of identity with the company. At the same time, the owner often has a sense of loyalty to the employees and would like to see them have a continuing role in the company.

For some business owners, the answer to these problems will be to turn over the company to an heir or sell to a competitor. But many owners do not have heirs interested in the business, and outside buyers are not always easy to find. Potential acquirers, such as private equity firms, competitors, or consolidators, might offer a good price, but the deal often comes with contingencies, such as earn-outs or requirements for the seller's role in the company that the seller may not want. These buyers often do not want to retain the entire workforce and may have values that differ from those of the owner.

ESOPs (employee stock ownership plans) can be an attractive and tax-favored alternative. For the owner of a C corporation, proceeds on the gain from the sale to the ESOP can be tax-deferred by reinvesting in the securities of other domestic companies. If these securities are not sold before the owner's death, no capital gains tax is ever due. If the company is an S corporation, LLC, or partnership, it can convert to a C corporation before the sale to take advantage of this tax deferral.

* Much of this material is from material written by the author for the website of the National Center for Employee Ownership.

DOI: 10.4324/9781003497462-5

If the company remains an S corporation, the owner does pay capital gains tax on the sale but reaps all the other benefits of selling to an ESOP. The most important of these is that the owner's shares are bought in tax-deductible dollars, either from company contributions or plan borrowings. Net interest deductions for businesses with more than $30 million in average annual revenue (as of 2024, as indexed for inflation) are limited to 30% of EBIT (earnings before interest and taxes), although, as shown later, this is not an issue for 100% ESOP-owned S corporations because they pay no taxes.

The sale can be all at once or gradual, for as little or as much of the stock as desired. For the employees, no contributions are required to purchase the owner's shares. The owner can stay with the business in whatever capacity desired. The plan is governed by a trustee who votes the shares, but the board appoints the trustee, so changes in corporate control are usually nominal unless the plan is set up by the company to give employees more input at this level.

An ESOP is a type of employee benefit plan, similar in many ways to qualified retirement plans and governed by the same law (the Employee Retirement Income Security Act). ESOPs are funded by the employer, not the employees. Stock is held in a trust for employees meeting minimum service requirements and allocated to employees based on relative pay or a more level formula, then distributed after the employee terminates. ESOPs cannot be used to share ownership only with select employees, nor can allocations be made on a discretionary basis. This chapter explores how ESOPs work, ways they can be used for business transition, and how to decide if they make sense. Palmieri and Cooper (Chapter 4) examined the evidence on how well employee ownership works.

Steps Involved in a Sale to an ESOP

The company first creates an employee stock ownership plan trust (ESOT), which is designed to hold the shares and allocate them to individual employee accounts. The trust is governed by a trustee appointed by the board (governance is discussed in more detail later in this chapter). The trustee hires an outside appraiser to determine the fair market value. A feasibility study is often done to determine the financial practicality of the transaction.

In the simplest approach, the company contributes cash to the plan annually. Each cash contribution buys shares from the seller. The annual contributions are usually based on some combination of how much the seller wants to sell and how much profit the company has available.

More often, the seller wants to sell a large block of stock or all the stock. If there are multiple owners, one may want to sell but the others may not. This kind of sale requires that the company borrow money to purchase the shares. The company can finance the sale with a bank loan, seller debt, non-bank financing, or some combination, and then reloan the money to the ESOT, normally on different terms. The loan to the company to buy the shares (the external loan) is usually paid in 5–7 years; the loan from the company to the ESOT (the internal loan) is usually for 10–20 years.

The trust holds the shares in a suspense account and allocates the shares as the internal loan is repaid. The suspense account is a mechanism for holding shares in the ESOP trust until they are paid. Each loan repayment triggers a release of shares to employee accounts equal to the percentage of the loan repaid. The released shares are allocated to the employees' accounts in the plan. The internal loan is really just an accounting mechanism—the company puts in cash to the trust and the trust sends it back to repay the loan. By doing this, the shares are allocated over a longer period of time, allowing future employees to obtain shares even after the external loan is repaid. Going forward, as employees leave the company, their shares will be repurchased and usually go back into the trust to be allocated to all the employees in the plan. Figure 5.1 provides a schematic of how this process works.

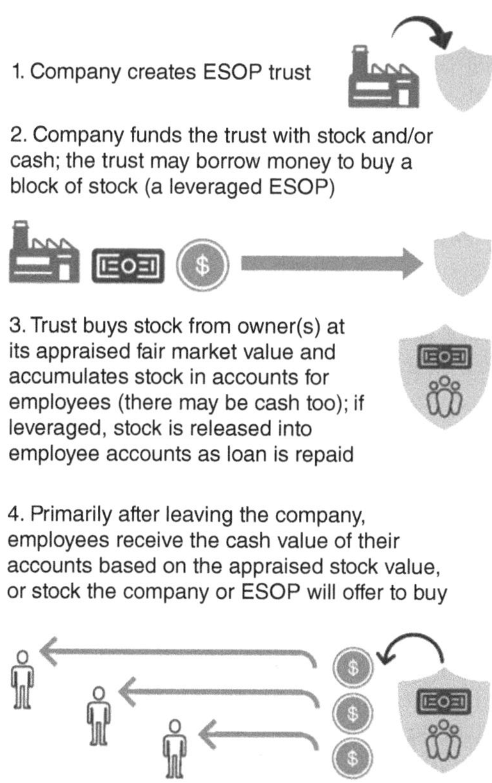

FIGURE 5.1 Tax Benefits of Selling to an ESOP.

Source: Rosen & Rodrick, 2024.

Compare the ESOP buyout with two other common methods of selling an owner's shares: redemption or sale to another firm. Under a redemption, the company gradually repurchases the shares of an owner. Corporate funds used to do this are not deductible. A $3 million purchase in a redemption would normally require more than $4 million in profits to fund, after taxes are paid. Moreover, the owner must pay taxes on the gain, at the capital gains or dividend rates. In a sale to a C corporation ESOP, the money made is considered a capital gain, not ordinary income, and taxes can be deferred. Even more important, the company needs only $3 million to fund the $3 million purchase, something that applies as well to sales to ESOPs in S corporations.

Or consider the second alternative, selling to another company or individual. In a cash sale, taxes would be due immediately. If the sale is for an exchange of stock in the acquiring company, taxes can be deferred until the new stock is sold, but 80% or more of the company must be sold all at once and the owner ends up with an undiversified investment for retirement.

If the company is a C corporation and the owner has held the shares for at least three years, once the ESOP owns 30% of the company's shares, the owner can reinvest the gains in the securities of other U.S. companies (other than real estate trusts, mutual funds, and other passive investments) within 12 months after or three months before the sale; no taxes are due until the replacement securities are sold. If the owner buys income-yielding securities and lives on the proceeds, giving them to an estate at death, no capital gains tax is due. If part of the securities are sold, tax is due only on a prorated basis.

If the company is an S corporation the tax deferral does not apply, but contributions to the trust used to acquire the shares are tax deductible. The company can convert to C first and then the seller would qualify for the rollover. S ESOPs have a very special tax benefit, however. S corporations are pass-through entities, meaning the company does not pay taxes. Instead, tax obligations are passed through pro rata to owners who pay taxes on their share of earnings based on their personal tax rates. Companies normally pay a distribution of earnings to owners, enabling them to pay taxes. Distributions must be made pro rata to ownership. But Congress decided that ESOP trusts do not have to pay any taxes. The Taxpayer Relief Act of 1997 changed the rules for S corporation taxation; U.S. Code § 512 exempted ESOPs from taxation. So, a 30% S ESOP pays no tax on 30% of its earnings; a 100% S ESOP pays no tax.

If the ESOP is less than a 100% owner, an interesting dynamic is created. Say the company is 30% ESOP-owned and makes $1 million in a taxable year. The 70% owner will want a distribution of earnings to pay taxes. Assume that owner receives $210,000 to do that. The ESOP then must raise $90,000 because it must get a pro rata distribution even though it pays no taxes. It can use this $90,000 to buy more shares, effectively using money that would have been paid in taxes to buy shares.

Many ESOPs are created as C corporations or in an S that converts to C, so that the seller can take a tax deferral on the sale. If it starts as a C, and becomes 100% ESOP-owned, it will convert to S status and pay no tax. If the company is an S corporation that converts to C, however, it cannot reconvert to S for five years.

Limitations on Contributions

ESOPs, as with other tax-qualified retirement plans, must comply with certain limits on annual contributions to the plan from the company. There are two limits to consider: the amount the company can contribute to the plan overall ("contribution limits") and the maximum annual addition to any one employee's account ("annual addition limits"). These contributions are fully deductible if they are within these two limits.

The maximum value a participant can receive in one year as an annual addition to their account is 100% of eligible pay or $69,000 (for 2024), whichever is less. For leveraged ESOPs: the limit calculation does not use the current value of the stock added to an employee's account when it was released from the suspense account. Instead, the limit applies to value of the shares at the time they were purchased using the loan. In other words, if the company's stock value were $20 when acquired in 2020, but rises to $27 in 2024, the contribution amount is still considered $20 per share.

Contributions are also limited to a maximum equal to 25% of the total eligible pay of ESOP participants. If the company has other defined contribution plans, company (but not employee) contributions to these plans will reduce this limit dollar for dollar. Eligible pay usually is under the annual compensation limit for all retirement plans ($330,000 in 2024). For instance, say ABC Company has 45 employees and 40 meet the eligibility rules for the plan with a total compensation of $4 million. The CEO makes $500,000 and the CFO $400,000. Only $660,000 of their pay counts as eligible pay, not $900,000.

Case Study of an ESOP[1]

Roger Ryberg founded Windings in New Ulm, Minnesota to provide engineered electromagnetic components for electric motors and generators for the aerospace, defense, medical, oil and gas, and factory automation industries. He started an ESOP in 1998. The ESOP trust bought a minority interest in the company in the first round and in 2008 bought the remaining shares. The ESOP has grown to more than 100 employees.

Ryberg, Windings's former owner, could have sold to other companies, but that never seemed right. As he approached 60, he knew having all his wealth tied up in the company was not prudent and so started to look at ways to diversify. Selling just part of a business is hard, though, and he wanted to remain for a while before getting out entirely.

He also wanted to make sure that whatever he did, the company could stay in New Ulm and reward the people who helped build the business. Looking back, he said this was the best choice he could have made. A retired supervisor said the culture used to be "here is what you have to do," but with the ESOP it became "here is what we need to do," so let's get people involved in sharing ideas on how to do it best. By aligning employee and company interests and giving workers a bigger role, he says the company saw a significant impact of recruitment, quality, profits, and sales.

Financing an ESOP

As noted previously, the simplest way to finance an ESOP to transfer ownership is to have the company make tax-deductible cash contributions to the ESOP trust, which the trust then uses to gradually purchase the owner's shares. When the seller wants to sell more all at once, then they have to seek financing.

The most attractive source of funds is senior bank debt. This source of funds allows the seller rapid liquidity and facilitates taking advantage of the tax deferral on the sale available for sales to ESOPs in C corporations (for reasons explored in detail later). Banks tend to view ESOPs very favorably since they very rarely default on acquisition loans.

A National Center for Employee Ownership [NCEO] (n.d.) study during the 2009–2013 period (which included a recession) found the default rate on ESOP acquisition loans was only two per 1,000 per year when default was defined as imposing a loss on creditors. Banks typically will finance up to an amount based on a multiple of EBITDA (earnings before interest, taxes, depreciation, and amortization) and/or some percentage of marketable assets.

Seller notes can be used to supplement the senior bank debt. Many sellers, however, prefer to finance the entire transaction with a note. The ESOP acquires the shares and then repays the seller at a reasonable rate of interest (not more than what a commercial lender would charge for subordinated loans of similar risk). Sellers often prefer this approach because not only are their shares sold, but they receive a reasonably high rate of return on the note.

Terms of seller notes are usually for 5–10 years with seven years being typical. Some notes have a balloon payment at maturity, meaning much of the note is paid off only at the end of the term, with interest accumulating over the term. If the company is doing well, however, the notes are often redeemed early. Seller notes are usually priced above senior debt rates, although some sellers choose to take a more modest return. Trustees must determine that the deal is not excessively favorable to the seller. Generally, loan rates on seller notes are a few points above the senior bank rate.

Some seller notes include warrants that give the seller the right to buy some number of shares at the transaction price for a specified number of years into the future. If the share price goes up, the warrants can be redeemed, so the seller receives the difference between the price of the warrants at the start of their term and at the end of their term. In other words, they function much like purchased stock options. Sellers who do this agree to a lower interest rate on the seller note. The present value of the foregone interest is calculated, and warrants with a calculated value equal to the value of the foregone interest are provided to the seller.

Companies can also use dividends to help finance an acquisition by the ESOP. In C corporations, reasonable dividends (a term that has never been defined, but should be taken to mean a percentage of earnings that does not impair the company's ability to grow) can be added to employee accounts each year to help repay a loan. The company can take a tax deduction for these dividends, and they do not count towards the annual contribution limits discussed above.

S corporations do not pay dividends; rather, they make a distribution of earnings. These can also be used to pay down debt, but are not deductible. In a 100% S ESOP, however, this is not an issue because the company pays no taxes anyway.

How the Price the Selling Owner Receives Is Determined

The price the ESOP will pay for the shares, as well as any other purchases by the plan, must be determined at least annually by an outside, independent appraiser. The process starts when the company's board hires a trustee to oversee the plan (see later in this article about how trustees are selected and their roles). The trustee then hires an appraiser. The firm should have a demonstrated expertise specifically in ESOP appraisals.

The appraiser's valuation will be based on several factors. Most appraisers try first to find comparable public companies and use their price/earnings ratio, price/assets ratio, and other guides in setting a price. That is often hard to do, however, for closely held companies, and is used as part of the appraisal only in some cases. The main focus is usually on discounted cash flow, book value, the company's reputation, future market considerations, cash in reserve above normal operating needs, debt, and other factors. The appraiser will try, as much as possible, to determine how much the business would be worth if there were a market for it. The appraiser is assessing what a financial buyer would pay, one who would operate the business as a stand-alone entity. A strategic buyer, such as a competitor, by contrast, might pay an additional premium because when the target company is acquired, there are perceived operational synergies that make the target more profitable to the buyer than it would be as a stand-alone entity. The ESOP cannot match this price because it cannot generate these synergies. Sales to synergistic buyers do trigger capital gains taxes, however, and often come with numerous contingencies.

Obtaining solid forecasts is critical to this process. There may be a temptation to be overly optimistic to arrive at a better price, but the trustee and appraiser must look carefully at forecasts to make sure they are reliable, preferably built from the ground up with several people at the company involved.

Reinvesting Gains from the Sale to an ESOP

One of the most attractive benefits of selling to an ESOP is that the seller can reinvest the gains in stocks and bonds of U.S. operating companies and not pay capital gains taxes until the replacement investments are sold. If the gains go into the seller's estate, the basis is stepped up and the estate pays no capital gains taxes.

This approach must meet several rules. Only owners of stock in closely held C corporations who have held that stock for at least three years prior to the sale qualify. The ESOP must own 30% of the total value of shares in the company after the sale. Corporations do not qualify, but partnerships, estates, taxable trusts, and individual owners do. The shares sold to the ESOP do not qualify if they were acquired as part of an employee benefit plan or through certain types of stock options. Sellers must buy stocks and/or bonds of U.S. operating companies, defined as companies that make not more than 25% of their income from passive investment (such as interest in loans or franchising fees). Companies can be public or private. The reinvested assets are called qualified replacement property (QRP).

The seller pays no tax on the sale to the ESOP until the qualified replacement property is "disposed of." Then the capital gain is calculated using the basis of the seller's shares in the company they sold to (usually zero). So, all gains from the sale to the ESOP, plus subsequent gains on the reinvested assets, are summed. Almost any transaction that results in the seller not owning the replacement securities any longer constitutes a disposition.

The seller could contribute the funds to a charitable remainder trust, which would take the value of the securities and give the donor an annual interest income that could be reinvested. The charity keeps the securities, however, so this works only for people with a charitable intent.

Case Study: Polyguard Products[2]

Polyguard, an Ennis, Texas-based manufacturer specializing in products that protect surfaces and structures from moisture, water, and other undesired substances, started an ESOP in 1986 when the owners who bought the company wanted employees to have a voice in how work was done and be rewarded for helping the company succeed. The ESOP bought a minority of their shares.

Years later, when they were ready to partially retire, the ESOP bought the rest of their stock.

Since then, the company has grown substantially, more than doubling capacity. Company president Shawn Eastham says about their success,

> I really believe the secret is employee engagement, and the fact we are an ESOP company. There's lower turnover, a better attitude, a better work ethic. It's people making sure the quality is good, going the extra mile for the customer.
>
> *(NCEO, 2023)*

Platitudes from the guy in the corner office, you might think. But then you start talking to shop-floor employees. "People work very hard and very fast," said one 30-year Polyguard employee. "People in one area, if they're caught up, will help in another area without being told to do it," added another veteran employee.

The ESOP "kind of ensures that everybody doing their job is doing it at 110 percent," is another comment heard. Hard work and a positive attitude aren't the whole answer, of course. Polyguard's astonishing track record can also be traced to its broad and diverse customer base, with three divisions selling into different markets in 31 countries. "When our pipeline division's business is down because the price of oil has plunged, commercial construction is usually up," says Eastham. "The divisions support each other." The company also capitalizes on innovation after innovation, with employee owners developing many of the products it sells.

How Employees Obtain Stock

Who Is in the Plan?

The rules for participating in an ESOP are the same as for other qualified employee benefit plans (pensions, profit sharing, etc.) and provide several tests to assure that plans meet minimum anti-discrimination requirements. Virtually all ESOP companies, however, cover at least all employees with 1,000 hours of service or more in a year who are 21 years of age or older and have at least one year of service. Employees covered by a collective bargaining agreement can be excluded from coverage, provided the company bargains in good faith about all retirement benefits. These are minimum requirements; companies can include more employees (such as part-time employees or more recent hires).

The law does provide several additional exceptions. For instance, the ESOP can include only employees in a separate line of business, such as a division or subsidiary with 50 or more employees. This does not apply, however, if the intent is to get around the coverage rules. For instance, a plan could not just cover a division comprised of management people and exclude a division that only has non-management employees.

Union employees may be covered by agreements that provide benefit plans different from those available to employees not covered by a collective bargaining agreement. The union may be reluctant to change any of these in return for an ESOP; the company may be unwilling or unable to add the ESOP to existing benefits. In multi-unit companies, moreover, an ESOP may be practical for one business division but not for another. The law allows an ESOP to be limited in this way, given the caveats above, and usually allows the business unit to offer either stock in the parent or itself.

How Is Stock Allocated?

Most companies allocate stock based on compensation (typically defined as the amount on an employee's W-2 tax form), plus elective deferrals under Section 401(k) plans and cafeteria plans. That is, each participant in the plan receives a percentage of the total shares allocated equal to that participant's percentage of total eligible pay. Eligible pay excludes pay in excess of $330,000 per year in 2024 (indexed for inflation in $5,000 increments each year). While W-2 compensation is the norm, compensation could also be defined to exclude bonuses or other "add-ons" to pay, provided the effect is not to push allocations more toward higher-paid people. About two-thirds of all ESOPs allocate on relative pay.

Several allocation approaches are possible. In the most general terms, all ESOPs must meet the basic test that no highly compensated person receives more than would be allocated under a straight pay basis. Alternatively, a formula can provide compensation that is eligible, can be capped at a lower level, or give points for tenure. Alternative allocation formulas should be discussed carefully with legal counsel to make sure they meet the rules.

Before selecting an approach, keep in mind that the payroll-based method is the only one that is a "safe harbor," i.e., it does not require any annual testing to make sure rules are not violated. It might seem that other formulas, such as giving one point for seniority and one for pay, would push distributions downward and therefore would more easily pass the test for being nondiscriminatory, but the situation is a little more complex.

If the effect of the formula is that only one highly compensated person gets more than would be allocated under straight pay, the whole formula is disqualified. In this example, a company could have a highly-paid, very senior person who would do better under this approach than a straight pay formula. A plan can be designed, however, with a fail-safe provision so that in any potential violation, the formula would revert to straight pay for those who would cause the violation.

Here, then, are some alternative approaches:

- ***Per capita*:** Everyone gets the same. The big disadvantage is that it caps the allocation at the pay of the lowest-paid participant (because no one can receive more than this person). This can be a major problem in leveraged plans because it excludes many of the payroll base from allocations, meaning less can be paid on the loan. For instance, if total pay is $3 million for 50 employees, but pay ranges from $40,000–$300,000, an equal allocation formula would make only $2,000,000 of payroll eligible (50 x $40,000). So, the maximum annual contribution would be 25% of $2 million, not $1 million.
- ***Points for seniority*:** Some companies allocate shares based on a percentage for pay and a percentage for seniority. This tends to push allocation downward, but in some cases can result in too much going to higher-paid people. One relatively easy solution is to put a rule in the plan that allocation is capped at what would be allocated on straight pay or at some dollar compensation limit. Any excess gets reallocated.
- ***Capping eligible pay*:** Federal law limits individual eligible pay for allocation purposes to $330,000 (this number is in 2024 dollars and is indexed annually); a company could choose to push this limit down even further. This can cause the same problem as in the first formula.
- ***Basing allocation on 401(k) contributions*:** Plans that combine an ESOP and a 401(k) can base the ESOP allocations on employee 401(k) contributions. The ESOP contributions become the 401(k) match. This can result in a very different allocation formula than under an ESOP, but the complex testing rules basically follow 401(k) rules. Thus, if the plan qualifies for 401(k) rules, as long as the ESOP match is the same percentage for everyone (e.g., 50 cents on the dollar), the ESOP allocation qualifies. This approach is often used in public companies, but only occasionally in closely held companies.

In a non-leveraged ESOP, allocations are made to employees based on how much the company contributes in cash to buy stock or in direct stock contributions. In a leveraged ESOP, each year, as the loan is repaid, a percentage of shares held in the ESOP trust equal to the percentage of the loan that has been repaid that year is released from what is called "the ESOP suspense account." The shares are then allocated to employee participant accounts (for allocation formulas, see the questions on allocation in this section).

Vesting Rules

In all defined contribution and defined benefit plans, vesting must be complete when the employee reaches normal retirement age, defined as the retirement age specified in the plan or the later of the time the participant reaches age 65 and with five years of participation in the plan.

Employees must also be fully vested in the case of a full or partial plan termination. Plans are not required to do so, but many provide for full vesting upon disability or death. Vesting must either be 100% after three years of service (cliff vesting) or start at not less than 20% per year after the second year of service and continue until 100% vesting is reached after six years.

How ESOP Accounts Are Distributed

If an employee leaves due to death, retirement, or disability, or reaches retirement age after termination but before an ESOP payout has started, distribution must start during the plan year following the plan year in which the event occurs, unless the participant elects otherwise. Otherwise, distribution must start within six years after the plan year of termination, unless the participant elects otherwise.

For instance, say an employee is fully vested and leaves the company at age 49 in 2024. The plan year is the calendar year. The payouts must start no later than 2029 and can be in installments for up to five years. Another employee also leaves in 2024 but is 65. Their payout starts in 2025. Many companies choose to pay out sooner, however, for both categories.

These rules interact with general retirement plan rules as well. For those who are not 5% owners, retirement distribution must start no later than the 60th day after the end of the plan year in which the later of these events occur: (a) the participant reaches age 65 or, if earlier, the plan's normal retirement age; (b) the calendar year in which the employee retires; or (c) the 10th anniversary of participation in the plan. These provisions can create somewhat complex interactions when employees leave prior to retirement age but after 10 years of service. Usually, in these cases, the normal ESOP rule would be trumped by the general rules and require a somewhat earlier distribution to begin. These rules would require distribution to start in the calendar year of departure for someone qualifying, not the following plan year.

However, if there is an outstanding ESOP loan, distributions to terminating employees do not have to start until the plan year following the plan year in which the loan is repaid. There are certain exceptions for death and retirement, and the interaction of this rule with installment distributions is complex. Once the distribution commences, it can be paid out in a lump sum or in equal installments, with interest, over a period not exceeding five years (or more for balances over $1,380,000 for 2024, indexed annually for inflation).

Companies can require employees to sell back their shares when they get a distribution or have rules stating that shares will be purchased prior to distribution within the plan just prior to distribution. This ability is limited to companies where: (1) either (a) company bylaws specify that all or substantially all the stock in the company be owned by employees or (b) the company is an S corporation; and (2) the plan document specifies that the company can offer the cash value of accounts instead. If the company is a bank and has a cash-only provision, it can also choose not to offer employees shares when they leave. Almost all ESOPs meet one or more of these definitions.

Employees can receive a distribution in cash or in stock. It can be paid out all at once or over up to five years in equal installments (with interest if in cash). Most ESOP companies buy the shares before making a distribution, then pay the employee the cash. If in cash, the employee can roll the proceeds into an IRA and not pay any tax until the money is withdrawn. If the employee does not do this, then taxes are due on the amount, plus a 10% penalty if before retirement age. If distributions are in shares, the employee has a put option to sell them back to the company at the most recent appraised value either when they are distributed or, if the employee prefers, one year later. Share distributions can be directly rolled into an IRA, but only some banks are willing to do this because the shares are not readily tradable.

Special Anti-Abuse S Corporation ESOP Issues

When S corporations were allowed to set up ESOPs in 1977, some companies and their advisors saw an opportunity to avoid paying taxes by the ESOP becoming a 100% owner of the company but structuring the deal so that few employees really benefited. There were several variations on this scheme, but most created a management company to have an ESOP and an operating company to have its own plan. The operating company would send all its profits to the management company, so the ESOP shares were worthless. In other cases, ESOPs were set up for professional firms (lawyers and dentists, for instance) with only a few participants. The IRS tagged these as "listed transactions," meaning they were simply tax-avoidance schemes and hence were subject to special penalties.

The ESOP community saw these schemes as inimical to what ESOPs were about and worked with Congress to create rules to prevent them (IRS). The rules are complicated, but basically are designed to make sure that a few employees in the company do not end up with the lion's share of the benefits. The structure of these rules means that S ESOPs are usually impractical in companies with fewer than 20 employees, but they do not create problems for companies using the normal approaches to ESOP eligibility, allocation, and vesting rules.

Governance

The trustee is the legal shareholder and typically votes the shares. Usually, the only issue that comes up is elections for the board. The board appoints the trustee, so the arrangement is very circular. All ESOP participants have at least some voting rights. In private companies, ESOP participants must be able to direct the trustee on the voting of allocated shares for sale of all, or nearly all, of the company's assets, merger, liquidation, recapitalization, reclassification, dissolution, or consolidation. Note that ESOP participants do not necessarily have the right to direct the trustee on votes regarding the sale of the company's stock.

A trustee should be an external, independent professional for any acquisition of shares by the ESOP or sales of ESOP shares to another buyer. On an ongoing basis, the trustee can be an outsider or one or more employees. A majority of ESOP companies have a committee of insiders acting as the trustee, but a growing percentage use an outside professional firm. That saves employee time and can help if there is litigation because the appearance of conflicts of interest is reduced.

ESOP companies have no specific legal requirements for boards, but approximately 75% have chosen to add outside board members because they believe it improves governance, enhances the credibility of the plan, and adds useful outside perspectives (NCEO, 2021a).

If an ESOP company receives an offer to purchase the company that is at a significant premium over current fair market value, the board must consider whether during the intermediate term employees would be better off as plan participants—not as employees—if the offer were accepted. So even though they might lose their jobs, if the offer increases their stock value enough (usually at least 30%–50%), the board must pass it on to the trustee to decide whether to pursue the offer, seek an even higher offer, or turn it down. This may seem counterintuitive, but flows from the fact that ESOPs are part of retirement law, which focuses on maximizing the value of plan assets.

Some owners worry they are giving up control with an ESOP, but, in practice, trustees do not want to be involved on management issues and do not impinge on management prerogatives.

Comparing an ESOP Sale to Other Ways to Sell a Business

When people list the pros and cons of ESOPs, often they note that the plans are complex. ESOPs are more complex than 401(k) and similar retirement plans and do cost substantially more to install and somewhat more to operate, mostly because an annual appraisal is required for closely held companies. Setting up a plan usually costs $150,000–$500,000 with ongoing costs typically in the $20,000–$30,000 range for most ESOPs but can be more for large companies and those that use external trustees.

But ESOPs are not more complex than selling to a third party. Table 5.1 compares issues that arise in the sale of a company to an ESOP compared with a sale to a third party. It was prepared with the advice of professionals who

TABLE 5.1 Selling to an ESOP Versus Selling to Another Buyer

	ESOP	*Sale to Another Company*
Key legal documents	• ESOP plan document • Trust agreement • Lender agreements • Corporate resolutions • Stock purchase agreements • Corporate governance agreements • Employee contracts/management incentives	• Detailed selling memorandum • Sale agreement (similar to stock purchase) • Non-compete agreements (often) • Liens, escrow, security agreement, and personal guarantees • Corporate resolutions • Employee contracts/management incentives
Feasibility studies and preparation	Feasibility studies assess whether the company has sufficient payroll and cash flow to buy the desired amount of stock. Can be performed internally or with expert advice. Forensic due diligence rarely needed.	Companies must prepare a detailed and accurate description of the firm and its finances, prospects, and risks. Buyers will want to do a forensic due diligence investigation and sellers should do the same to assess the financial soundness of the buyer and the terms of the offer.
Valuation	Outside appraisal required; valuation based on fair market value.	In smaller deals, outside appraisal not required but recommended; in larger deals price usually set by controlled auction.
Terms and risks	Plans can be structured in a variety of ways: • Flexibility in financing. • Rules for operating the plan must comply with ERISA, but there is lots of flexibility in design. • Escrow may be, but usually is not, required.	• Buyers will typically have multiple contingencies: • Earn-outs often required, often in the 10%–20% range. • Escrow held back. • Purchase price adjustments in companies that underperform post-transaction may be required based on working capital or earnings requirements. • Buyers prefer to purchase assets, with potential tax and liability implications for sellers. • Financing may fall through.
Time to sell	Once the seller has decided on doing an ESOP and its basic structure, four to six months.	Median formal offer to sale time is 10 months for companies in the small to mid-market range.
Role of seller post-transaction	Flexible depending on seller interests.	Buyer will usually determine role in smaller deals; in large deals role is usually negotiable.
Sale of minority interest	ESOPs can buy any percentage of stock from any number of sellers.	Buyers almost invariably want to buy the entire company.
Success rates	If an ESOP is determined to be feasible, only rarely do transactions fall through once a decision to proceed has been made.	Overall, only about 25% of privately held businesses put up for sale are sold and only about 50% of businesses with 100 or more employees are sold.

(*Continued*)

Table 5.1 (Continued)

	ESOP	*Sale to Another Company*
Transaction costs	• For most closely held companies, transactions cost between $150,000–$400,000, with some larger and more complex transactions priced significantly higher. Fees include feasibility studies ($10,000–$40,000), plan documentation ($20,000–$50,000), valuation ($15,000–$25,000), trustee fees if using an outside trustee ($25,000–$70,000 in most deals but much more in larger deals), plus any corporate legal fees and personal financial advisor fees for seller. • Some ESOPs, especially larger deals and those where the seller is considering other sale options, will require investment banking assistance to raise financing, adding to costs. In these cases, an M&A advisor will normally charge a success fee similar to that charged in a sale to another buyer. • The ESOP pays the diligence, financing, and legal fees out of contributions from the company. • If the ESOP is not leveraged but rather acquires shares through company contributions over time (either from cash contributions to the trust or stock contributions), costs can be a great deal lower, often under $100,000.	• Legal costs may be somewhat lower. • Feasibility and due diligence comparable to or higher than ESOPs, and considerably higher in larger deals. • Legal costs are similar for smaller sales and much higher for large sales. Appraisal costs, if needed, would be similar. • The buyer usually pays the diligence, financing, and legal fees. Broker success fees are generally 5%–12% of the sale price in sale prices under $5 million and drop as low as 1%–3% in larger transactions. These additional fees mean, for instance, that a $5 million sale might require about $300,000 in broker or investment banker fees; a $10 million sale would require $500,000 in these fees. These fees are in addition to other costs.
Tax Issues	If the company is or becomes a C corporation at the time of sale, and the plan acquires 30% or more of the shares, then that sale, plus any subsequent sales, qualify the seller to defer capital gains taxes by reinvesting in stocks and bonds of U.S. operation companies. No taxes are due until the replacement investments are sold.	Sales to third parties generally are taxable as capital gains.

Source: Compiled by author.

have done both types of transactions. The table shows that the overall level of complexity is similar, but ESOPs are much less risky in terms of the likelihood of finding a buyer. They are often considerably less costly, mostly because in the case of a sale to a third party, in addition to substantial legal, accounting, and sometimes other fees, the price paid to the seller is usually reduced by brokerage commissions paid by the buyer. ESOP companies do not have to pay this "success fee," although some companies will do this if they hire an M&A firm that looks at selling to an ESOP as well as other buyers. Sales to third parties also do not qualify for special tax benefits, as is the case with ESOPs.

This comparison focuses on leveraged ESOPs. If the ESOP is based instead on periodic cash or stock contributions to the plan that are used to buy stock over time, the cost can often be less than $100,000 to set up the plan.

Making the Decision

All of this may sound appealing, but it is not feasible for every company. Several factors must, at a minimum, be present:

- ***The company is making enough money to buy out an owner***. The company must be generating sufficient cash to buy the shares from selling owners, conduct its normal business, and make necessary reinvestments. That means ESOPs are not a good fit for companies with uncertain future profits, much less those in economic distress.
- ***Payroll must be adequate to cover the purchase***. Because there are some limits (albeit generous ones) on how much can go into the ESOP each year, if a business has an exceptionally high value relative to its payroll, it may not be a good ESOP candidate, although this is an unusual scenario.
- ***If the company is borrowing to buy the shares, its existing debt must not prevent it from taking out an adequate loan***. Likewise, the company must not have bonding covenants or other agreements that prohibit it from taking on additional debt.
- ***If the seller wants to take the tax-deferred rollover, the company must be a regular C corporation or convert from S to C status***. S corporations can establish ESOPs, but their owners cannot take advantage of the tax-deferred rollover described above.
- ***The seller must be willing to sell their shares at fair market value, even if the ESOP pays less than an outside buyer would***. An ESOP will pay the appraised fair market value based on a variety of factors, but sometimes an outside buyer can pay more for a company if it has a particular fit that creates synergies that go beyond what the company is worth on its own.

- ***Management continuity must be provided.*** Banks, suppliers, and customers will all want to be persuaded that the company can continue to operate successfully. It is essential that people be trained to take the place of departing owners to assure a smooth transition.
- ***Sellers and leaders must be comfortable with the eligibility and allocation rules.*** ESOPs must operate in a way that is equitable for all employees. If owners want to pick and choose who gets stock, an ESOP is not the right tool. Note, however, that ESOP companies can provide any employee with other forms of equity or equity rights (such as stock options or stock appreciation rights) outside the ESOP.
- ***The governance rules must be acceptable.*** The trustee will not normally want to be involved in business decisions, but must make the ultimate decision if the company receives an offer to buy the company at a very substantial premium.
- ***The company must be willing to devote the time and resources to developing in-house expertise on the ESOP.*** Because these plans are complex, one or more people in the company must develop appropriate expertise on administrative and fiduciary issues.

Conclusions

For many owners of closely held companies, an ESOP is an ideal solution. For others, it simply will not work. There are many steps involved, and the process will take many months to complete. A good first step is to become educated about how the plans work. The National Center for Employee Ownership (NCEO) and other nonprofits in the field offer articles, books, webinars, and live meetings to help in this process. These groups can also help identify other ESOP companies which can assist.

If an ESOP seems like a choice worth exploring in more detail, the next step is a feasibility study. Professionals in this field can conduct an analysis of how the finances would work, alternative funding approaches, and different plan structures. If this is promising, then the company should hire an ESOP attorney and a trustee. The trustee will hire the appraiser. Once a fair value has been determined under one of the processes described earlier, the company can work to obtain financing and put the plan in place.

Selling a company will always involve a complex process no matter how it is done. It is one of the most serious decisions in a seller's (and company's) life, so deserves to be done carefully, considering all the financial, personal, and legacy issues that a sale entails. The materials presented in this chapter can provide some guidance.

Notes

1 Part of this case study is in a video produced by the National Center for Employee Ownership (2021b).
2 The narrative of this case study is adapted from National Center for Employee Ownership (2017, p. 6).

References

National Center for Employee Ownership. (2017). *Employee ownership* [Booklet]. https://www.nceo.org/assets/pdf/misc/Employee-Ownership-NCEO.pdf

National Center for Employee Ownership. (2021a, August). *Report on the ESOP corporategovernancesurvey*. https://www.nceo.org/data/report-esop-corporate-governance-survey

National Center for Employee Ownership. (2021b, August 20). *Why an ESOP was right for Windings, Inc.* [Video]. YouTube. https://www.youtube.com/watch?v=567VF-_DNJA

National Center for Employee Ownership. (2023, December). *Who should own your business after you? Why thousands of business owners sell to their employees* [Booklet]. https://www.nceo.org/sites/default/files/2024-02/WhoShouldOwn_EN_low-res_2024feb8.pdf

National Center for Employee Ownership. (n.d.). *Default rates on ESOP loans, 2009–2013*. https://www.nceo.org/articles/default-rates-esop-loans-2009-2013

Rosen, C., & Rodrick, S. (2024). *Understanding ESOPs* (2nd ed.). National Center for Employee Ownership.

6

UTILIZING PURPOSE TRUSTS FOR RURAL SUCCESSION AND COMMUNITY RESILIENCE

Mark C. Hand, Tiffany Vargas, and Zoe Schlag

Introduction

Small businesses represent 43% of the U.S. GDP and employ 61.7 million workers—over 46% of private sector employees (Office of Advocacy, 2023). Meanwhile, an estimated 12 million baby boomers hold ownership in privately held businesses, and as those baby boomers approach retirement in what some call the "silver tsunami," they need a liquidity solution to exit their businesses (Dodd & Beaulieu, 2022). Consequently, more than 5 million businesses holding over $10 trillion in assets will likely sell during the next decade (Cohan, 2022). However, the buy side market is simply not prepared to absorb this turnover with current deal volume. In 2023, the U.S. private equity deal count in the M&A market totaled just under 6,000 (Geoghan et al., 2024). Meanwhile, 5,723 business brokers in the U.S. in 2023 averaged two to four deals annually. The Exit Planning Institute (EPI) notes that only 30% of small businesses go on through a successful sale, leaving 70% of the market without a buyer (EPI, 2023a, 2023b).

This problem is even more stark for rural businesses, which "often lack access to business brokers or other intermediaries between the seller and the buyer" (Templin et al., 2017, p. 287). Private equity is likewise less likely to pursue targets in rural contexts due to the growth constraints a rural business may face, such as the ability to attract talent and access a growing market of consumers. Meanwhile, for businesses seeking to sell through a business broker or an online platform, there is a difficult multi-sided matching problem with talent, where businesses must find qualified executive talent both well suited to run the business and willing to move to a rural area. However, the risk of not developing affordable, feasible sale options for businesses in a rural context is

DOI: 10.4324/9781003497462-6

that without a buyer, they will simply go out of business. Such losses are of great consequence in rural communities (Beach, 2024).

Employee ownership, which businesses are increasingly using purpose trusts to achieve, offers a compelling solution to meet this opportunity. By leveraging the existing talent base in a business as well as seller financing, employee ownership buyouts represent a scalable approach to developing sale options for rural businesses across America to ensure their continuity after an owner's retirement.

Businesses in rural areas are already open to employee ownership; some 16% of all employee stock ownership plans (ESOPs) in the U.S. are based in rural counties (Kruse et al., 2024), and advocacy groups have also identified the potential for worker cooperatives in rural areas (Democracy at Work Institute, n.d.). But the potential impacts of the silver tsunami far outpace the demonstrated capacity of those alternatives. ESOPs hit a plateau in the 2000s (Rosen, 2015), and the number of worker cooperative members declined in 2022 (Kahn, 2022).

Purpose trust ownership offers an emerging corporate form that promises to be a good fit for many rural, employee-centered, and community-rooted companies that ESOPs and cooperatives have been unable to reach. By the end of 2023, there were an estimated four dozen companies across the U.S. owned by a purpose trust for the benefit of their employees and/or other stakeholder groups (Broughton et al., 2022).

In the U.K., since the establishment of tax incentives in 2014, the use of employee ownership trusts (EOT) has grown tenfold (Pendleton & Robinson, 2023). In Canada, employee ownership advocates have succeeded in establishing them as legal entities, with an eye toward similar incentives. This shift is part of a broader reimagining of business ownership and governance through the lens of shared ownership. In the U.S., adoption is accelerating using the legal structure of purpose trusts, in the context of employee ownership as an EOT, community ownership of real estate as a neighborhood trust, and more broadly through multi-stakeholder trusts.

This chapter introduces purpose trust ownership, the history of its development, and recent related scholarship on this approach. It then examines current purpose trusts to demonstrate characteristics that make them especially suitable for rural areas—namely their flexibility, low cost, and long-term ownership structure. We close with recommendations for policymakers and researchers interested in learning about and promoting purpose trust ownership.

Literature Review

This section examines research on the potential application of purpose trusts to sustain rural businesses and economies in the U.S., divided into three parts: challenges facing rural communities; the impending wave of small business closures; and the existing literature on steward ownership itself.

On the Present and Future of Rural Economies

Rural areas in the U.S. face long-term transitions that present both challenges and opportunities for development (Walzer & Merrett, 2022). These areas were already recovering from the Great Recession when the COVID-19 pandemic struck, further exacerbating their struggles (Sanders, 2023). Rural areas have experienced population decline due to aging populations and lower birth rates, and job growth has lagged behind that in urban centers (Heinrich, 2017; Soergel, 2016). Additionally, reliance on a small number of industries, underinvestment in infrastructure, and external pressures like globalization have contributed to economic disparities (Goetz et al., 2018). Healthcare challenges, including opioid use and mental illness, are prevalent in rural areas that are losing healthcare providers (Sanders, 2023).

Despite these challenges, there is potential for rural areas to thrive. The growing renewable energy industry and initiatives like the Inflation Reduction Act offer opportunities for growth (Walzer & Merrett, 2022). Remote work, accelerated by the pandemic, allows rural areas to attract workers, and the migration of retirees could bring new economic opportunities (Brown, 2021). Entrepreneurship and business succession programs that introduce alternatives like ESOPs will be key to fostering resilience (Walzer, 2004; Walzer & Merrett, 2022).

On the Silver Tsunami and Its Potential Impact on Rural Areas

The silver tsunami refers to the anticipated retirement of many baby boomer business owners, particularly in rural areas, resulting in a potential wave of business closures. This shift will affect approximately 2.34 million businesses and 24.7 million employees during the 2020s and 2030s (Hatcher, 2020). However, many owners lack succession plans—fewer than one in five have a clear plan (Business Enterprise Institute, 2016) and passing ownership to children has a low success rate (Hatcher, 2020). Many businesses close due to the difficulty of finding buyers, often leading to acquisitions by out-of-area buyers who prioritize profits over community interests. The pandemic has exacerbated these issues, with permanent closures increasing in hard-hit sectors (Brown, 2021; Crane et al., 2022).

Rural businesses are especially vulnerable due to their smaller size and the fact that they represent a larger share of employment in rural areas compared to urban areas (Wilmoth, 2023). Rural business owners are often unaware of alternative ownership models, such as employee ownership, and face challenges in securing transition financing or finding successors due to limited local talent and social capital (Ip & Jacobs, 2006; Templin et al., 2017). These businesses also play vital roles in their communities, providing employment, services, and social connections, which are crucial for rural resilience (Steiner & Atterton, 2015). When they close, they take with them not only jobs but also the social and civic networks that help rural communities thrive (Halseth & Ryser, 2006; Lovell et al., 2018).

The challenges for rural businesses are compounded by the limited access to private equity. Many rural areas have seen minimal private equity transactions, and fewer than 10% of rural business owners use business brokers, making transitions even harder (Black, 2014; Templin et al., 2017).

The Rise of Purpose Trust Ownership in the United States

Alternative ownership structures, including purpose trusts, gained attention in the 2010s as mechanisms to organize companies around goals beyond profit maximization (Kavadis & Thomsen, 2023; Mayer, 2021). Changes to the Uniform Trust Code in 2000 allowed for the creation of long-term, non-charitable purpose trusts, which have been explored increasingly for use in business ownership (Ausness, 2016; Gary, 2019). This model enables companies to be owned by a trust that holds the business's mission at the core, rather than focusing solely on profits. In Europe, purpose trusts have been utilized for mission-driven ownership, including foundation ownership (Schroeder & Thomsen, 2023).

In the U.S., the concept of stewardship ownership gained traction through initiatives like The Purpose Foundation, which promotes mission-centric governance (Sanders, 2022). In the U.K., purpose trusts have been widely used for employee ownership since the mid-2010s, spurred by tax incentives and government support (Pendleton et al., 2023). The U.K. model of employee ownership trusts (EOTs) has seen significant growth, with over 1,300 EOTs by 2022 (Employee Ownership Association, 2021). Although the U.S. lacks similar incentives, purpose trusts are emerging as an alternative ownership model, particularly for businesses transitioning away from private equity or traditional forms of ownership (Michael, 2018).

While the U.S. does not have the same legislative framework or tax incentives for purpose trusts as the U.K., the concept is growing. Purpose trusts are being explored in Canada and other countries as a model for transitioning businesses and preserving local community interests (Olijnyk, 2023; Shell, 2024).

As of 2021, trust codes in four U.S. states allow the formation of such trusts in perpetuity; others, in line with legacy rules against perpetuities, have default fixed timelines for the legal duration of a purpose trust (Bove & Langa, 2021). Oregon enshrined a corporate form—the stewardship trust—that can be used to establish a trust to employees' or other stakeholders' benefit (Gary, 2020, 2023). As of May 2024, Illinois was set to do the same with what advocates have called virtuous trusts.

Not long after converting companies to EOTs, businesses began to use purpose trusts to benefit other stakeholders as well. Organically Grown Company, an Oregon-based food distributor, became what they termed a perpetual purpose trust in 2018, benefiting the growers, customers, employees, and local community in addition to providing a return to its investors (Gary, 2019).

Since then, the field has expanded. Common Trust, an organization co-founded by one of the authors in 2022 to support businesses to exit to EOTs, launched the first capital vehicle dedicated to financing these types of buyouts (a critical component of supporting businesses to unlock liquidity), and now other capital providers are following suit. As of April 2024, scholars had identified 48 U.S. companies that had used non-charitable purpose trusts, a majority of which were located on the east or west coasts (Broughton et al., 2022; Hand, 2024). See Figure 6.1.

By industry, the highest concentrations of EOTs and other purpose trusts are in food and agriculture (10), followed by manufacturing and software. In total, those companies employed 4,000–12,500 individuals.[1] California accounted for 11 trusts, followed by Oregon (7) and Washington (4), combined representing 40% of identified purpose trusts. The most high-profile purpose trust conversion to date has been outdoor clothing company Patagonia, whose founder gifted the company to a purpose trust in 2022.

In the U.S., purpose trusts are the newest entry in a rich and increasingly dynamic tradition of employee ownership. The dominant form of employee ownership in the U.S. is the employee stock ownership plan (ESOP), in which a trust holds individual retirement accounts on behalf of a company's employees, who have "beneficial ownership" but not voting rights or tradable shares in

FIGURE 6.1 Purpose Trusts in the U.S. as of April 2024 (n=48).

Source: Compiled by authors.

the company. ESOPs grew in number through the 2000s before plateauing in the 2010s at between 6,000–7,000 U.S. companies (National Center for Employee Ownership, 2024).

Worker cooperatives, today numbering between 600–700, have a much longer history in the U.S., stretching back to its founding (Mackin, 2023). In a worker cooperative each employee ("member") has an equal vote in how the cooperative is run, and its profits are shared among members on a regular basis.

Purpose Trusts: The Basics

Regardless of the specific label, each model uses the same underlying structure: a non-charitable trust established for the benefit of a purpose rather than a person (Groff & Gary, 2023). The trust is dedicated to achieving a specific purpose, usually to protect the mission of the company, and operates based on this mission or objective. This characteristic makes purpose trusts an important tool for owners looking to create a legacy that upholds their company values. By establishing a purpose trust, individuals or businesses can ensure that their assets are dedicated to achieving specific long-term objectives across generations. The trust may also include employee control of the business and an emphasis on sharing profits and benefits with employees.

Depending on state legislation, a purpose trust may exist indefinitely, continuing its mission long after the death of the person who established the trust and the trustees. These trusts are governed by a Trust Agreement, which outlines the fiduciary duties of the trustees (also known as the trust stewardship committee). This legal document ensures that the trust assets are managed in accordance with the specified purpose. Purpose trusts have jurisdictional variation across the U.S. Only a few states, including Delaware, New Hampshire, Wyoming, Oregon, and Maine, have enacted trust laws that fully accommodate the requirements for perpetual purpose trusts. These laws allow the trust to function without beneficiaries.

Of central importance in the use of purpose trusts for corporate ownership is the role of trustees, who are legally responsible for ensuring that the company fulfills the purpose of the trust, including balancing the interests of the stakeholders laid out in the trust (e.g., employees, community members, the company itself) and whatever other purposes are specified in the trust documents.

A Brief Typology of Purpose Trusts

A clarification of definitions is needed before continuing the discussion. The growing field of alternative ownership uses a wide array of contested terms, as is often the case in nascent industries in which individual players work to define terms to their advantage (Santos & Eisenhardt, 2009).

Legally speaking, the examples used below all have the same legal structure: a non-charitable purpose trust with no ascertainable beneficiaries. This structure was made possible starting in the 2000s by changes in the Uniform Trust Code (Hirsch, 2009).

In this emerging industry, stakeholders have pushed forward a variety of definitions, each with its own clarity, ambiguity, and contest. They variably refer to legal structures, philosophical commitments, branding choices, or have simply spread as marketing terms used by advocates. They include:

- Philosophical ownership approaches
    - **Steward ownership**. A set of ownership principles advocated for by Purpose Foundation and its global affiliates, which can be achieved through multiple legal forms, including purpose trusts.
    - **Employee ownership**. An approach toward ownership of corporate assets that typically allows the broad base of employees to participate in the financial success of the business and have a say in how it is run. This can be achieved through a variety of legal structures, and the level of economic benefit and governance rights varies by legal design.
- Legal definitions
    - **Perpetual purpose trusts**. A non-charitable trust with no ascertainable beneficiaries established for the benefit of its purposes. In the U.S., purpose trusts are often used as employee ownership trusts.
    - **Employee ownership trusts**. A recognized legal form in the U.K., and which has worked its way into some U.S. state laws.[2] In the U.S., this phrase is used to describe purpose trusts whose structure is designed to hold assets for the benefit of employees of the business owned by the trust.
    - **Stewardship trusts**. A recognized legal form in Oregon; also used as an umbrella term to include different types of purpose trusts.
    - **Virtuous trusts**. A pending recognized legal form in Illinois similar to stewardship trusts in Oregon.
- Other non-legal use cases of various ownership structures
    - **Neighborhood trusts**. A non-legal term that refers to purpose trusts being used to hold ownership of real estate assets to support place-based economic development (Schneider, 2024).
    - **Christian purpose trusts**. A non-legal phrase for purpose trusts set to sectarian purposes (Simmons, 2019).
    - **Ownership trusts, trust ownership, and purpose trust ownership**. Non-legal umbrella phrases that include different types of purpose trusts. They vary in focus, e.g., *trust* versus *purpose* as the salient feature of ownership.

This chapter does not attempt to resolve the conceptual confusion, anticipating that these terms will continue to be "essentially contested concepts" (Gallie, 1955). We use the following definitions in this chapter:

- **Purpose trust** and **purpose trust ownership**. Umbrella terms that loosely include all types of purpose trust-based ownership of companies and real estate assets for the benefit of employees, local communities, and other stakeholders, often with features of steward ownership.
- **Employee ownership trust**. A company owned by a purpose trust primarily for the benefit of employees.
- **Neighborhood trust**. Real estate owned by a purpose trust to the benefit of its local community.
- **Multi-stakeholder trust**. Companies owned by a purpose trust for the benefit of multiple stakeholders, often but not always including employees.

Purpose Trust Ownership as a Tool for Rural Economic Growth

Because the concept of ownership via purpose trust is so novel, their full benefits have not yet been realized. This section points to three key features of purpose trusts that will be of special benefit to rural areas: (a) their flexibility; (b) their relatively low cost; and (c) their potential perpetuity. Examples of existing purpose trusts, rural and otherwise, demonstrate those potential benefits.

The Flexibility of Trust Ownership

The first feature of purpose trusts that make them suitable for application to rural areas is that they are remarkably flexible vehicles. Built from the same legal foundation that enables wealth holders to provide for cemetery plots and pets (Cuccinello, 2023), purpose trusts offer an open platform for owners to decide how the trust is established, for what purpose, and for whose benefit (Michael, 2017; Rosen & Case, 2022).

The most common use of purpose trusts that own corporate assets is for the benefit of employees, as in the U.K. There, scholars have suggested that EOTs offer several benefits. They can offer more scope for democratic participation, to the degree that owners consider trust deeds as a constitutional document (Cathcart, 2014). That participation can include worker directorships, employee councils, employee trustees, and employee shareholder meetings (Pendleton & Robinson, 2023). Through these mechanisms, employees can establish greater voice in the strategic direction of the company, including in the decision of whether and when to sell the company (Cathcart, 2014). In the U.K., this promise of participation is baked into the law governing EOTs, where employee ownership must be both significant (which at least some authors interpret to mean "financially significant") and meaningful (to include democratic participation) (Pendleton et al., 2023). So far, the U.S. has established no U.K.-style incentives, which also means no U.K.-style requirements, leaving owners in the driver's seat as they establish a trust.

Employee benefit is only one of the purposes for which purpose trusts can be used. The flexibility of purpose trusts means that owners can extend benefits to other stakeholders, including employees, suppliers, customers, communities, defined neighborhoods (called neighborhood trusts), or social, environmental, or even spiritual causes (Simmons, 2019). The Organically Grown Company, for example, established what they termed a stewardship trust overseen by five separate groups: employees, farmers, customers, community allies, and investors (Gary, 2020).

This diversity of causes directly reflects the hybrid motivations of many rural business owners, for whom benefiting a local community is often a priority (Bosworth, 2012; Smith, 2008). Steiner and Atterton (2015) argue that

> in entrepreneurial decisions, profit is often not the most important factor considered by rural business owners, who may be motivated by other considerations, such as growing the local economy and supporting local businesses … there is a growing body of evidence suggesting that rural businesses are more than just "money making machines" and that rural business owners extend their desires above and beyond pure profitability.
>
> *(p. 9)*

A recent survey of Minnesota small business owners bears this out: "rural business owners were highly correlated with increased concern for keeping the business in the community" (Darger et al., 2024).

Case Study 1: Clegg Auto

In addition to holding multiple *purposes*, purpose trusts are also flexible enough to hold multiple *companies*. For instance, in 2022, Clegg Auto transitioned its four subsidiary businesses to a single EOT (Price, 2023). Clegg Auto represents a group of four auto repair and body shops located in Utah. Originally founded and led by two brothers, the owners sought to transition the businesses to employee ownership in 2022. After reviewing the various approaches toward employee ownership—including an ESOP and a worker cooperative—Kevin Clegg chose to pursue a buyout of the four businesses utilizing an EOT. They were attracted to that model due to its flexibility and simplicity when compared with the ESOP.

In addition, Kevin Clegg was especially attracted to the concept of steward ownership, and the ability to establish a long-term ownership structure able to protect key company values and ensure that employees benefit from the companies' success. Clegg was doubly attracted to the EOT as a legal vehicle to protect and enshrine the companies' commitment to high-quality customer service.

In 2022, the shareholders of Clegg Auto combined all four subsidiaries into a single EOT. Employees at all four companies participate in a profit-sharing program and employee participation in governance is protected in the trust. The new ownership structure brought promising results, even in the early years. In addition to strong company performance, and being able to share profits with employees, the companies recorded their highest customer satisfaction rating in the company history.

The use of purpose trusts as a roll-up vehicle presents a unique opportunity in the rural context. For the subset of rural businesses that are profitable but much smaller (i.e., 10–50 employees or fewer), a key barrier in any sale process will be the cost of the transaction. Because purpose trusts represent a lower-cost pathway to employee ownership, they offer a more accessible exit strategy to smaller businesses that might be dissuaded by the costs of establishing and administering an ESOP (Michie, 2017).

Furthermore, given the ease of successive mergers and acquisitions, EOTs offer a unique roll-up opportunity to offer liquidity to selling business owners, establish a long-term ownership structure for rural businesses that do not require a future sale, and build resilience across smaller businesses through a holding company structure, owned by the EOT.

Case Study 2: Kensington Corridor Trust

Purpose trusts are flexible enough to establish the purpose not only of companies, but also of real estate assets. For instance, in 2019 the Kensington Corridor Trust (KCT) was established to acquire and redevelop real estate in the Kensington Corridor of Philadelphia. The trust structure was pursued to address vacancies and speculative development within the Kensington Corridor. Through acquisition and redevelopment of real estate, the KCT sought to place local real estate assets into long-term community control, while preserving affordability (Black, 2024). Under this model, the trust owns real estate assets, and the governance of the trust is overseen by community members and small business owners to ensure that assets held by the trust are governed for the benefit of the local community as opposed to speculative investors.

While the KCT offers a unique example of using purpose trusts in an urban context, it offers lessons and tools for use in rural areas as well. KCT offers a blueprint for how commercial districts can be improved while also ensuring that the needs of residents are recognized in that process. For rural towns seeking to pursue redevelopment of commercial districts, the purpose trust structure offers an alternative to traditional real estate development that can ensure that the priorities and needs of residents will be protected through that redevelopment process.

Case Study 3: ACP International

The flexibility of purpose trusts allows owners to separate economic and governance rights in the company. This benefits owners in two ways. First, it allows owners to stage ownership transitions and leadership transitions over time. Second, it shifts the focus from share ownership as the mechanism for driving wealth, to profit-sharing.

An example of a company taking advantage of both features is ACP International in Arlington, Texas. ACP, which manufactures signs and safety equipment, converted to an EOT in 2022. One selling owner remained as the company's CEO, with plans to slowly transition responsibility to his leadership team, and expanded the company's profit-sharing with employees as part of the sale (Hand et al., 2023).

Case Study 4: Berrett-Koehler Publishers

Finally, the separation of economic and governance rights possible through a purpose trust means that owners have many more options available to them in terms of how they reward employees. Most purpose trusts have profit-sharing programs, with the formula for that distribution spelled out in the purpose trust documents. But a business owned by a purpose trust can issue equity to employees, establish ESOPs, issue 401(k)s, or incorporate other long-term asset-building programs. For example, Berrett-Koehler Publishers was founded in 1992 with "a deep sense of responsibility to administer the publishing company for the benefit of all of our 'stakeholder' groups—authors, customers, employees, suppliers and subcontractors, owners and the societal and environmental communities in which we live and work" (Berrett-Koehler Publishers, n.d.). During the company's history, the company was able to incorporate several components to pursue successively more aligned ownership and governance. For instance, "the company created an ESOP and raised capital directly from authors, readers, service providers and other community members, so that Berrett-Koehler would be owned by its stakeholders and their interests represented" (Jorgensen, 2020). In 2011, the company became a Certified B Corporation. And yet still, because the company's founder remained the largest shareholder, the company sought to find a liquidity solution that would structurally preserve the company's mission and independence after his exit. To do so, the company established a perpetual purpose trust to eventually become the largest shareholder of the company, safeguarding its mission and purposes over the long term.

Berrett-Koehler's example provides unique insights and opportunities for rural businesses. First, given that exit options are more limited in rural areas, the unique features of purpose trusts as a long-term ownership structure for businesses is an attractive offering in a rural context because the business won't need to be resold again. Secondarily, because purpose trusts and steward ownership can be established in conjunction with other forms of employee ownership such as an ESOP, companies that may already have an ESOP can establish a purpose trust for its governance benefits.

The Low Cost and Ease of Transitioning to Purpose Trust Ownership

A second feature of purpose trusts is that they are relatively inexpensive and easy to initiate and implement relative to ESOPs (Michie, 2017; Patton Power, 2021). This is mainly thanks to being regulated at the state level as trusts, rather than at the federal level as retirement accounts that require annual valuations (Michie, 2017; Rosen & Case, 2022). Purpose trusts, by contrast, separate stakeholder benefits (protected by the trust) and stakeholder participation in decision-making (established separately in the trust documents). As a result, stakeholder participation in the governance of purpose trusts can be established over time, as suits each individual company. This relative inexpensiveness makes them more appropriate for small businesses in which rural areas over-index (Wilmoth, 2023).

In addition to the relatively low cost to establish a purpose trust or EOT as an exit strategy, the most common capital structures utilized for these transactions are uniquely scalable within a rural context, where liquidity is more limited. An EOT buyout functions through the purchase of shares of a selling owner through a leveraged buyout. This is typically capitalized either through a mix of bank debt, mezzanine debt and/or seller financing, or entirely through seller financing. Through this structure, selling business owners can access liquidity while lenders are paid back through company cash flow during the term of their loan. Because most EOT buyouts transact through a combination of third-party debt and seller financing, business owners can sell their business to an EOT using entirely local sources of capital, such as bank debt from a local bank and seller financing from the selling owner.

Case Study 5: Text-Em-All

While 100% seller-financed transactions are relatively rare in the world of leveraged buyouts, most of the EOTs established in the U.K. have been established with majority, if not 100% seller financing (Gateley Legal, 2021).

This transaction structure offers a unique liquidity solution for selling business owners in rural areas who may not be connected to sources of capital to support a sponsored transaction, or, as discussed earlier, are hesitant to disclose to anyone that they are putting the business up for sale, for fear of losing employees or customers.

Text-Em-All is a Software as a Service (SaaS) business founded in 2002. In 2023 its founders converted the company to an EOT using principles of steward ownership. The transaction was financed 100% through seller financing, allowing the selling owners to be bought out progressively over time through company cash flow. While the selling owners would have had a range of financing options had they chosen to pursue that pathway, they chose to pursue seller financing for a variety of reasons, including that the selling business owners were not ready to transition out operationally, but wanted to begin the process of transitioning to employee ownership to unlock the performance gains that come with it (Razo, 2024).

A unique liquidity challenge for rural businesses is that they may struggle to access equity financing, and, in the case of smaller businesses, they may not be able to access bank debt for a transaction. As a result, a 100% seller-financed transaction where a selling owner is bought out over time offers a uniquely scalable liquidity solution for healthy, profitable businesses that may otherwise lack access to capital.

A Long-Term Ownership Structure

A third major advantage of EOTs for rural areas is that they offer a long-term ownership structure for rural businesses. The combination of using perpetual purpose trusts coupled with the capital structure used at the time of the buyout, with cash flow deleveraging the business over time, results in the business now existing under an ownership structure that is not required or inherently incentivized to seek a future sale in subsequent years. Unlike other buyers of businesses (such as private equity, search funds, or other equity sponsors) who must exit the business to realize the value of the appreciated shares, EOTs do not require the future sale of the business. Rather, the trust is intended to be the long-term owner of the business, allowing it to operate with an orientation toward long-term firm survival rather than preparing the business to be marketable for a future sale (Blasi et al., 2013).

Case Study 6: Organically Grown Company

Furthermore, purpose trusts can be designed in such a way to offer a protective mechanism against a future sale of the business if certain conditions are not met. This is especially important in a rural context where the survival of local firms that provide local jobs and that reinvest in the community is of particular importance. This was a primary concern of the Organically Grown Company (OGC), which had previously established an ESOP. As Gary (2020) writes, OGC's executives

> knew that the financial success of the company made it attractive to external buyers. They feared, however, that outside buyers might not care about OGC's mission. They also worried that the financial success of OGC made it an attractive target for a corporate takeover, and that the fiduciary duties of the directors to maximize benefit for shareholders might make it impossible to resist a takeover attempt.
>
> *(p. 711)*

That legacy, argues Michie (2022), is also central to stakeholders' sense of ownership over the firm. In the John Lewis Partnership in the U.K., for example, Michie argues that employees' drive to contribute is sustained in part by their knowledge that the firm is legally protected from takeover by an outside group not committed to the firm's goals and the benefit of future employees.

This advantage does involve a tradeoff. Because a purpose trust may contain certain provisions around when a sale can be approved, a business that is owned by a trust and needs to raise additional equity financing to finance growth may find itself with a smaller market of equity providers from which to raise capital, because these types of provisions are to date quite new, and therefore not yet familiar or market standard with equity providers.

Purpose Trust Ownership as an Opportunity for Policymakers and Researchers

As covered in this chapter, purpose trust ownership offers a unique set of advantages to rural business owners looking for ways to transition out of their business. This section suggests ways that federal, state, and local policymakers might support this nascent field, and the paths forward it offers to scholars focused on rural development and employee ownership. As demonstrated, because purpose trusts are uniquely flexible and can be utilized for a wide range of ownership goals, policy is most likely to develop around the specific use cases of purpose trusts.

Recommendations for Rural Policymakers

Policymakers have long played a central role in the diffusion and dynamics of employee ownership around the world, and they have ample reasons for doing so. Businesses that successfully transition from the original owner not only remain in local hands, but tend to expand, hire more employees, and increase sales (Darger et al., 2024; Templin et al., 2017), especially to the degree that they reflect the community-mindedness of their environment (Birkhead et al., 2024). Early signs indicate there is serious demand among rural business owners for new options. When Colorado established tax incentives to support conversions to employee ownership writ large, for example, 60% of calls asking for more information came from business owners located in rural counties (Heffernan, 2024).

Policymakers interested in encouraging the spread of purpose trusts have many tools at their disposal, including increasing awareness and education of the model, offering tax incentives, and reducing the technical and administrative burdens of conversion (Nuttall, 2012).

In a recent white paper, purpose trust advocates offered recommendations to policymakers at both the federal and state/local levels (Hand et al., 2024). At the federal level, recommendations include the reorientation of the Small Business Administration (SBA) programs and its SCORE Mentor program toward business retention and transition, including to purpose trust transition; the exploration of the Department of Agriculture's 26 business support programs to determine which could develop a focus on purpose trust ownership; the easing of community development financial institution (CDFI) lending to purpose trusts; and incorporation of purpose trust ownership into workforce development programs.

On the state level, advocates recommended waiving rules against perpetuities and allowing trusts without ascertainable beneficiaries; exploring state-specific legislative models for purpose trusts; extending employee ownership conversion tax credits to purpose trusts; and prioritizing purpose trust businesses for state contracts. They also advocated for the establishment of state-level employee ownership offices or commissions within economic development agencies, to provide transition resources and connections, which could boost awareness and adoption through local campaigns, workshops, and incentives.

Each state also has agencies focused on small business, labor, workforce development, agriculture, and banking; each of these are potential homes for initiatives in support of trust ownership. Most locally, chambers of commerce and county-level economic development agencies are natural homes for programs that would boost retention of local businesses.

Implications for Research

This chapter highlights several directions for future research regarding the role of business succession in rural economies and employee ownership more generally. First, we underline the potential impact on rural areas of the coming wave of retirements by baby boomer business owners. Rural businesses are often deeply embedded in their communities, serving as important sources of employment, goods and services, and social connection. Their closure could lead to a loss of jobs, a decline in the availability of essential goods and services, and a weakening of social ties. Future research could examine not only how business closures affect different types of rural communities, but also how some communities are preparing for and responding to the silver tsunami.

Second, the dearth of research on EOTs, neighborhood trusts, multi-stakeholder trusts, and steward ownership is important. In this chapter we discussed mainly the *potential* for this type of ownership to contribute to rural economic development, borrowing theory from research on other forms of employee ownership, and leaning on non-academic writing for examples of existing trusts. Missing so far is theoretically rooted empirical research of steward ownership in the U.S., including how and why owners choose from among ownership options; how those companies are set up during the transition; the impact of new organizational form on the management and performance of the company; those companies' impact on employees, stakeholders, and communities; and the legal and regulatory frameworks around them.

Conclusions

In many important ways, rural economies are struggling. At the same time, recent trends, such as the rise of remote working and increased internet infrastructure spending, offer unique opportunities to rural business owners and communities. But one trend threatens this rural renaissance: in the next ten years, a disproportionate number of baby boomer business owners will retire, leaving the future of small and medium-sized businesses in question. Those retirements, if they lead to closures, will deeply affect rural communities, in which businesses often serve as social as well as economic centers of gravity.

Converting these businesses to purpose trust ownership offers one promising option for transitioning businesses from original owners to a form of ownership well-suited to rural areas with primary features that benefit rural owners and their communities. These trusts are remarkably flexible, meaning they can be used for a wide variety of purposes, and can hold different combinations of corporate and real estate assets, tailored to fit the needs of the diverse businesses and communities in rural America.

Second, purpose trusts are relatively inexpensive to set up and transact with capital structures that are widely accessible in a rural context, and as a result more suitable for the smaller businesses often found in rural communities. They offer the potential of perpetuity, a core value of rural American communities.

Just as rural business owners should consider purpose trust ownership as an exit option, rural policymakers should consider how they might support the growth of trust ownership in their communities, through advocacy programs, tax incentives, and other policies. Researchers also can use purpose trust ownership as a testbed for theories of rural development and employee ownership, contributing to the resilience of rural American communities for future generations.

Acknowledgments

The authors thank Simon Pek for feedback on previous drafts.

Notes

1 This number excludes the nearly 45,000 employees of Hobby Lobby, which the authors have not been able to confirm operates under a perpetual purpose trust. According to Penley (2022), "100% of the company's voting stock has been moved to a trust where the 'stewardship' can continue to pass on to one person from another."

2 Scholars question whether employee ownership trust is an appropriate name, given the lack of actual employee ownership—direct or indirect—in the model. At least one has proposed using employee-centered purpose trust as an alternative (Gary, 2023). We use employee ownership trust here, as it remains the most-used phrase.

References

Ausness, R. C. (2016). Non-charitable purpose trusts: Past, present, and future. *Real Property, Trust and Estate Law Journal 51*, 321.

Beach, B. (2024, July 1). *A "silver tsunami" is hitting rural America as small business owners retire without replacements*. Harvest Public Media & National Public Radio. https://www.kcur.org/news/2024-07-01/silver-tsunami-rural-america-small-business-owners-retire

Berrett-Koehler Publishers (n.d.). *About Berrett-Koehler Publishers*. Retrieved October 1, 2024, from https://www.bkconnection.com/home/bk-community-menu/about-berrett-koehler-publishers

Birkhead, C., Gibson, N., & Hand, M. C. (2024). Where employee ownership works best. *International Review of Applied Economics, 38*, 1–13. 10.1080/02692171.2024.2410227

Black, G. (2014, August 6). *The geography of U.S. PE investments*. PitchBook. https://pitchbook.com/news/articles/the-geography-of-u-s-pe-investments

Black, K. (2024). *Kensington Corridor Trust: The first four years*. Nowak Metro Finance Lab, Drexel University. https://drexel.edu/nowak-lab/publications/case-studies/kensington-corridor-trust/

Blasi J., Kruse, D., & Weltmann, D. (2013). Firm survival and performance in privately held ESOP companies. In D. Kruse (Ed.), *Sharing ownership, profits, and decision-making in the 21st century* (pp. 109–124). Emerald Group Publishing. 10.1108/S0885-3339(2013)0000014006

Bosworth, G. (2012). Characterising rural businesses—Tales from the paperman. *Journal of Rural Studies, 28*(4), 499–506. 10.1016/j.jrurstud.2012.07.002

Bove, A. A., Jr., & Langa, M. (2021). The perpetual business purpose trust: The business planning vehicle for the future, starting now. *ACTEC Law Journal, 47*(1), Article 3. https://scholarlycommons.law.hofstra.edu/acteclj/vol47/iss1/3

Broughton, A. C., Blasi, J., Schlag, Z., Razo, D., Hand, M. (2022). *Employee ownership trusts and perpetual purpose trusts in the United States* (Version 5) [Data set]. Harvard Dataverse. 10.7910/DVN/EYGHCW

Brown, R. (2021). How to save jobs and build back better: Employee ownership transitions as a key to an equitable economic recovery. *Maine Policy Review, 30*(2), 111–115. 10.53558/hoze8462

Business Enterprise Institute. (2016). *2016 business owner survey report*. https://web.archive.org/web/20170710233039/https://www.google.com/recaptcha/api2/anchor?k=6LeDgCMUAAAAAAMQyQbYomnsv5fQ2ohSrFvcLH5D&co=aHR0cHM6Ly9leGl0cGxhbm5pbmcuY29tOjQ0Mw&hl=en&v=r20170629165701&theme=light&size=compact&cb=jg4x7n75l68n

Cathcart, A. (2014). Paradoxes of participation: Non-union workplace partnership in John Lewis. *The International Journal of Human Resource Management*, *25*(6), 762–780. 10.1080/09585192.2012.743476

Cohan, T. M. (2022, July 27). *The current rise in small businesses being sold over the next 10 –15 years*. SCORE. https://www.score.org/princeton/resource/blog-post/current-rise-small-businesses-being-sold-over-next-10-15-years

Crane, L. D., Decker, R. A., Flaaen, A., Hamins-Puertolas, A., & Kurz, C. (2022). Business exit during the COVID-19 pandemic: Non-traditional measures in historical context. *Journal of Macroeconomics*, *72*, 103419. 10.1016/j.jmacro.2022.103419

Cuccinello, H. (2023, July 28). Inheritance for your dog: How the rich put millions into trusts with very specific purposes, from taking care of pets to cryogenically freezing their bodies. Business Insider. https://www.businessinsider.com/purpose-trusts-estate-planning-wealth-management-2023-7

Darger, M., Petel, A., Hebeisen, J., Reed, C., & Dragotta, J. (2024, March). What new University of Minnesota Extension research reveals about business owners' plans for the future transition of their firms. *Minnesota Economic Trends*. https://mn.gov/deed/newscenter/publications/trends/march-2024/transition.jsp

Democracy at Work Institute. (n.d.). *Rural development*. Retrieved October 1, 2024, from https://institute.coop/rural-development

Dodd, T., & Beaulieu, B. (2022, July). *The "silver tsunami" and its effect on the M&A landscape* [White paper]. Butcher Joseph & Co & ITR Economics. https://butcherjoseph.com/wp-content/uploads/2022/05/Silver_Tsunami_White_Paper.pdf

Employee Ownership Association. (2021). *What the evidence tells us: Employee ownership performing well on ESG objectives*. https://web.archive.org/web/20200104033001/http://employeeownership.co.uk/resources/what-the-evidence-tells-us/

Exit Planning Institute. (2023a). *2023 national state of owner readiness*. https://exit-planning-institute.org/2023-national-state-of-owner-readiness

Exit Planning Institute. (2023b). *2023 state of owner readiness report*. https://exit-planning-institute.org/state-of-owner-readiness

Gallie, W. B. (1955). Essentially contested concepts. *Proceedings of the Aristotelian Society*, *56*, 167–198.

Gary, S. N. (2019). The need for a new type of purpose trust, the Stewardship Trust. *ACTEC Law Journal 45*(1), Article 8. https://scholarlycommons.law.hofstra.edu/acteclj/vol45/iss1/8

Gary, S. N. (2020). The Oregon stewardship trust: A new type of purpose trust that enables steward-ownership of a business. *University of Cincinnati Law Review*, *88*(3), 707–733.

Gary, S. N. (2023). The changing landscape of business succession: How and why purpose trusts matter. *Ohio State Business Law Journal*, *18*(1), 41–98. 10.2139/ssrn.4551502

Gateley Legal. (2021, January 7). *A practical guide to employee ownership trusts*. Gateley. https://gateleyplc.com/insight/article/a-practical-guide-to-employee-ownership-trusts/

Geoghan, S., Glick, S., Hodell, J., Moss, S., Batchelor, G. T., & Smith, C. (2024, February 2). *Private equity 2023 year-in-review and 2024 outlook: Clearer skies emerge for private equity amidst challenges*. Cherry Bekeart. https://www.cbh.com/guide/reports/private-equity-industry-report-2023-trends-and-2024-outlook/

Goetz, S. J., Partridge, M. D., & Stephens, H. M. (2018). The economic status of rural America in the President Trump era and beyond. *Applied Economic Perspectives and Policy*, *40*(1), 97–118. 10.1093/aepp/ppx061

Groff, B., & Gary, S. (2023). Patagonia, purpose trusts, and stewardship trusts: Business with a purpose. *Probate and Property*, *37*(1), 36–41.

Halseth, G., & Ryser, L. (2006). Trends in service delivery: Examples from rural and small town Canada, 1998 to 2005. *Journal of Rural and Community Development*, *1*(2), 69–90. https://journals.brandonu.ca/jrcd/article/view/40

Hand, M. (2024, April 11). *The state of the field of purpose trust ownership* [Presentation]. Purpose Trust Ownership Convening, Employee Ownership Ideas Forum, Aspen Institute, Washington, DC, United States.

Hand, M., Everett, J., Garvey, M., & Raafat, S. (2024, May 24). *Our policy recommendations on purpose trust ownership*. Employee Ownership + Workplace Democracy. https://www.eowd.org/p/our-policy-recommendations-on-purpose

Hand, M., Watson, W., Storkan, S., Nussbaum, J., Whittaker, C., Cinatl, F. (2023, March 30). *Employee ownership lunch panel* [Video]. Employee Ownership + Workplace Development, Labor and Employment Law Association, & The Texas Center for Employee Ownership. Southern Methodist University, Dallas, Texas. https://www.eowd.org/p/video-employee-ownership-at-smu

Hatcher, D. (2020). Rethinking options for retiring entrepreneurs. *ProfitWise News and Views*, No. 3. https://www.chicagofed.org/~/media/publications/profitwise-news-and-views/2020/pnv3-2020-rethinking-options-for-retiring-entrepreneurs.pdf

Heffernan, N. (2024, May 2). *Innovations in state employee ownership policy* [Video]. The Aspen Institute. May 2, 2024. https://www.aspeninstitute.org/videos/innovations-in-state-employee-ownership-policy/

Heinrich, M. (2017, May). *Understanding economic challenges in rural America*. U.S. Congress Joint Economic Committee. https://www.jec.senate.gov/public/_cache/files/fe1f3a2f-f89c-4628-ac6a-0e3b5fb8fafc/rural-economy-report-final.pdf

Hirsch, A. J. (2009, November). Delaware unifies the law of charitable and noncharitable purpose trusts. *Estate Planning*. FSU College of Law, Public Law Research Paper No. 402, FSU College of Law, Law, Business & Economics Paper No. 09-30. https://ssrn.com/abstract=1481977

Ip, B., & Jacobs, G. (2006). Business succession planning: A review of the evidence. *Journal of Small Business and Enterprise Development*, *13*(3), 326–350. 10.1108/14626000610680230

Jorgensen, M. (2020, May 29). *A mission-driven publisher's succession to shared ownership*. Purpose Foundation. https://www.purpose-us.com/writing/the-life-of-an-idea-an-independent-publishing-company-transitions-to-steward-ownership

Kahn, K. (2022, February 11). Latest worker co-op survey shows more co-ops but fewer workers. *Fifty by Fifty: Employee Ownership News*. https://www.fiftybyfifty.org/2022/02/latest-worker-co-op-survey-shows-more-co-ops-but-fewer-workers/

Kavadis, N., & Thomsen, S. (2023). Sustainable corporate governance: A review of research on long-term corporate ownership and sustainability. *Corporate Governance: An International Review*, *31*(1), 198–226. 10.1111/corg.12486

Kruse, D., Blasi, J., & Moriarty, J. (2024, April 8). *ESOPs in rural areas* [Issue brief]. Aspen Institute Economic Opportunities Forum & Institute for the Study of Employee Ownership and Profit Sharing at Rutgers University. https://www.aspeninstitute.org/publications/esops-in-rural-areas/

Lovell, S. A., Gray, A., & Boucher, S. E. (2018). Economic marginalization and community capacity: How does industry closure in a small town affect perceptions of place? *Journal of Rural Studies*, *62*, 107–115. 10.1016/j.jrurstud.2018.07.002

Mackin, C. (2023). Defining employee ownership: Four meanings and two models. *Journal of Participation and Employee Ownership*. Advance online publication. 10.1108/JPEO-10-2022-0019

Mayer, C. (2021). The future of the corporation and the economics of purpose. *Journal of Management Studies*, *58*(3), 887–901. 10.1111/joms.12660

Michael, C. (2017). *The employee ownership trust: An ESOP alternative*. Employee Ownership Trust Advisors. https://eotadvisors.com/the-employee-ownership-trust-eot-an-esop-alternative (Reprinted from "The employee ownership trust: An ESOP alternative," Jan/Feb 2017, *Probate & Property*, *31*[1], 42–47).

Michael, C. (2018, December 28). The British are coming—ESOPs and perpetual trusts. *Fifty by Fifty: Employee Ownership News*. https://www.fiftybyfifty.org/2018/12/the-british-are-coming-esops-and-perpetual-trusts/ (Reprinted from "The British are coming—ESOPs and perpetual trusts," December, 2018, Employee-Owned America, https://employeeownedamerica.com/2018/12/10/the-british-are-coming-esops-and-perpetual-trusts/).

Michie, J. (2017). The importance of ownership. In J. Michie, J. R. Blasi, & C. Borzaga (Eds.), *The Oxford handbook of mutual, co-operative, and co-owned business* (online ed., pp. 3–13). Oxford Academic. 10.1093/oxfordhb/9780199684977.013.1

Michie, J. (2022). "Forms of ownership for sustainability and resilience: The need for biodiversity and corporate diversity." In P. Arestis & M. Sawyer (Eds.), *Economic policies for sustainability and resilience* (pp. 91–133). Palgrave Macmillan. 10.1007/978-3-030-84288-8_3

National Center for Employee Ownership. (2024). *Employee ownership by the numbers*. https://www.nceo.org/articles/employee-ownership-by-the-numbers

Nuttall, G. (2012, July). *Sharing success: The Nuttall review of employee ownership*. Crown. https://assets.publishing.service.gov.uk/government/uploads/system/uploads/attachment_data/file/31706/12-933-sharing-success-nuttall-review-employee-ownership.pdf

Office of Advocacy. (2023, March 7). *Frequently asked questions about small business, 2023*. U.S. Small Business Administration. https://advocacy.sba.gov/2023/03/07/frequently-asked-questions-about-small-business-2023/

Olijnyk, Z. (2023, March 31). New employee ownership trusts provide an option in succession planning, but not hoped-for tax breaks. *Canadian Lawyer*. https://www.canadianlawyermag.com/news/general/new-employee-ownership-trusts-provide-an-option-in-succession-planning-but-not-hoped-for-tax-breaks/374859

Patton Power, A. (2021). *Adventure finance: How to create a funding journey that blends profit and purpose*. Palgrave Macmillan. 10.1007/978-3-030-72428-3_27

Pendleton, A., & Robinson, A. (2023, January 14). *Employee ownership trusts: A new era in British employee ownership* [Google slides]. Google Docs. https://docs.google.com/presentation/d/1GJjbuH-iQBoCVTWVo0dB5Sq4_pZFo6TY/edit#slide=id.p1

Pendleton, A., Robinson, A., & Nuttall, G. (2023). Employee ownership in the UK. *Journal of Participation and Employee Ownership*, *6*(3), 194–214. 10.1108/JPEO-11-2022-0030

Penley, T. (2022, October 23). *Hobby Lobby CEO inspires with faith-over-fortune message after giving up company: "Wealth can be a curse"*. Fox News. https://www.foxnews.com/media/hobby-lobby-ceo-inspires-faith-fortune-message-giving-company-wealth-curse

Price, D. (2023, May 24). *A Utah auto shop demonstrates a pathway to worker ownership via a perpetual purpose trust*. ImpactAlpha. https://impactalpha.com/a-utah-auto-shop-demonstrates-a-pathway-to-worker-ownership-via-a-perpetual-purpose-trust

Razo, D. (2024, April). *Text-Em-All embarks on a revolutionary journey with its transition to an employee ownership trust*. Common Trust. https://www.common-trust.com/blog/text-em-all-employee-ownership-trust

Rosen, C. (2015, February). *Why has the total number of ESOPs gone down but participation and assets gone up?* National Center for Employee Ownership. https://www.nceo.org/observations-employee-ownership/c/ESOP-numbers

Rosen, C., & Case, J. (2022). *Ownership: Reinventing companies, capitalism, and who owns what*. Berrett-Koehler Publishers.

Sanders, A. (2022). Binding capital to free purpose: Steward ownership in Germany. *European Company and Financial Law Review*, *19*(4): 622–653. 10.1515/ecfr-2022-0020

Sanders, A. (2023, November 24). *Rural employment and unemployment*. Economic Research Service, U.S. Department of Agriculture. https://www.ers.usda.gov/topics/rural-economy-population/employment-education/rural-employment-and-unemployment/

Santos, F. M., & Eisenhardt, K. M. (2009). Constructing markets and shaping boundaries: Entrepreneurial power in nascent fields. *Academy of Management Journal*, *52*(4), 643–671.

Schneider, K. (2024, May 13). Priced out of housing, communities take development into their own hands. *The New York Times*. https://www.nytimes.com/2024/05/13/business/gentrifying-neighborhoods-community-coops.html

Schroeder, D. J., & Thomsen, S. (2023). Foundation ownership and sustainability. *Academy of Management Proceedings*, *2023*(1). 10.5465/AMPROC.2023.12206abstract

Shell, J. (2024, May 9). *Employee ownership trusts: What they mean for Canadian business owners*. Medium. https://jonshell.medium.com/employee-ownership-trusts-what-they-mean-for-canadian-business-owners-15bb71157cf0

Simmons, T. E. (2019). Christian purpose trusts. *Creighton Law Review*, *53*, 643–657. https://cdr.creighton.edu/items/80f3198a-7c53-4a9d-a223-0a8f3ad0789f

Smith, R. (2008). "Zzzz……some reflections on the dynamics of village entrepreneurship". *International Journal of Entrepreneurship and Small Business*, *6*(3): 370–389. 10.1504/IJESB.2008.019133

Soergel, A. (2016, December 8). In America's rural–urban divide, age, earnings and education are prominent. *US News & World Report*. https://www.usnews.com/news/articles/2016-12-08/in-americas-rural-urban-divide-age-earnings-and-education-are-prominent

Steiner, A., & Atterton, J. (2015). Exploring the contribution of rural enterprises to local resilience. *Journal of Rural Studies*, *40*, 30–45. 10.1016/j.jrurstud.2015.05.004

Templin, E., Chazdon, S., Muske, G., Barroso, F. D., Osborne, L., & Craig, W. (2017). The silver tsunami and rural small business retention: What can communities do? *Community Development*, *48*(2), 282–298. 10.1080/15575330.2017.1287110

Walzer, N. (2004). Introduction: Entrepreneurship in community development. *Community Development: Journal of the Community Development Society*, *35*(1), 1–4. 10.1080/15575330409490118

Walzer, N., & Merrett, C. (Eds). (2022). *Rural areas in transition: Meeting challenges & making opportunities*. Routledge. 10.4324/9781003280620

Wilmoth, D. (2023, August). *Small business facts: Small businesses in rural areas*. U.S. Small Business Administration, Office of Advocacy. https://advocacy.sba.gov/wp-content/uploads/2023/08/Fact-Sheet-Small-Business-in-Rural-Areas-508c.pdf

7

EMPLOYEE OWNERSHIP TRUSTS IN THE U.K.

Graeme Nuttall

Introduction

Employee ownership has proven astonishingly successful in the U.K. This is because of a model of employee ownership, the employee ownership trust (EOT), which became a mainstream idea within a decade.

Under the EOT model, a trustee holds a majority or a 100% shareholding in a trading company, collectively and indefinitely on behalf of all the current and future employees of that company (or group), without any share allocations to individual employees. This concept can be difficult to understand, at first, especially for those steeped in models that depend on employees owning a share or shares personally.

Background to EOT Legislation

What follows is an explanation of how the EOT model works and why it is successful, starting with the background to the U.K.'s enactment of its pivotal EOT legislation in 2014.

Employee Trusts and Other Initiatives

Employee trust ownership of a company is not a novel concept in the U.K. The flagship John Lewis Partnership has been employee trust-owned since the 1920s. Before 2014, there were dozens of companies wholly or partly owned by employee trusts. This was a tried-and-tested model (Nuttall, 2014). It was one of a range of employee ownership models (Nuttall, 2022). Organizations existed to promote employee ownership, including the U.K.'s Employee

DOI: 10.4324/9781003497462-7

Ownership Association (EOA), Co-Operative Development Scotland, and Wales Co-Operative Centre (now Cwmpas). Between 1978 and 2000 the U.K. developed a full range of tax-advantaged share and share option plans. Other measures had sought to grow employee ownership, including through worker cooperatives in the mid to late 1970s, in privatizations especially in the bus industry, through a (now-abolished) tax-advantaged "statutory ESOP" and in public service mutuals initiatives (Pendelton et al., 2023).

Notwithstanding a generally favorable regulatory framework, example employee-owned businesses (EOBs), and periodic initiatives, only the occasional U.K. private company was converting to employee ownership before 2014.

The Nuttall Review of Employee Ownership

In 2012, the U.K. government investigated why there was not more employee ownership of private companies. Graeme Nuttall was appointed as its independent adviser to identify the barriers and help find solutions to knock them down. The Nuttall Review of Employee Ownership (Nuttall, 2012) made 28 recommendations to promote employee ownership in all its forms, which were accepted wholly or in part by the government. The Nuttall Review moved employee ownership in private companies from a lobbying topic into government policy (Nuttall, 2013).

The government's support for the Nuttall Review provided official recognition of key points, namely that:

- employee ownership is distinct, from a policy point of view, from employee engagement and employee financial participation;
- employee ownership is capable of being a business model in its own right and not just an "add-on" to other ways of owning and managing a business;
- there are benefits from employee ownership for a business and its employees;
- the obstacles to promoting employee ownership were a lack of awareness of the concept, a lack of resources to support it, and the need to reduce its actual or perceived complexities; and
- tax rules have a key role in overcoming obstacles.

This set a firm base on which to grow employee ownership.

A Definition of Employee Ownership

The acceptance of the Nuttall Review's definition of employee ownership was fundamental to shaping government policy. The Nuttall Review defined employee ownership as:

> … a significant and meaningful stake in a business for all its employees… What is "meaningful" goes beyond financial participation. The employees' stake must underpin organizational structures that ensure employee engagement…
>
> This review has a particular emphasis on the employees' stake being a substantial or controlling stake. There is no set rule as to what percentage of issued share capital is a substantial stake. Over 25% is substantial from a company law perspective…
>
> References to share ownership by all employees assume such ownership is voluntary. Share ownership must be made available to all employees on the same or similar terms but this can be subject to a minimum period of employment or other reasonable qualifying conditions. Entitlements often vary on a fair basis according to length of service, remuneration or similar factors…
>
> *(Nuttall, 2012)*

This definition deliberately linked significant employee share ownership with employee engagement. It also emphasizes a key concept, that of "all-employee" participation. This contrasts with participation on a "discretionary" basis, when only selected employees or certain groups of employees participate. This definition is in general use across the U.K.

The Additional Characteristics of an Employee-Owned Private Company

While EOBs can take on the characteristics of a social enterprise or worker cooperative, the Nuttall Review considered employee ownership is best understood as a "for-profit" business model, that is, one using conventional management and organizational structures.

U.K. private companies with employee ownership are, in many respects, the same as companies that operate without this business model. But such companies with employee ownership have additional characteristics, consistent with the meaning of employee ownership, namely that:

- all employees have a direct or indirect share ownership stake; and
- there are organizational structures that promote employee engagement and other features of employee ownership.

The Types of Employee Ownership

The Nuttall Review categorized employee ownership according to the type of share ownership employees have in a company:

- Direct: where employees become individual owners of shares through one or more tax-advantaged or other share plans;
- Indirect: where shares in a company are held collectively on behalf of employees in an employee trust (the trust model); and
- Hybrid: where there is a combination of direct and indirect employee ownership.

Key Difference between Direct and Indirect Employee Ownership

The key difference between direct and indirect employee ownership is there are no individual allocations or awards of shares with indirect ownership. Instead, shares are held on behalf of all current and future employees of a company as a discretionary class of potential beneficiaries. A new joiner automatically becomes a member of that class of beneficiaries, subject to any qualifying period of employment, without paying anything. One who leaves employment stops belonging to the class of beneficiaries, without receiving any payment, unless former employees are allowed to remain as beneficiaries. The trustee has a fiduciary responsibility to act always in the interests of the beneficiaries of the trust.

For anyone familiar with only share and share option plans, the idea of holding shares collectively on behalf of employees as a way of providing employee ownership can be contrarian or even anathema. In a direct model, employees buy shares or are awarded shares for free or at a discount. They then sell those shares on leaving a company or at other times. Instead, with the trust model, the company's shares remain owned indefinitely on behalf of all employees.

The intention of the Nuttall Review was to promote employee ownership in all its forms. For example, company law changes were made following one recommendation regarding share buy-backs and treasury shares, to help private companies operate an internal share market. Instead, one model, which was intentionally brought to the fore by the Nuttall Review, the indirect or trust model, became the dominant U.K. model.

Impact of Codification of the Trust Model

In 2014, because of the Nuttall Review (HM Treasury, 2013), the trust model was partly codified in that year's Finance Act, in the form of the EOT. The EOT was introduced after two years of sustained support from the U.K. Government for employee ownership as a good business model (Fieldfisher, 2021a). The EOT helped overcome the obstacles identified in the Nuttall Review. In essence, it did this by focusing on business succession as the key opportunity to convert a business to employee ownership (Pendelton et al., 2023). The EOT raised awareness of employee ownership as a business succession solution, generated the professional and other resources to support it, and reduced the actual or perceived complexities of employee ownership.

The Success of the EOT in Growing Employee Ownership

The EOT has propelled employee ownership into the mainstream, and at scale. The EOT is the dominant model of employee ownership in the U.K. (Pendleton et al., 2023).

In the decade following the enactment of the EOT legislation, some 1,800 companies transitioned to employee ownership using the EOT model (Mathieu, 2024). This total is highly significant in an employee ownership context. It exceeds the number of U.K. worker cooperatives, which decreased to 365 in 2024 from 392 in 2023 (Co-operatives UK, 2024). After 10 years, the U.K. is more than halfway to matching the estimated 3,500 companies majority-owned by U.S. employee stock ownership plans (ESOPs), a model celebrating its 50th year in 2024.[1]

On average, a U.K. worker cooperative has around six to seven worker-owners (Co-operatives UK, 2024). Eighty-three percent of EOT-owned companies have between 10 and 250 employees, with an average of 120 and a median of 32 employees (Pendelton et al., 2023). The U.K. EOT is a small-to-medium-sized enterprise phenomenon, although larger companies also adopt the EOT model.

The U.K.'s 2024 EOT Top 50 required 277 employees to be included (RM2, n.d.). These 50 companies employed 125,114 employees and had combined sales of £16.01 billion. When the largest employer, the John Lewis Partnership, is excluded, these companies employed 52,214 or on average 1,065 employees.

These new EOBs are spread across different sectors. The top five sectors are professional services (37%), information and communication (15%), wholesale and retail trade (14%), manufacturing (9%), and construction (7%) (WPI Economics, 2023).

This increase in number and size of companies has not been achieved by any reduction in the size of the employees' shareholding. As explained next, an EOT will, in practice, always have a controlling shareholding.

How an EOT Works

The following summarizes the steps to implement a transition to employee trust ownership, as a business succession solution, and to maintain that ownership. It is important to appreciate the EOT legislation does not prescribe an entire model. It provides key design features that are, in effect, overlaid on the pre-existing trust model. The differences made by the EOT legislation are emphasized.

Feasibility

The assumption is that advice has been taken regarding the advantages and disadvantages of employee ownership among other succession solutions and a decision was made to proceed with employee ownership using an employee trust. This advice will have considered business culture, finance, design, tax, other regulatory aspects, implementation, and how to make employee ownership work in practice (Fieldfisher, 2021c). These considerations are largely the same regardless of the model of employee ownership.

Typically, a business converting to employee ownership must be self-reliant. There is no outside party to bring in cash or other resources, such as a new management team. The business must be stable with adequate cash flows and profitability. Without these characteristics, it cannot generate the profits to finance the buyout of the current owners, unless either or both management and other employees invest their own money. This is a distinctive feature of employee buyouts: if employees cannot afford to invest, then a company's profits are used to finance its change in ownership.

Moreover, it is likely that several years' profits will be needed, especially if a majority or 100% shareholding is bought. The accepted way to achieve this is for sellers to receive deferred consideration in the form of installment payments. The average U.K. deferred consideration period, when a controlling interest is bought, has been calculated as 6.8 years (WPI Economics, 2023). Some elderly shareholders and others who need payment quickly may not agree to this. There is also a risk of not getting paid in full, which can make deferred consideration unacceptable to some.

There are other potential difficulties. Paying deferred consideration may restrict investment. The company commits to a new ownership structure, which can be difficult but not impossible to change. This may make the business less attractive to third-party investors if equity investment is required.

Activities before moving to employee ownership may include management changes and perhaps recruitment, to adjust for the retirement or reduced involvement of selling shareholders. Management must support employee ownership by embracing participative styles of management.

The trust model involves the trustee of an employee trust becoming a long-term shareholder. There are two main aspects to this: establishing the trust and arranging for the trust to acquire its shareholding. Once the trust has its shareholding, the ongoing administration is then relatively straightforward.

Many aspects of establishing an EOT are the same as for establishing other forms of trust, which made it possible for advisers in the U.K. to become familiar quickly with the EOT model, although it remains important to obtain advice from expert employee ownership practitioners. Concerns have been raised about newcomers to advising on employee ownership lacking the experience to provide bespoke advice and relying on template documents to set up an EOT (Mitchell & Bell, 2024).

Establishing an Employee Trust

Any trust needs someone to create the trust (usually the employer company). There must be a trust fund (i.e., the property held in the trust) and a trustee to administer the trust. The terms of the trust must be clear.

Tax rules impact on how the document that sets out the terms of the trust, the trust deed, is drafted. Understanding these rules and especially the significance of the "all-employee benefit requirement" is key to understanding what distinguishes an EOT from other types of employee trust.

Until April 5, 2014 an employee trust would be drafted to satisfy the requirements of Section 86 of the Inheritance Tax Act (1984) (a "Section 86 trust"). An EOT must be drafted to satisfy the all-employee benefit requirement in Section 236J of the Taxation of Chargeable Gains Act (1992). There are reliefs from inheritance tax charges that generally apply to trusts for both a Section 86 trust and an EOT (HM Revenue & Customs [HMRC], 2024d).

Under a Section 86 trust a trustee may make a distribution on bespoke terms to a selected beneficiary or beneficiaries. In contrast, an EOT requires, with only limited exceptions, all employees to benefit from any distribution. Moreover, any such distribution must be "on the same terms." These requirements follow the Nuttall Review definition of employee ownership. An EOT distribution (if ever made) either must be of the same amount for all employees or differ only by reason of their remuneration, length of service, or hours worked.

The trustee of an EOT must not be permitted, at any time, to make loans to beneficiaries of the EOT. This is another material difference from a Section 86 trust but there are others as well. The all-employee benefit requirement helps prevent abusive tax avoidance behaviors associated with some uses of the more flexible Section 86 trust (HMRC, 2024c; Loan Charge Review, 2019).

Those who want long-term trust ownership of shares are prepared to accept these additional EOT restrictions. The trustee of an EOT will have less flexibility to respond to changes in circumstances than it would for a Section 86 trust, but in many ways the EOT requirements make the indirect employee ownership proposition much more straightforward to explain and understand. An EOT is designed to retain shares indefinitely and is not primarily a vehicle through which financial benefits are provided to employees. Once this is understood, the additional EOT restrictions are acceptable.

In order to be an EOT a trust must satisfy the all-employee benefit requirement. However, there are EOT-related capital gains tax (CGT) and income tax exemptions and, in order to benefit from these, additional requirements must be met. If these tax exemptions are not wanted, a more flexible Section 86 trust might be established instead of an EOT (for example, as at Zaha Hadid Architects).

These additional requirements, for the first decade of the EOT's existence, did not regulate how an EOT was governed or the process an EOT trustee had to follow to buy shares. The employee ownership sector wished to pre-empt potential abuse, especially of the CGT exemption. The government was lobbied for additional regulation to bring more elements of best practice into law (EOA, 2024). Further requirements were announced on October 30, 2024, with immediate effect (HMRC, 2024b).[2]

The trustee is typically a company established solely for the purpose of acting as trustee of the employee trust (Pendleton et al., 2023). Such a company is simple to administer with minimal regulatory requirements. This approach also provides limited liability with freedom to choose a board of directors for the trustee company that is best suited to achieving the purpose of the trust.

The articles of association of the trustee company usually set out the required composition of the trustee's board of directors and include additional procedural requirements to support decision-making, especially on major issues. A composition that is seen as best practice is the so-called paritarian composition. This is where:

- some directors are appointed by the board of directors of the employer company;
- the same number are selected (or elected) from the employees as a group; and
- there are one or more independent directors (such as a professional adviser) (Nuttall, 2021).

From October 30, 2024, in keeping with best practice, a new trustee independence requirement ensures former owners cannot claim the CGT exemption and, in effect, keep control of the company post-sale by retaining control of the EOT (HMRC, 2024b). Previously former owners could be in the majority on the trustee's board of directors.

An alternative to establishing a trustee company is for individuals to act as trustees. However, there are administrative complications (and potential personal liabilities) if an inevitably changing group of individuals acts personally as trustees. If a professional trustee company is appointed there will be restrictions on who may be on the board of directors, as well as professional fees to pay. A non-U.K. tax resident trustee company would be outside the scope of U.K. CGT if it sold shares (HMRC, 2024a). Because the trust is intended to retain shares indefinitely, this option was discounted by most companies. From October 30, 2024 it is a requirement for anyone claiming the CGT exemption that the trustee of the EOT is a U.K. tax resident (HMRC, 2024b).

There are other technical and practical aspects to establishing an EOT and a trustee company that are not covered in this summary.

Arranging for the Trust to Acquire Shares

Tax reliefs encourage the gift of a controlling interest into a Section 86 trust or an EOT. But the usual scenario is that family or founder shareholders wish to move to employee ownership by selling their shares. Typical key documents to do this include:

- a share purchase agreement between the sellers and the trustee (probably with the employer company as a party);
- amended articles of association for the employer company, to reflect its new status as a majority trust-owned company (these articles should provide formal mechanisms for employee engagement, such as an employee committee to work with the board of directors and/or the right to employee representatives on the board of directors); and
- a shareholders' agreement, if there are other shareholders alongside the trustee with rights and responsibilities additional to those in the company's articles of association.

This list assumes no bank finance or other source of external finance is involved. In some cases, the company (occasionally the trustee) may borrow from a bank (either with or without security) to provide funds for the trustee to accelerate payment to the selling shareholders.

There are other important arrangements, including the trustee satisfying itself that the proposed purchase price is not too high by obtaining independent valuation advice. From October 30, 2024, there is a requirement when claiming the CGT exemption that action is taken to ensure the consideration paid on disposal of shares to the trustee does not exceed market value (HMRC, 2024b). Checks must be made that contributions to the trust are not unlawful distributions under company law and also on the appropriate accounting treatment for the arrangements (Employee Share Ownership [ESOP] Centre, 2017). Careful cash flow projections will ensure the company's business is not adversely affected by the planned deferred consideration payments and that it can afford to pay all-employee bonuses during the deferred consideration period.

The employee buyout will require a communications program with employees to explain the changes and other impactful practices (DJS Research, 2023). There would be consultations with any trade union.

Tax Considerations

There are important tax considerations to any form of employee trust buyout. This section is not comprehensive and only highlights key points. Once the idea of an employee trust buyout is accepted commercially, the basic tax proposition needs agreement. This is (in the U.K.) that:

1 the employer company will not get a tax deduction for payments it makes to the trustee to enable the trustee to buy a permanent shareholding;
2 the payments are received tax-free by the trustee (HMRC, 2024a);[3]
3 there are no employment-related tax liabilities for either the employer or employees from the ownership of shares in a discretionary trust; and
4 the owners realize a capital gain, when they are paid by the trustee for their shares. In the U.K., capital gains treatment has historically been a more favorable tax treatment than receiving income.

If an owner wishes to pursue an employee trust buyout then an application to HM Revenue & Customs (HMRC) for clearance under Section 701 of the Income Tax Act (2007) is advisable. This is to confirm the proposed payment or payments by the trustee company to the owner will not be considered, in effect, as disguised dividends (and therefore taxed as income). An array of anti-avoidance provisions can be used to tax the employer company, the trustee, or the sellers as if they had received a distribution. This is if HMRC doubts the bona fides of the financing arrangements (Chartered Institute of Taxation [CIOT], 2021).

Purchases of existing shares incur a stamp duty liability at 0.5% of the consideration with no allowance for any installment payments.

The key change in the trust model from 2014 is that if an EOT is used to acquire a controlling interest in a trading company (or group), then an unlimited CGT exemption should be available to the seller (if they are a person other than a company).

The EOT CGT Exemption

A U.K. individual will usually expect to pay CGT at a reduced rate when selling their company because of business asset disposal relief (previously known as entrepreneurs' relief). In broad terms, if a controlling interest (as defined) is sold into an EOT, then after April 6, 2014 there is a complete exemption from CGT (Section 236H of the Taxation of Capital Gains Act, 1992). The comparative saving this unlimited exemption provides on larger-value transactions rose in 2020 because an individual's lifetime limit for business assets disposal relief was reduced from £10 million to £1 million, and from October 30, 2024 following an increase in the rate of CGT on disposals of shares.

Claiming the EOT CGT exemption under Section 236H is relatively straightforward. The main conditions have already been mentioned. The exemption is only available for disposals in the tax year (April 6 to April 5) in which the trustee of the EOT acquires its controlling interest. What happens in response to this is that instead of selling a minority interest to the EOT trustee, owners agree to sell a controlling interest into an EOT in one event to obtain the benefit of the exemption. Another condition is the "limited participation requirement." This may be an obstacle in companies with relatively few employees in comparison to the number of shareholders who are employees or office-holders and who would benefit from the CGT exemption. Broadly, this requirement denies the CGT exemption in certain cases where the ratio of those who benefit from the EOT exemption to employees is greater than two-fifths.

Assuming a claim for the CGT exemption is made (in the required way) then certain disqualifying events (for example, ceasing to meet the controlling interest requirement, the employer company ceasing to trade or the trustee becoming a non-U.K. tax resident) will trigger a deemed disposal and reacquisition by the EOT trustee of the relevant shares. Avoiding these events and the consequent "catch up" tax charge is, for the most part, within the trustee's control and so these risks are acceptable to a trustee.

Prior to October 30, 2024 there was a relatively short "clawback period" during which a seller's CGT exemption claim would fail if there were a disqualifying event. From October 30, 2024, the period during which tax can be recovered from a former owner is extended to the end of the fourth tax year the year of disposal. This means sellers must be confident a disqualifying event can be avoided during this long period.

Administering the Trust

Once a trust has acquired a long-term shareholding, maintaining that situation is relatively straightforward.

There is some flexibility to define the role of the trustee. The purpose of the trust model is to provide long-term employee ownership of the underlying company. This was stated expressly in Parliament during the passage of the Finance Bill 2014, as being to provide "employees, the business and the economy the long-term benefits of employee ownership" (Gauke, 2014). The trustee's board of directors will meet periodically to check that the company (or group) they control is meeting this aim. Typically, this means ensuring a company is an independent, professionally managed enterprise with an employee ownership ethos, such that employees are provided with good work, have individual and collective voice, and hold a financial share in the company's success (Fieldfisher, 2021b).

The articles of association of the employer company may require certain major decisions to be approved by the trustee of the employee trust, in addition to those requiring members' approval under company law. In some cases, the trustee may be more closely involved in corporate decision-making and management responsibilities may be shared between the board of directors of the employer company and that of the trustee.

One responsibility of the trustee is to ensure the employer company's remuneration policies are consistent with the principles of all employee ownership.

All-employee profit sharing is a characteristic of EOBs of whatever type. In addition to a specific employee receiving a salary and benefits and, possibly, performance-related remuneration, they will share, together with all employees, in company profits. This may be achieved through regular awards under an employee share plan or through cash bonuses. If a company has only indirect employee ownership, then it will have to operate a cash profit sharing plan.

A company controlled by the trustee of an EOT will want to take advantage of an income tax exemption for certain bonus payments, to the extent possible.

The EOT Income Tax Exemption

Since October 1, 2014, an income tax exemption provides a tax incentive for companies to become controlled by an EOT (Income Tax [Earnings and Pensions] Act, 2003, Part 4, Chapter 10A).

If an EOT has a controlling interest in a company, there is an income tax exemption of up to £3,600 per employee each tax year on certain qualifying bonus payments (with national insurance contributions liabilities continuing to apply). It is the employer company and not the trustee of the EOT that must pay the qualifying bonuses.

The income tax exemption requirements are relatively straightforward, especially if the scheme formula is kept simple. The bonus must be a genuine bonus. Broadly, it must be awarded to everyone in employment with the employer (or in the relevant group) when the award is determined, including any non-U.K. employees. Although recent joiners may be excluded, by setting a minimum qualifying period not exceeding 12 months, and employees can be excluded in limited circumstances involving disciplinary matters.

Participation must be on the "same terms." An award must be of the same amount for everyone or determined by reference to remuneration, length of service, or hours worked. If more than one factor is used, each must give rise to a separate entitlement and the total entitlement must be the sum of those entitlements and not the product. Also, the scheme must not disproportionately benefit any one group of eligible employees.

Other qualifying conditions relate to the employer and its ownership and governance arrangements. Briefly, the employer (which cannot be a service company) must:

- be controlled by an EOT throughout a qualifying period of normally 12 months;
- be a trading company throughout the qualifying period; and
- the "office-holder requirement" must be met when payments are made and throughout the qualifying period (except for up to normally 90 days).

The office-holder requirement prevents the income tax exemption applying where the ratio of directors and other office-holders (and connected employees) to employees and office-holders is greater than two-fifths. The 90-days exclusion allows for recruitment to overcome temporary defaults.

Hybrid Employee Ownership

Some companies adopt a hybrid form of employee ownership. This is to achieve the benefits of both the direct and indirect forms of employee ownership.

Either at the outset or later, an element or elements of direct employee share ownership can be added to trust ownership. This could be on an all-employee basis and/or for selected key individuals. If a selective plan is in keeping with a company's employee ownership ethos there is no objection, in principle, to rewarding individuals for personal performance.

If a majority of a company's shares are held in an EOT, the remainder could be held directly by employees through one or more share plans. A typical hybrid model is that a tax-advantaged share incentive plan (SIP) is introduced. This will provide all employees an opportunity to acquire and dispose of shares in a tax-efficient way. The plan would usually be operated as a tax-efficient financial incentive, perhaps in addition to paying income-tax-free bonuses. Although it could also provide employees with individual votes (each employee could instruct the trustee of the SIP trust that holds their shares how to vote on them).

Why EOTs Are Popular

Having outlined how the trust model works, and the distinguishing features of an EOT, what follows is an explanation of why this model is successful, from the point of view, in turn, of employees, managers, and owners, and how it benefits a business, again highlighting EOT differences over other models.

Employees

The purpose of an EOT is to provide long-term employee ownership of a company. The benefits to employees from the EOT model are therefore, unsurprisingly, broadly the same as for any model of employee ownership. From an employee's point of view, that includes improved health and well-being, quality of life, a fairer basic wage, job security, better health and safety, and enhanced training and skills (EOA, 2023).

The structural difference of the trust model for employees (as distinct from other models) is that there are shares held on their behalf in the trust on a long-term basis. This means employees: (a) may receive cash profit shares without the need to hold or sell shares personally to receive a financial benefit; and (b) have a collective voice, through the trustee of that trust, in how the company is owned and governed.

The permanence of the shareholding in an EOT can be seen by employees as a benefit, especially if it were preceded by an unsettling period during which the long-term prospects for a business were uncertain. Such a shareholding underpins many of the benefits of employee ownership for employees, including job security.

As highlighted, the tangible financial benefit, in addition to market rates of pay and benefits, and possibly individual performance bonuses, is an all-employee profit share. This is the approach taken by the John Lewis Partnership. Its annual cash bonuses in the 50 years to 2020 averaged 14.8% of salary (Nuttall, 2024).

Some non-EOBs operate profit-sharing plans, but these are at the discretion of their owners. What employee ownership means is that profit sharing is part of how the company operates. It does not cost an employee anything to be a potential beneficiary of a discretionary trust and this is not a taxable benefit. And with the EOT model, bonuses can be free of income tax.

Profit-sharing is not exclusive to the trust model. An EOB with direct employee ownership using a SIP can pay out profits, tax-free, to employees by way of share awards under the SIP. However, if there is a share plan, such as a SIP, there must be a repurchase plan to ensure liquidity to buy shares from departing employees. In addition, there are annual costs and administration, including regular share valuations that do not arise with EOT income-tax-free bonuses. Companies that, pre-2014, used a SIP as their employee ownership model have been known to convert to EOT ownership (for example, at Childbase Partnership).

Profit sharing provides a way to reduce income inequality and is associated (as are share plans generally) with improved employee financial health, through increased personal savings and reduced credit payments (Nuttall, 2024).

Employee engagement is key to accessing the benefits of employee ownership and this is something appreciated by employees (Stern, 2020b). Companies without employee ownership can have very good employee engagement but employee ownership is a profound enabler of employee engagement (MacLeod & Clarke, 2009).

Employees in an EOB should have both an individual and a group voice. Research shows that as well as financial participation and participative mechanisms, the best outcomes also involve an ownership culture encompassing a collective voice (Postlethwaite et al., 2005). What the trust model ensures is that there is a collective voice at the highest level of corporate governance, as a shareholder. With an EOT this will be a controlling shareholding.

Employee-trust-specific research shows how the model upholds values such as fairness and trust at all seniority levels and supports "meaningful work" (Lewis & Yeoman, 2016; Steare et al., 2015). There are a few areas in which

EOTs out-perform other employee ownership models (although the differences are not statistically significant). EOTs are the most likely to offer paid annual leave above the statutory minimum, and to provide access to private health care and hold accreditations for employee welfare, employee diversity and inclusion, and health and safety (WPI Economics, 2023).

Management

In addition to the benefits available to all employees, there can be additional benefits from trust ownership for managers, especially those aspiring to senior management.

Owners discussing business succession usually talk about who will take over as owner. In a family business that might mean finding family members who will inherit. In other cases, it means who will buy the business. In an small and medium-sized enterprise (SME), these questions are frequently tied to who will take over its management.

Some companies require a share purchase as a condition of promotion. The financial benefit of this depends mainly on the difference between the share price when the manager is promoted and when they leave. To participants, it can seem a matter of good fortune or bad luck as to whether they make money or not. Some may be lucky because they have bought low and sold high; others may have the misfortune to buy high and sell low.

Participants have limited choice as to when to buy, unless they wish to try to defer promotion. And anyone buying shares cannot know how well the company will be performing when they leave. Another difficulty with this model is that if a share price increases, the investment required by new managers to maintain parity with others can become prohibitively expensive. With an EOT, employees may be promoted on merit and not because of their ability to take on financial risk or to afford to buy shares.

And any concerns that managers may struggle to do their job in an EOB are misplaced. Interviews with managers of EOBs reveal an impressive picture of effective leadership in action (Stern, 2020a).

Owners

Having considered benefits for employees and managers of the EOT model, it is time to consider the benefits for an owner. In the U.K., after family succession, an EOT is the next most popular option for business succession (Tawfick, 2024).

Any private company owner considering a move to employee ownership, of any type, will appreciate the advantages this offers compared to, say, a trade sale. It avoids sharing trade secrets with competitors and gives control over timing. But the advantages for some owners are broader.

The three most popular aims of those choosing an EOT in 2023 were (in order of significance): to ensure the business remains independent; to protect and promote the livelihoods of current and future employees; and to protect and sustain the core values, culture, and ethos of the business (WPI Economics, 2023). Other reasons include the tax relief on sales for previous owners and protecting long-term legacy. A similar set of reasons is found in other surveys, again with non-tax reasons taking priority (Ownership at Work, 2023; Pendleton et al., 2023). The specific values-based aims are particularly well served by the trust model (including hybrid versions).

The trust model helps fulfill these specific aims because they can be written into the trust deed. The terms of the trust can reflect the extent to which a former owner, and the company's management and employees, wish a company to remain independently owned and what happens to any sale proceeds if there is an onward sale. In the U.K., there are trustees that do not have a power of sale without a court order and that require any sale proceeds to be paid to charity rather than employees, as deterrents from selling out. The trust model allows the company's ethos to be maintained and developed. A company that wishes to embrace wider corporate purpose can also use the trust model to uphold this aim (McDonald, 2022; Nuttall, 2020).

What is also attractive to owners is that the buyout arrangements are straightforward to understand and implement. The practical success of the trust model as a business succession solution is largely attributable to important characteristics. It provides a buyout "vehicle" designed to acquire an employer company's shares for the benefit of participating employees and to provide financial benefits to those employees on a fair basis. Continuity of the existing business is assumed, without a subsequent restructuring or merger with a larger enterprise as may happen with a trade sale. Professional management of the business will continue. The board of directors and senior management team will continue to be appointed because of their experience and expertise, and a move to employee ownership will not fundamentally change this situation. Employees do not invest their own money. Negotiations are with a single trustee (that is, with its board of directors) rather than directly with a large group of employees. These can be partial or complete sales of a company. Selling shareholders, who are also managers, do not have to leave the business immediately: they can stay on the trading company board and they may retain some shares. Indeed, these core characteristics are the same for the U.S. ESOP (Nuttall & Hoffmire, 2024).

However, when a shareholding is held indefinitely in an employee trust, there are marked differences with direct employee ownership models (Nuttall & Hoffmire, 2024). These differences are seen as important advantages by many owners:

- There can be a single lead adviser, working with an independent expert share valuer and any other advisers needed to deal with conflicts of interest. These advisers can arrange transfers to trust ownership relatively quickly.

- Once the trustee has paid for its shareholding there is no further need to finance share purchases. Long-term trust ownership avoids the challenges of financing an internal market on an ongoing basis.
- The trust model provides a stable and long-term method of ownership. This helps maintain the independence of the company. Instead of a decision to sell shares in the EOB being made by individuals (acting according to their own wishes) it is made by a trustee of a trust that exists to preserve long-term employee ownership (and not with a purpose of providing financial or retirement benefits as with a SIP or ESOP). The trustee can take a broader view of what is in the interests of current and future employees if an offer is received.
- The complexities of operating direct employee ownership are avoided. The tax position of shares held long term in a trust is straightforward. The main ongoing administrative matter is deciding who should be on the board of directors of the trustee company.
- There is clearly a collective voice on the part of employees, through the trustee of the trust. The trustee acts as a collective voice for all employees and, given owners' priorities, as custodian of the company's employee ownership ethos.

In contrast to selling to the trustee of a Section 86 trust, the EOT provides a more tax-efficient exit for an owner. Concerns over anticipated CGT changes caused a noticeable increase in new EOTs prior to the 2024 Budget (see Figure 7.1). But the CGT EOT exemption is unlikely it seems, from survey results, on its own to make an owner choose an employee trust buyout over an alternative exit route, although it certainly draws attention to the idea (Pendleton et al., 2023). This awareness-raising feature of the tax exemption was one reason for introducing the exemption (HM Treasury, 2013).

The CGT exemption helps sellers in other vital ways. It makes deferred consideration more workable. Without it, there could be CGT to pay up front on the entire consideration, notwithstanding full payment may not be received for many years. It helps a seller accept the delay and credit risk in getting paid.

There is a shortcoming in the model under English trust law. A non-charitable trust can only exist for 125 years, not forever. The Nuttall Review recommendation to exempt employee trusts from this limitation was put on hold pending further evidence (Department for Business, Innovation & Skills [BIS], 2014; Fieldfisher, 2014). Owners take a pragmatic view that 125 years is sufficiently long term.

The Business

The qualities of the trust model as a practical business (and management) succession solution mean it gets support from management teams. The lower establishment costs for employee trusts, in contrast to say a trade sale or other succession solutions, are another reason to support the model, as well as the low operating costs for the model. There should be a fee for an independent trustee director. Otherwise, there are negligible running costs because there are none of the complexities and costs of administering a share plan.

From a business point of view, employee ownership's proven positive impact on business results is another attraction (EOA, 2023). Most notably, EOBs are 8%–12% more productive than non-EOBs (calculated on a gross value added per employee basis).

Consistent with the above overall results, EOT-controlled companies show strong financial outcomes. A majority increased their gross operating profit (65%) and turnover (73%). Furthermore, they are more likely to have increased, rather than decreased, their investment in R&D or their capital expenditure, expanded their employee headcount, and appear more financially resilient in turbulent times than other ownership models. They are the least likely model to have increased their level of debt (WPI Economics, 2023).

The Future for EOTs

The number of U.K. EOBs continues to grow. In 2021, the annual total of new U.K. EOBs of all types (excluding worker cooperatives, which are not increasing in number) was 285 (Kahn, 2022). By October 2024, the European Federation of Employee Share Ownership confirmed to Graeme Nuttall a creation rate in the U.K. of 450 new EOTs a year. This momentum is supported by other data.

The number of Wales-based businesses under employee control doubled two years ahead of target (Business Wales, 2024). There was a 47% increase in the number of EOBs operating in Scotland in 2022–2024 (Co-operative Development Scotland, 2024). The number of advance tax clearance applications for EOT transactions increased 27% to 542 in 2023 (Williams, 2024). This is a strong prediction of further growth. The potential for even more significant growth exists with roughly 120,000 U.K. SME businesses likely to experience ownership transition in the decade 2024–2034 (Ownership at Work, 2023).

Events such as the COVID-19 pandemic's impact on attitudes or the 2020 change in business assets disposal relief may have added to overall momentum. However, the progressive increasing annual growth in U.K. employee ownership (Figure 7.1) suggests several factors provide constant momentum. Practices suggest that each employee-ownership transition adds to this growth pattern. There are hundreds of new companies and thousands of employee-owners acting as advocates for employee ownership. Every new EOT-owned company informs a wider group about employee ownership, leading especially to former owners talking to other business owners about their positive experience of the model. Advisers on a transaction gain knowledge and confidence to advise other clients on the model.

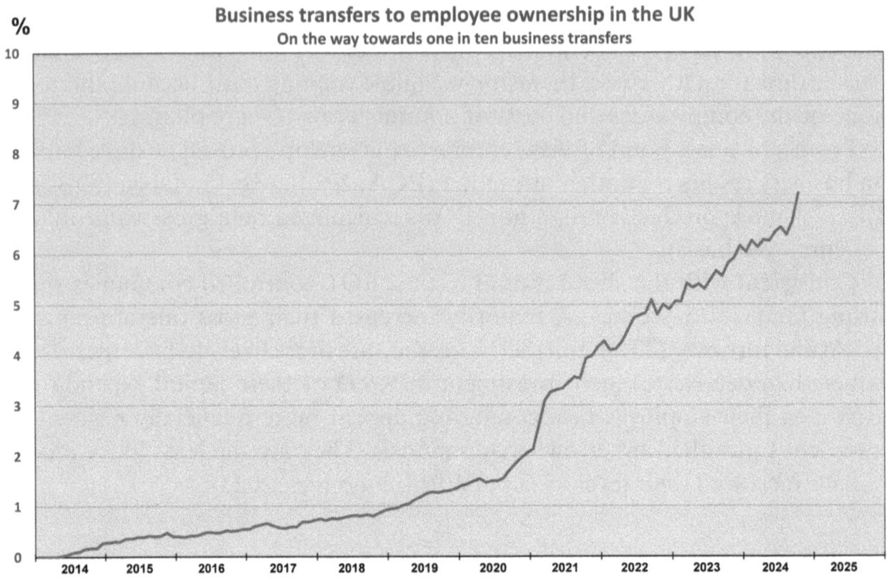

FIGURE 7.1 Cumulative New EOTs.

Source: Mathieu, 2024.

Occasionally a well-known name that adopts employee ownership will increase national awareness (e.g., Aardman Animations, Riverford Organic Farmers, and Richer Sounds). Sector-based momentum is an important factor. The move of a major construction company, Erith, to EOT ownership in 2017 was the start of others in the sector adopting this model (Morby, 2020). EOT ownership for a large architecture practice in 2017 similarly attracted attention to this model (Marrs, 2018). By early 2022, 110 of the Royal Institute of British Architects' chartered practices were EOT-owned (Waite, 2022). The creation in 2018 of the first 100% EOT-owned English law firm showed regulatory obstacles could be overcome for English (and Welsh) firms (Fieldfisher, 2018). By 2024, there were 30 employee-owned law firms (Postlethwaite, 2024). Geography is another factor. Regional initiatives to promote employee ownership, such as by Cwmpas in Wales, have created momentum.

Publicity for the results of U.K. employee ownership research also contributes. The 2017–2018 Ownership Effect Inquiry convinced 20 independent U.K. business organizations to support employee ownership (EOA, 2018).

U.K. Government support propelled the trust model to the fore. A decade on there remains official support across the U.K. (and Ireland) for more EOTs. The Scottish Government has an ambition for 500 EOBs in Scotland by 2030 (Co-operative Development Scotland, 2024). The Welsh Government has a commitment to support buyouts by workers (Business Wales, 2024). Research by Northern Ireland's Department for the Economy supports more employee ownership (Mitchell & Bell, 2024). A report for the Irish Department of

Finance recommends reforming the taxation of employee trusts in line with the U.K. (Indecon, 2024). The U.K. Government's 2024 reform of the EOT legislation was to "ensure that the reliefs remain focused on the intended purpose of encouraging and supporting employee ownership" (HMRC, 2024a).

In Summary

Employee ownership is a mainstream business model in the U.K. The 2012 Nuttall Review created a framework for employee ownership policy, including recommendations to raise awareness of the trust model as a business succession solution. Because of the Nuttall Review, this model is partly codified in law in the form of the EOT. The EOT helped overcome the obstacles to private company employee ownership. There is a CGT exemption for individuals and trustees selling a controlling interest to an EOT trustee. This is a valuable ingredient in the EOT's success. It nudges consideration of an employee buy-out, informs what this looks like, and helps overcome doubts about deferred consideration. The relative simplicity of implementing and operating the EOT model also contributes to its success.

The trust model is set to remain a mainstream business model in the U.K., as the government in Westminster and leaders in Scotland, Wales, and Northern Ireland continue to support its growth.

Fundamentally, it is good design that makes the EOT an attractive business succession solution. An EOT is designed to retain shares indefinitely, to provide long-term employee ownership in a practical way that meets the aspirations of many owners for an exit, one that maintains their business as independently owned, protects employees, and preserves a company's culture and an owner's legacy.

Notes

1 Estimate provided by Joseph Blasi, 2024, via personal communication; based on an estimate prepared by Corey Rosen and Nancy Wiefek, the National Center for Employee Ownership, and Joseph Blasi, Institute for the Study of Employee Ownership and Profit Sharing.
2 These changes were subject to consultation at the time of going to print and may be subject to substantive changes before enactment.
3 The October 30, 2024 announcements left unclear the tax free treatment of receipts where the EOT CGT exemption is unavailable.

References

Business Wales. (2024, June 21). *Employee ownership day 2024*. Welsh Government. https://businesswales.gov.wales/news-and-blog/employee-ownership-day-2024

Chartered Institute of Taxation. (2021, September 13). *Employee ownership trusts: Enhancement and anti-abuse measures, funding and other tax issues*. https://www.tax.org.uk/ref833

Co-operative Development Scotland. (2024). *Scottish employee-owned business census 2024*. https://cdsblog.co.uk/eob-census-2024

Co-operatives UK. (2024). *Co-operative and mutual economy 2024*. https://www.uk.coop/sites/default/files/2024-09/Co-operative_Mutual_Economy_2024.pdf

Department for Business, Innovation & Skills. (2014, July 30). *Consultation outcome: Amending the perpetuities rule and simplifying employee ownership*. United Kingdom. https://www.gov.uk/government/consultations/amending-the-perpetuities-rule-and-simplifying-employee-ownership

DJS Research. (2023). *Good employee ownership: A guide to effective & impactful practices in employee owned businesses*. Ownership at Work. https://ownershipatwork.org/wp-content/uploads/2023/12/EO-Knowledge-Programme-Good-Employee-Ownership-Report.pdf

Employee Ownership Association. (2018, June 8). *The ownership dividend: The economic case for employee ownership*. Employee Ownership Association & LID Publishing Ltd. https://issuu.com/revistabibliodiversidad/docs/eoa_full_book

Employee Ownership Association. (2023). *EO knowledge programme 2023: People powered growth*. Employee Ownership Association & Ownership at Work. https://ownershipatwork.org/wp-content/uploads/2023/10/People-Powered-Growth.pdf

Employee Ownership Association. (2024, October 30). *Policy win that builds on a decade of EO growth and impact*. https://employeeownership.co.uk/Site/content/News-and-Insights/News/Policy-Win.aspx

Employee Share Ownership Centre. (2017, January 12). *EOT accounting*. Understandings. https://esopcentre.com/metapages/understandings/

Fieldfisher. (2014, January 26). *Tomorrow's trust—employee trust owned companies need a trust that lasts indefinitely, not just 125 years*. https://www.fieldfisher.com/en/services/tax-structuring/tax-deductions-blog/tomorrows-trust-employee-trust-owned-companies-need-a-trust-that-lasts-indefinitely-not-just-125-years

Fieldfisher. (2018, December 6). *Fieldfisher advises on first major UK law firm's move to employee ownership*. https://www.fieldfisher.com/en/insights/fieldfisher-advises-on-first-major-uk-law-firms-move-to-employee-ownership

Fieldfisher. (2021a, March 31). *Nuttall review of employee ownership—a guide to source materials including the employee ownership tax exemptions introduced in the Finance Act 2014*. https://www.fieldfisher.com/en/services/tax-structuring/tax-deductions-blog/nuttall-review-of-employee-ownership-quick-guide-to-source-materials

Fieldfisher. (2021b, May 14). *An introduction to the employee ownership trust*. https://www.fieldfisher.com/en/insights/eot-introduction

Fieldfisher. (2021c, November). *How to prepare for EO—a practical guide for business owners*. https://res.cloudinary.com/fieldfisher/image/upload/v1646316552/PDFs/Guide_-_How_to_prepare_for_EO_nkq7ui.pdf

Gauke, D. (2014, July 2). *Further consideration of Bill, as amended in the Public Bill Committee*. Finance Bill, HC Deb (2 July 2014), Vol. 583, Col. 966. https://hansard.parliament.uk/Commons/2014-07-02/debates/14070260000001/FinanceBill

HM Revenue & Customs. (2024a, October 30). *Taxation of employee ownership trusts and employee benefit trusts* [Consultation outcome]. https://www.gov.uk/government/consultations/taxation-of-employee-ownership-trusts-and-employee-benefit-trusts/taxation-of-employee-ownership-trusts-and-employee-benefit-trusts

HM Revenue & Customs. (2024b, November 6). *Changes to the taxation of employee ownership trusts and employee benefit trusts* [Policy paper]. https://www.gov.uk/

government/publications/changes-to-the-taxation-of-employee-ownership-trusts-and-employee-benefit-trusts

HM Revenue & Customs. (2024c, December 5). *Current list of named tax avoidance schemes, promoters, enablers and suppliers* [Corporate report]. https://www.gov.uk/government/publications/named-tax-avoidance-schemes-promoters-enablers-and-suppliers/current-list-of-named-tax-avoidance-schemes-promoters-enablers-and-suppliers

HM Revenue & Customs. (2024d, December 5). IHTM42995—Employee benefit trusts: employee ownership trusts: introduction. *Inheritance Tax Manual*. https://www.gov.uk/hmrc-internal-manuals/inheritance-tax-manual/ihtm42995

HM Treasury. (2013, July). *Supporting the employee ownership sector*. https://assets.publishing.service.gov.uk/government/uploads/system/uploads/attachment_data/file/210661/supporting_employee_ownership_sector.pdf

Income Tax (Earnings and Pensions) Act, c. 1 (2003). (Eng.). https://www.legislation.gov.uk/ukpga/2003/1/contents

Income Tax Act, c. 3 (2007). (Eng.). https://www.legislation.gov.uk/ukpga/2007/3/contents

Indecon. (2024). *Indecon Review of the Taxation of Share-Based Remuneration.*

Inheritance Tax Act, c. 51 (1984). (Eng.). https://www.legislation.gov.uk/ukpga/1984/51/contents

Kahn, K. (2022, July 5). *UK announces surge in employee-owned businesses*. Fifty by Fifty. https://www.fiftybyfifty.org/2022/07/uk-announces-surge-in-employee-owned-businesses/

Lewis, P. N., & Yeoman, R. (2016, November). *Busting the millennial myth—The power of purpose*. Fieldfisher. https://res.cloudinary.com/fieldfisher/image/upload/v1574346398/PDF-Files/PDFs%20from%20old%20website/eo-millennia_web_lngewp.pdf

Loan Charge Review. (2019, December). *Independent loan charge review: Report on the policy and its implementation*. https://assets.publishing.service.gov.uk/media/5dfca55d40f0b6661e94aa1b/Independent_Loan_Charge_Review_-_final_report.pdf

MacLeod, D. & Clarke, N. (2009). *Engaging for success: Enhancing performance through employee engagement*. Department for Business Innovation and Skills. https://engageforsuccess.org/wp-content/uploads/2021/02/Engaging-for-Success.pdf

Marrs, C, (2018, January 12). *Power to the people: The rise of the employee-owned practice*. Architects' Journal. https://www.architectsjournal.co.uk/news/power-to-the-people-the-rise-of-the-employee-owned-practice

Mathieu, M. (2024, September). Celebrations. *EFES Newsletter*. European Federation of Employee Share Ownership. https://www.efesonline.org/EFES%20NEWS/2024/EFES%20NEWSLETTER%20-%209-2024%20EN.htm

McDonald, C. (2022, September). *How to measure the social and environmental impact of employee ownership*. Ownership at Work. https://ownershipatwork.org/wp-content/uploads/2022/09/How-to-measure-the-social-and-environmental-impact-of-EO-Sept-2022.pdf

Mitchell, R., & Bell, F. (2024, August). *The employee ownership model in Northern Ireland.* Research Bulletin 24/1. Department for the Economy. https://www.economy-ni.gov.uk/sites/default/files/publications/economy/Research-Bulletin-24-1-Employee-Ownership.pdf

Morby, A. (2020, May 13). *McGee ownership shifts to employee trust*. Construction Enquirer. https://www.constructionenquirer.com/2020/05/13/mcgee-ownership-shifts-to-employee-trust/

Nuttall, G. (2012, July). *Sharing success: The Nuttall review of employee ownership*. U.K. Department for Business, Innovation & Skills. https://assets.publishing.service.gov.uk/government/uploads/system/uploads/attachment_data/file/31706/12-933-sharing-success-nuttall-review-employee-ownership.pdf

Nuttall, G. (2013, March 13). *Making it mutual: Seizing the decade for employee ownership*. Fieldfisher. https://www.fieldfisher.com/en/insights/seizing-the-decade-for-employee-ownership

Nuttall, G. (2014, October). Tried and tested. *Tax Adviser Magazine*, pp. 43–45. https://res.cloudinary.com/fieldfisher/image/upload/v1574944186/PDF-Files/PDFs%20from%20old%20website/SME-Nuttall-Trusts_y2y4iw.pdf

Nuttall, G. (2020, October 2). *EO v3.0—Employee ownership with added Gandhian purpose*. The Gandhi Foundation Annual Lecture 2020. Fieldfisher. https://www.fieldfisher.com/getattachment/7a1e544f-15fc-40c0-9b9a-20ed155aa397/The-Gandhi-Foundation-Annual-Lecture-2020-Graeme-Nuttall-OBE-01-10-2020.pdf?lang=en-GB

Nuttall, G. (2021, June). *How Robert Oakeshott made paritarian governance good practice for employee ownership trusts*. Ownership at Work. https://ownershipatwork.org/wp-content/uploads/2021/06/Graeme-Nuttall-June-2021-How-R-Oakeshott-made-partitarian-governance-good-practice-for-EOTs.pdf

Nuttall, G. (2022, July 5). *Celebrating the 10th anniversary of the Nuttall review*. Employee OwnershipWales & Cwmpas. https://employeeownershipwales.co.uk/wp-content/uploads/2022/09/2022-08-31-Nuttall-G.-_Celebrating-10-years-of-employee-ownership.pdf

Nuttall, G. (2024). Shared success: Employee ownership as a supercharged "all-party" solution to bolster wealth. In T. Nurcombe & R. Shorthouse (Eds.), *A wealth of opportunities: A centre-right prospectus for spreading wealth* (pp. 97–102). Bright Blue. https://www.brightblue.org.uk/wp-content/uploads/2024/03/BB-Essay-Collection-March2024_PRF08-Interactive.pdf

Nuttall, G. & Hoffmire, J. S. (2024, August). *Comparing EOTs and ESOPs as employee ownership models in the US* [Presented article]. Second Annual Rutgers–Oxford Employee Ownership Research Symposium. https://smlr.rutgers.edu/sites/default/files/Documents/Centers/Institute_Employee_Ownership/Rutgers-Oxford/Hoffmire_Nuttall_Comparing_EOT_ESOPs_US_Rutgers_Oxford_2024.pdf

Ownership at Work. (2023, November). *Generation EO: The great employee ownership succession opportunity*. Ownership at Work & DJS Research. https://ownershipatwork.org/wp-content/uploads/2023/11/Generation-EO-The-Great-Employee-Ownership-Succession-Opportunity.pdf

Pendelton, A., Robinson, A., & Nuttall, G. (2023). Employee ownership in the UK. *Journal of Participation and Employee Ownership*, *6*(3), 194–214. 10.1108/JPEO-11-2022-0030

Postlethwaite, R. (2024). Employee ownership in law firms: A growing trend? *Solicitors Journal*. https://www.solicitorsjournal.com/sjarticle/employee-ownership-in-law-firms-a-growing-trend

Postlethwaite, R., Michie, J., Burns, P., & Nuttall, G. (2005, October). *Shared company: How employee ownership works*. Job Ownership Limited. https://employeeownership.com.au/eoa/wp-content/uploads/2012/01/Shared-Company-UK.pdf

RM2. (n.d.). *Employee ownership trust top 50* 2024. Retrieved October 31, 2024, from https://www.rm2.co.uk/resources/eot-top-50/

Steare, R., Stampoulidis, P., Lewis P. N., & Woodman, P. (2015, September). *The MoralDNA of employee-owned companies*. Chartered Management Institute. https://www.managers.org.uk/~/media/Files/MoralDNA/The_MoralDNA_of_Employee-Owned_Companies.pdf

Stern, S. (2020a) *Redesigning the CEO: How employee ownership changes the art of leadership*. Ownership at Work. https://ownershipatwork.org/wp-content/uploads/2021/01/Redesigning-the-CEO-how-employee-ownership-changes-the-art-of-leadership-1.pdf

Stern, S. (2020b). *Redesigning work: Employee owners speak*. Ownership at Work. https://ownershipatwork.org/wp-content/uploads/2021/01/REDESIGNING-WORK-PDF-0720-1.pdf

Tawfick, E. (2024, October 17). *Nearly one in three UK business owners have fast-tracked exit strategies over past 12 months as possible CGT Budget raid looms*. Today's Wills &Probate. https://todayswillsandprobate.co.uk/nearly-one-in-three-uk-business-owners-have-fast-tracked-exit-strategies-over-past-12-months-as-possible-cgt-budget-raid-looms/

Taxation of Chargeable Gains Act, c. 12 (1992). (Eng.). https://www.legislation.gov.uk/ukpga/1992/12/contents

Waite, R. (2022, October 17). Shedkm switches to employee ownership. *Architects' Journal*. https://www.architectsjournal.co.uk/news/shedkm-switches-to-employee-ownership

Williams, M. (2024, October 7). 27% increase in businesses transferring ownership to employees in a year to 542. *IFA Magazine*. https://ifamagazine.com/27-increase-in-businesses-transferring-ownership-to-employees-in-a-year-to-542/

WPI Economics. (2023, October 17). *Exploring the potential of the employee ownership business model—A deep dive into the economic, people, societal and environmental benefits*. https://ownershipatwork.org/wp-content/uploads/2023/10/Exploring-the-potential-of-the-Employee-Ownership-business-model.pdf

8

RETAINING BUSINESSES USING COMMUNITY-SUPPORTED ENTERPRISES

Norman Walzer and Ben Doyle

Previous chapters demonstrate that many small and rural communities are challenged when long-term business owners plan to retire and/or leave the community without obvious replacement strategies. It is also clear that community leaders have several options or approaches available to transition a business to new owners and perhaps make the business better suited to meet local demands and needs. In many cases, local leaders have pursued innovative strategies and implemented them successfully to help retiring business owners continue operations in their communities. In these cases, they often worked with nonprofits or statewide groups in adapting to changing conditions.

Hiring a broker and selling an operating business is often the first option considered by retiring business owners but long-term population declines, shrinking markets, and increased competition, including the internet have made private sales of these small businesses more difficult. Likewise, aging local populations and loss of possible heirs to other careers mean fewer people available and willing to take on the full-time commitment required to operate a small business successfully.

A second option may involve transferring an operating business to current employees, but, as shown in other chapters, that approach requires sufficient employees in an age group that is willing to take on the additional management or ownership responsibilities. Changing demographics make it more difficult to hire employees and cause older employees to work longer. Thus, small businesses or stores, especially in rural areas, often operate with relatively few full-time employees, many of whom are near retirement age.

When a direct sale or an employment ownership approach is not viable for whatever reason, community leaders have found ways for residents to pool funds, purchase a business or real estate, and then hire or contract with a

DOI: 10.4324/9781003497462-8

manager. This approach, especially when used by nonprofits, can bring access to sources of funds to modernize the building or restock inventory when that cost would have been prohibitive to a private owner. Such a strategy may be needed to retain a business that provides services required to maintain a high quality of life or viability of the city or place.

Fortunately, small rural communities often include a population base with lasting ties to the area plus financial wealth to invest in projects that not only make the area more livable but also foster its longevity. This commitment can be both financial and time spent volunteering. A challenge, however, may be to identify a suitable project or to find residents willing to invest.

There is growing evidence that residents value social interactions and personal involvement in community affairs, both of which are more readily available in smaller places, which can reduce the potential issue of loneliness (Saad, 2021; Auma, 2024). Local groups both in the U.S. and around the world have found ways to translate this support by residents into efforts that involve pooling funds to purchase and/or retain local businesses (Walzer, 2019 and 2021).

Increasingly, local leaders and residents recognize the importance of quality of life, which sometimes may literally determine the continued viability of a place in the future. This situation means that groups or organizations that are not always active economic agents have found ways to undertake new endeavors that even involve managing for-profit enterprises. The ventures expand the resources available to local leaders in helping with the business transition process and maintain and/or boost the attractiveness and longevity of the area.

This chapter examines strategies used by various groups that used investments by residents to help retain businesses. Of special interest is the role(s) that nonprofit organizations play to stimulate, support, or even guide local groups through the transition process. Nonprofits with a statewide mission are increasingly important in building local capacity. Agencies focusing on historic preservation find that retaining local businesses is key to their success, especially when threatened businesses are long-standing ventures in the community.

The Preservation Trust of Vermont (PTV) is a prime example of a statewide nonprofit agency that works successfully with community leaders to preserve businesses. It has a long history of helping to revitalize or transition businesses on the verge of closing. While local groups spearhead the efforts, the PTV provides information, guidance, technical support, training, and help to arrange funding that in many cases were key to the successful outcomes.

Local agencies have used a variety of approaches unique to their situations that might be difficult to replicate elsewhere, but most have core components that can be modified or adjusted to meet other situations. Walzer (2021) describes these strategies in more detail. Especially important are essential elements that must be recognized in designing a local approach. Subsequent discussions will highlight these components along with descriptions of actions taken in the business transition processes.

The discussion starts with a brief overview of important considerations in selecting possible strategies and then provides examples of how local agencies and groups organized and launched business ventures. The potential role(s) of nonprofits is highlighted with a discussion of ways the Preservation Trust of Vermont has worked with these groups to preserve historic structures and transition businesses since 1980.

Background Issues and Future Options and Need

Many rural areas have lagged metro areas in population growth or, in some cases, have even declined in population for many years. Rural areas, overall, declined in total population for the first time in history between 2010 and 2020 (Johnson, 2022). While alarming at first glance, a closer examination finds these changes to be more complex than initially thought.

From a national perspective, declines in the overall rural population stem partly from the way in which rural areas are defined and tabulated. For example, standard metropolitan areas, as defined by the Office of Management and Budget (OMB), include a core county including a city or cities of 50,000 or more plus adjoining counties where a large percentage of residents are linked to the core county by commuting patterns (United States Census Bureau, 2023). In addition, the OMB groups counties with a city of 20,000 or more, but less than 50,000 population, as micropolitan statistical areas. Nonmetropolitan areas are often viewed as the remaining counties.

A result of these definitions is that as a metropolitan or micropolitan area expands economically, it attracts commuters from surrounding small towns to work. The increase in commuting patterns has two effects. First, it strengthens the link between the core county and surrounding counties, which may then be reclassified from rural to a metro or micro area. This reclassification shows a decrease in the rural population even when the populations of the formerly rural counties did not change (Deller & Conroy, 2022; Winchester, 2010).

A second, and possibly more significant, outcome of the core county expansions is that increased commuting patterns may negatively impact businesses in the surrounding small towns as residents purchase goods and services near where they work. The outcome is that businesses are adversely affected and may be less profitable. Spending less time in their home community may also mean residents are less socially engaged and less likely to invest time and resources in making the community a better place to live.

While reclassification is one explanation for slow growth or declines in rural population nationally, another factor is the natural aging process. Deaths of long-term residents mean a natural population decline when they are not replaced by births or in-migration. In cases of two-person households, a surviving family member may continue to reside in the same house, which limits available housing for residents possibly interested in moving to the city or town.

Many rural towns and counties have declined in population, some for decades. This situation combined with declines in business activities led to business closures and erosion in tax bases, adversely affecting living conditions. Currently facing a potential business closure due to a pending retirement, relocation, health conditions, or other factors, the preferred response is to pass the business to the next generation. However, many likely heirs have pursued higher education and/or work opportunities in larger areas, so they are not available or not interested in continuing the business.

Even more difficult is when current owners experience burnout from difficulties in hiring workers and long hours involved in managing the business so they no longer operate the business as aggressively as in the past. They may defer maintenance and reduce inventory to save money since the business operates on a thin profit margin. If the business represents a large component of their assets, an inability to sell the business can create financial difficulties with increased pressures to find some alternative.

Another option may involve selling or transferring the business to employees with several approaches discussed in other chapters. Some alternatives, however, may require more employees or other conditions that a small business does not meet. The number of employees may be too small, and/or they may not be interested in pursuing ownership. In these circumstances, community leaders must consider other innovative approaches, such as gaining control of the business, accessing additional funds, and then making the venture financially attractive to buyers.

After trying other options, residents in several small Kansas communities successfully operated grocery stores as municipal-owned ventures (Procter, 2021). Although this structure requires allowance by state statutes, it has been shown to work. In Sheffield, Illinois, a nonprofit agency acquired a grocery store and operates it as a for-profit business within the broader mission and scope of the host. These alternatives are discussed in more detail in this chapter.

Roles of Nonprofits or State Agencies

States and regional governments have a role in helping local groups transition businesses. First and foremost is that a state has a healthy investment climate that fosters private sales of businesses when owners retire or sell for other reasons. Competitive tax rates and regulatory policies are important in fostering business growth and expansion, especially in rural areas with declining populations.

Second, incentives and/or grants from state agencies that not only allow, but also encourage, small business development are key. Rural areas may pose special needs due to the small size of the businesses and the limited staff available in many rural places to pursue grants and/or manage development programs. Thus, state governments that understand and accommodate the needs of small towns or places are more likely to succeed in retaining small business post-retirement.

A third and more direct approach is for either a state agency or a nonprofit with access to necessary resources to work directly with local groups in managing the transition. State-funded agencies often have resources available to work with newly formed businesses. These programs may involve working with the U.S. Small Business Association, the U.S. Economic Development Administration, or other federal agencies. Low-cost loans may be an option in some cases. Likewise, entrepreneurship development initiatives can help identify or attract new entrepreneurs and these types of support are included in many state or federal programs. Tourism and recreation are also important local economic development considerations that provide other state agencies with incentives to support these initiatives.

Likewise, nonprofit 501(c)(3) organizations have access to a wide array of financial and marketing resources. Historic preservation programs, for example, have a vested interest in working with local groups to stabilize the economy by preserving local buildings or monuments that celebrate important historical events or sites. These agencies recognize the importance of maintaining a viable economic environment so that their investments in historic buildings or properties can have strong impacts.

Preservation Trust of Vermont

The Preservation Trust of Vermont (PTV) is a successful example of this approach with its broad support of local groups trying to maintain businesses that have served the community for many years. Its broad-based support ranges from helping groups organize as a group, designing strategic plans, supporting potential ventures with technical and management assistance, or helping raise funds to operationalize local initiatives. The support and assistance are flexible enough to work with diverse volunteer organizations using locally designed strategies and approaches tailored to local needs.

The aim of PTV is to build community by preserving historic buildings, villages, and downtowns to help make the communities vibrant places to live. The programmatic efforts have focused on small communities due to the rural nature of Vermont as a state. Statewide population declines generated interest in finding novel and innovative ways to help towns and places maintain a tourist trade as well as provide suitable and attractive living environments for potential newcomers. The state has been aggressively trying to attract residents with relocation incentives since 2018 (Agency of Commerce and Community Development, 2023).

Of special interest in current discussions is the broad base of support for local economic development approaches provided by PTV. While a focus is on preserving buildings and structures, local groups also receive assistance in learning about strategies employed elsewhere. This support is especially important for local leaders who have limited exposure and experience using development strategies. By contacting an agency such as PTV, these leaders obtain help in organizing groups, identifying feasible options, exploring alternate strategies, and raising funds.

Finding ways to transition and preserve a local business has been the motivating factor in the cases described later. Continuing the business is seen as a way for the community to remain vibrant and preserve a past way of life. Retaining these businesses also affects the surrounding area because, without them, the area may become a food desert or be without other essential services.

State- and federal-funded programs can support specific local initiatives to help transition businesses, including during a retirement phase. However, local groups, including mainly volunteers with limited experience on these issues, may have difficulty accessing these programs without guidance and technical assistance provided by intermediary agencies or nonprofits such as PTV. Past leadership and programming by late preservation leader Paul Bruhn to help small communities undertake historic preservation and local development led to the National Park Service (NPS) launching a Paul Bruhn Historic Revitalization Program that provides grants to communities for a broad range of local initiatives. This is but one example of the resources available.

PTV also offers a Village Trust Initiative, which is available to 20 towns with fewer than 2,500 residents (PTV, 2024). This program is offered in collaboration with the Vermont Council on Rural Development (VCRD) and the Vermont Community Foundation (VCF) to encourage communities to have, or start, a 501(c)(3) along with a project of interest. Once again, while small amounts of funds are available, the program builds local capacity to undertake initiatives that involve preservation as well as local prosperity.

Likewise, the PTV collaborates with national and private organizations, such as the 1772 Foundation that supports rehabilitation and repair to historic structures, and also provides needed local services such as daycare, food pantries, and so on. People and groups interested in supporting these restoration and revitalization initiatives can donate funds as well.

Many people select an area or location in which they wish to live and then find suitable employment, which makes focusing on place to live an essential community development strategy (Austin et al., 2022). This approach makes it even more important that rural places have an authentic sense of place that potential residents find attractive. An historic presence, well-maintained downtown, affordable housing, access to natural resources, high-quality educational opportunities, and a safe environment are all factors considered in selecting where to live. This is even more important when higher-quality internet access provides educational, shopping, and entertainment opportunities. The PTV, as a historic preservation agency, has helped local groups find ways to emphasize local advantages and build a positive future for the community.

Historic structures can also be a rallying point in a community and enhance the social capital so important in retaining and/or increasing population. Long-time residents consider these structures or institutions an essential part of the community (past and present) and important to preserve. Likewise, the events and activities help integrate current and incoming residents into social activities, another important aspect of building social capital. Thus, preserving and enhancing the local structures, including long-standing businesses that provide important services, is a development strategy, especially with population declines and shrinking local markets.

Agencies such as PTV recognize the importance of preservation in local development and help local groups create and implement effective strategies. The vision of PTV is:

> By taking a broad view of preservation, PTV nimbly and creatively supports locally led efforts to save and revitalize historic buildings, gathering places, villages, downtowns, and local economies. Empowering community champions with skills, resources, and connections, PTV helps Vermont realize a dynamic and hopeful future.
>
> *(Preservation Trust of Vermont, 2024)*

Several key points in this stated vision are worth highlighting. First, PTV builds or strengthens local capacity by providing access to financial resources or technical assistance. Local groups identify people willing to initiate and/or support the effort with assistance or guidance from external agencies. Several examples are described in more detail in Walzer (2019).

Second, PTV recognizes that preserving a long-standing local business updated to meet current market demand is an essential component of making a community viable. For this reason, some projects have involved helping local groups work with business owners to find new and innovative ways to restart closed businesses or those on the verge of closing. In these cases, the goal is a positive long-term future for the community without continued reliance on state government support.

Third, the PTV recognizes the importance of viable rural communities (including municipalities, towns, and unincorporated entities called gores) in an overall vision for the State of Vermont. This approach is essential to Vermont as a small rural state where preserving and enhancing rural places is key to its future. Its liberal stance on policy issues makes finding ways to support local initiatives a natural fit.

The Plunkett Foundation in the U.K. is another example of a foundation helping to support local groups reopen businesses and revitalize social gathering places. Pubs in many small rural communities had closed, or were on the verge of closing, leaving residents without social gathering places, which contributed to rural loneliness (Plunkett UK, n.d.). By working with Plunkett, local groups could expand operations and include other local services. These efforts in more than 700 communities not only stabilized the population base in many cases but also improved quality of life. McCusker (2021) describes other similar efforts in the U.K.

Creating inclusive, accessible villages and downtowns through a variety of approaches addresses another issue of growing importance, especially in more rural areas. Aging residents may have difficulties finding suitable living arrangements when family members move to other locations for better employment opportunities. Residents left behind must be able to purchase food and other necessities, which makes an accessible downtown with at least basic services necessary. Without these services, elderly residents may move to places with better health facilities or living accommodations, further threatening the long-term viability of the town or place.

A broad vision of quality of life in economic development also encompasses preserving agricultural buildings and connecting to outdoor recreation, which is a major industry in Vermont and many other places. Access to natural resources is a major, and sometimes overlooked, economic development attraction. Surveys of factors considered important in selecting a place to live often list entertainment as a relatively high priority (Auma, 2024). While a small rural place may not contain many local entertainment options, access to a lake or other natural amenities can make a serious difference, as noted later in the Elmore Store discussion. In some instances, these recreation facilities are owned and/or managed by a state or private agency, which means that incorporating them into a local development strategy may involve minimal local costs beyond infrastructure facilities to accommodate traffic and so on.

Innovative Transitioning Approaches

Previous discussions focused on how local groups can revitalize their communities by helping to transition businesses when a retiring owner is unable to transfer ownership to heirs or another buyer. This section examines instances when a local group, mostly having worked with PTV or another nonprofit, implemented an action plan that financed and reopened a business important to the future of the community.

The approach used in each community is unique and is driven by both the proposed venture and availability of resources. These discussions highlight not only the projects but also how local organizers marshalled resources to make the project succeed. The broad approaches are similar in many ways because the overall aim is to have a sustainable business enterprise. The organizational structure and strategies used, however, differ due to the local resources available and the interests of potential investors.

In subsequent discussions, the terms community-supported enterprise (CSE) and community-owned businesses (COB) are interchangeable. In each instance residents pool funds to purchase a building, real estate, or business inventory, with possible rehabilitation, and then either hire or contract with a manager to operate the venture. This differs from the approach used in Kansas and other states where a municipal corporation owns and manages the venture. The CSEs can be organized as a for profit, not-for-profit, cooperative, or LLC.

Also important are the differences in the motivations of local groups for launching these enterprises. Most often, residents faced immediate closure of a grocery store, causing significant travel to purchase basic grocery items. In these cases, the focus may be on just replacing the store under the threat of closing. Other groups took a longer-term view by expanding the offerings to include other daily necessities, locally produced crafts, and/or other services bought by residents, tourists, and other groups. This broader approach increases the profitability and viability of the business.

In some cases, a previous owner may have disinvested in the building or inventory because of limited profits and funds available. With access to a broader set of resources, the CSE can improve the property, update inventory, and make other investments so that the business can be affordable and profitable again. The intent is that the business operates profitably rather than annually asking for contributions from investors. Several examples of these efforts are described next.[1]

Royal Super Mart (Sheffield, IL)

The Village of Sheffield, IL (pop. 821 in 2020) is in rural Bureau County in the Ottawa, IL micropolitan statistical area. With a population of 926 in the 2010 Census, Sheffield had a 11.3% population decline during the 2010s. However, the 2020 population counts were not always reliable due to COVID-19 issues so the 2020 figure may be an undercount. Nevertheless, local retail markets had shrunk in size.

The population is mostly White (92.9%), with a median household income of $68,250 and a 5.2% unemployment rate. The median age of residents was 41.0 years according to the 2021 American Community Survey, with 19.5% of residents 65 years or older (Neilsburg Research, 2024). Older residents, especially those with limited mobility, depend on local access for groceries, especially health items, so having a store was important.

The Village has an active one-block-long downtown with most buildings occupied by a variety of retail and service businesses. Lack of a large employer means that many residents commute to surrounding employment centers, and they likely patronize businesses in those areas, further eroding markets for local businesses. Vacant residential space and older houses in need of repair are available in Sheffield to potential in-migrants or businesses, along with vacant land that could be developed.

Recognizing the need for capital reinvestment in infrastructure, the Village of Sheffield launched a strategic planning initiative and in 2018 created a Tax Increment Finance District (TIF), including most of the land within the corporate limits. The TIF was designed to expand the local real estate tax base; eliminate blighted areas; construct, improve, and maintain public infrastructure facilities; improve employment opportunities; and attract new retail and commercial businesses (Lanham & Pratt, 2024).

As an example of efforts to help sell vacant lots, the Village implemented an action plan that reimbursed qualified builders of single-family homes on vacant lots for $10,000 using funds from real estate tax increment funds. Another TIF initiative involved repair and/or replacement of the public infrastructure in the downtown. These projects included making disabled parking areas ADA-compliant; raising and repairing sidewalks; improving and repairing streets; and other activities to make the business district both more attractive and conducive to shopping.

At the same time, high importance was placed on linking the downtown environment to the past. For instance, the downtown area middle of the street parking was favored by residents and made the downtown area unique, so it was maintained along with other features. These downtown rehabilitation efforts were undertaken between May and December 2021. The TIF program was effective in adding several stores, including a remodeled restaurant, an insurance agency, and a construction and consulting office.

In 2022, the owner of a local family-owned grocery (since 1950) and hardware store (since 1977) approached retirement age with no detailed succession plan. He decided to sell the grocery business but could not find a suitable buyer using a private broker. Closing the store meant residents had to travel 15 miles each way to purchase groceries. While many residents work outside the community, the local demand for groceries was sufficient to make the business profitable, partly due to customers' allegiance to the long-time owners. The store was a gathering place for Sheffield residents, so it was important to community development. A long history of service in the community made retaining the name of the store and the current location important in considering possible options such as the Village community development initiative using TIF funds.

A non-profit Corner Wellness Center (CWC) has operated in Sheffield near the downtown area since 2015, providing counseling, a gymnasium, support groups, and educational programs. The Center provides opportunities and an environment in which residents can grow in "physical, emotional, and spiritual health." The owners, as residents in the community, recognized the importance of local access to healthy foods for overall community wellness. They started an initiative to create a for-profit grocery store, managed by a Board of Directors, under the auspices of their nonprofit organization. The store opened in 2023 as a social enterprise. Profits after taxes are reinvested in the store and related programs such as youth mentoring, nutrition, education, and other initiatives that support the community health mission. See Figure 8.1.

The importance of grocery stores as downtown anchor institutions has been well-documented (Bailey, 2010). Transitioning the Royal Super Mart to new ownership generates sales taxes, property taxes, and employment opportunities in the Village. Purchasing from local suppliers, whenever possible, also supports surrounding areas and builds allegiance to the store. It also generates foot traffic downtown and expands the customer base for other businesses. The store provides fresh food options and basic groceries, along with space for customers to meet and socialize.

FIGURE 8.1 Royal Super Mart. Photo by Norman Walzer.

Recognizing that many residents commute to work in surrounding communities, the store provides an after-hours self-access checkout available for members who live in Sheffield or in a 10-mile surrounding area. Shopping during regular hours does not require a membership, but annual memberships are $40 for the primary household member and $5 for each additional family member over 16 years of age (Lanham & Pratt, 2024). The after-hours access allows members to shop from 5 a.m. to 11 p.m. daily and the store has the usual surveillance and alarm systems for security.

To finance this initiative, the CWC launched a fund-raising campaign that generated approximately $540,000 from contributions of $5 to $50,000. It also obtained grants (approximately $80,000) from utilities and other agencies. The building underwent a nearly total remodeling effort during the transition process. The new owners purchased up-to-date refrigeration equipment at favorable prices, so the store is well-equipped to provide a variety of fresh foods.

Since it is part of a local overall community development project, the Village of Sheffield will reimburse the Cornerstone Wellness Center up to 50% of the project with a maximum of $557,000 during the remainder of the TIF program, until 2042. The annual Village share will be obtained from the net real estate tax increment. In essence, the village rewards investors by repaying its portion of the costs from funds raised by the project.

This transition example has several important attributes that can be applied elsewhere. First, the motivations and purposes of the Royal Super Mart are closely aligned with the long-term development and vitality of Sheffield. The Village government was already engaged in major capital improvements to the downtown area, including streets and parking. The grocery store is part of an active and viable downtown area. By using TIF funds, elected leaders can financially support the store project using revenues generated by growth in the property tax base with a minimal immediate drain on local funds.

Second, the business transitioning endeavor was launched by an established community-based wellness center with a solid reputation for advancing overall community health. Thus, launching a grocery initiative was a logical next step in generating community support and retaining an important existing business with which residents identify and will support.

East Calais Community Trust

East Calais is an unincorporated village in Calais, VT (pop.1,867) on the National Register of Historic Places. It is in rural Washington County (pop. 59,807) with a median age of 44 years and 29% of the population 60 years or older (United States Census Bureau, 2022). The median household income in 2020 was $82,558, well above the approximate average ($74,014) for Vermont. The mean travel time (29.6 miles) to work for Calais residents is well above the average in Vermont and 18% of residents reported working from home.

East Calais is advantaged by its location on VT Route 14, approximately 10 miles from Montpelier (the state capitol), which offers employment opportunities. When the East Calais General Store, which had provided groceries and other items since the 1850s, closed in December 2019, like country stores in nearby Woodbury and North Montpelier, the 18.6-mile stretch of Route 14 from East Montpelier to Hardwick became a food desert.

In response, East Calais residents organized the East Calais Community Trust (ECCT) in 2019 to reconstruct the historic building, including the three apartments on the second and third floors. The Trust, a nonprofit agency managed by a board of directors and an advisory committee, launched fund-raising efforts in 2020 with a loan of $50,000 from a financial institution for acquisition purposes. This is one of the earliest efforts by a nonprofit in Vermont to undertake this type of endeavor. PTV was a fiscal sponsor initially, which allowed ECCT to jumpstart the fund-raising efforts. Later, the group raised $2.7 million, including a Paul Bruhn Historic Revitalization grant and a Community Supported Enterprise Grant/HUD, both of which PTV initially helped administer along with other grants and donations (Community Capital of Vermont, 2024). See Figure 8.2.

While the store was closed during the pandemic, it continued to serve the community from a front porch that also was a drop-off location for the Kellogg–Hubbard Library; a source of free food in the "Everyone Eats" program; and a barbeque truck that sold meals. Each Saturday during the summer the ECCT hosted "Extra Row," where community residents provided produce from their gardens to share.

The building, in continuous operation since 1850, was in significant disrepair with antiquated systems, a deteriorated interior, and underground fuel tanks that required remediation. The Trust arranged for site inspections, removed gas tanks, and purchased the building in June 2020 with more than $160,000 in local support. The condition of the building created many hurdles in meeting current building codes as well as modernizing and making the building an attractive venue suitable for planned uses. Extensive restoration, deep energy retrofits, and ADA upgrades, resulted in the state's first all-electric, fossil fuel-free general store. The remodeled three affordable housing units are managed by Downstreet Housing and the store once again serves as a hub for the community.

ECCT is committed to reviving the store as a local source for food including fresh produce, with a kitchen offering a deli and grab-and-go meals for both residents and people traveling through. Besides offering food and household staples, the general store has a gathering area with Wi-Fi and a coffee bar featuring locally roasted coffee where customers can visit and socialize while shopping, which helps build social capital in the community. It has a well-designed kitchen offering family-style meals and other facilities plus the three apartments.

FIGURE 8.2 East Calais General Store. Photo by Jude Domski for the Preservation Trust of Vermont. Used with permission.

Since opening, the store provides daily breakfasts, an assortment of deli items, baked goods such as burritos, assorted beverages, and a variety of locally made items. Locally grown honey, maple candy lollipops, chocolates, clay mugs, and pots are also available. A wall in the store displays local artwork. These features provide multiple profit centers that attract tourist dollars when people visit the area for recreational and other purposes.

Raising and managing funds from many diverse sources involved serious oversight and accounting responsibilities. While many challenges had to be overcome, those involved in this project were innovative and thoughtful in working with local groups. The costs of materials and labor increased substantially during the pandemic, but some work and materials were donated by residents or local businesses to help with the project. These efforts also built buy-in from residents, making them an integral part of the success. ECCT and the store manager pursued grants and donations to keep the cost feasible and PTV played a significant role in guiding and administering the overall efforts.

A crucial step in the success of this endeavor involved finding someone with the same vision as ECCT to organize and manage the store. Fortunately, an East Calais resident expressed an interest in leasing and managing the store. She responded to a newspaper announcement, was interviewed by the ECCT Board, and accepted a lease for the store operation. Her previous management experience was with a farm market in Maine where she had lived on site. Past activities as kitchen manager and chef for a senior center provided needed insights to managing takeout food operations. The ECCT applied for grants and used a GoFundMe campaign to purchase equipment and inventory, which met the intent of ECCT to reduce the cost to residents by minimizing debt when possible.

The East Calais General Store opened in late 2023 as part of a broad community development initiative that benefitted from a recognition that without the store, the area would be a food desert. The project was fortunate in finding an experienced person to lease and manage the store. Purchasing from local suppliers builds allegiance to the operations as well as stimulating the local economy. For instance, the store works with a local supplier, Pete's Greens, a Community Supported Agriculture organization, to distribute produce to customers. The store employs several local workers and generates income in the community. It also serves both residents and visitors, which broadens its customer base and profitability. ECCT is exploring other ways to offer local sites where store customers can hold activities at a nearby location.

The Elmore Store, Lake Elmore, VT

The Elmore General Store, in Elmore, VT (pop. 1.075), illustrates some of the complex obstacles that local groups face in trying to reopen a closed country store. The building is on highway VT-12 next to Lake Elmore, used by residents and tourists for water sports. The median age in Elmore is 44.7 years, slightly older than Lamoille County (41.0), with 28% of residents 60 years or older. The median household income is $104,500, which is 1.5 times that of the County ($69,886) and substantially above Vermont ($74,014). Thus, the area has financial resources available for projects.

The Elmore General Store has operated since the 1840s in its current location adjacent to the town hall and across from an elementary school. The store provides postal services and banking services, making it a convenient place to purchase general groceries and convenience items while conducting other activities. See Figure 8.3.

The couple who had owned the store since the 1980s decided to retire but had difficulty finding a suitable buyer. They not only managed the store but were also actively engaged in community events, which made the store a community center and meeting place. The fact that locally-produced foods and merchandise were sold also strengthened the linkage between the store and the community.

The structure and age, septic system, and the HVAC of the building and facilities limited the types of services and activities it could support. The structure foundation needed attention after many years of use, and required significant outlays not supported by revenues generated from current store operations.

Likewise, as with many older buildings, the facilities and equipment in the store were dated with some in need of serious repair or additions. A small commercial kitchen needed expansion to accommodate additional value-added food or deli operations. Thus, without significant investment, the store was limited in the variety of services it could provide. This condition made the business less attractive to potential buyers who were unlikely to be able to afford the improvements needed and still be profitable.

FIGURE 8.3 Elmore Store. Photo by Jude Domski for the Preservation Trust of Vermont. Used with permission.

Elmore Community Trust (ECT)

The potential closing of this store and community asset led residents to contact the PTV to explore other options. In response, 10 Elmore and nearby residents created the Elmore Community Trust, a 501(c)(3) nonprofit, and with coaching from PTV, raised approximately $400,000 from grants, donations, and other sources including help from professional fund-raising groups.

The stated goal of the Trust is to "care for the places that make Elmore special, and to support businesses, organizations, and residents that contribute to our vibrant community" (Elmore Community Trust, 2022, p. 2). Much of the money was from local donors and others interested in access to services at the store but also in promoting the future of the community. In 2022, the Trust purchased the store and inventory from the previous owners.

A local couple was interested in managing the store through a lease with their LLC, so the Trust sold them the inventory for a nominal fee. They reopened the store, providing a variety of convenience items and services including newspapers, locally raised and produced products, access to Wi-Fi, banking services, and postal services through a contract with the U.S. Postal Service.

Shortly after opening the store, the Postal Service announced it would discontinue its contract with the store, a potential setback to operations. While the contract did not generate large revenues, residents using these services also purchased other merchandise. The community responded to the potential loss of postal services with an aggressive letter-writing campaign to elicit support from Congressional representatives. This effort led to the Postal Service reversing its decision and the store continuing to provide these services.

After slightly more than one year of operations, the store managers decided the capacity of the store would not support their business interests, including pretzel making and plans for additional services, so they announced that they would leave in early 2023. This situation forced ECT to reopen the search for a manager. Fortunately, a town resident with experience as a chef and caterer, stepped forward and leased the store as a manager. ECT sold the inventory for a minimum amount to help the new manager restock inventory and reopen (May 2023) with the Trust owning the store.

The long-term prosperity of the store will depend on substantial investments in the structure and facilities, which the Trust plans to address. In 2022–23, improvements to the electrical system, a new generator, hazardous tank removal, and septic system improvements were made, allowing it to hold a variety of events during the year. The estimated cost of renovation ranged from $80,000 to $1.2 million. The Trust raised $67,000 in 2022.

Funds raised in 2023 were used to renovate a downstairs apartment to public use space with restrooms that will allow the store to expand activities. An option to sell state tax credits to businesses was also considered to provide direct financial benefits to contributors. Other strategies such as finding monthly donors and continuing past fund-raising efforts are underway, along with state and federal grants (Elmore Community Trust, 2022).

An expanded deli will provide prepared foods plus beverages in a lunch venue. Serving pizza several nights per week is also an option. The back bedroom section of the building could be renovated and converted to selling space. Also under consideration is a summer concert series on the property to help attract patrons. These efforts will continue the tradition of making the store a community center that residents will patronize, support, and help expand. While the Elmore Community Trust faced significant obstacles reopening the store, it also built community support and solidified a strong clientele, which helps explain its successes.

While this project is still in its early stages, it illustrates several important components. First is the importance placed on community development with a driving force being to improve quality of life in the community. The store is a focal point not only for purchasing groceries but also as a meeting place and source of entertainment for residents in the surrounding area.

Second, the Trust is exploring plans to partner with other agencies in enhancing use of the adjacent state park. The park is a major tourist attraction in the region and by tailoring the lines of merchandise sold, the ECT could possibly expand its clientele and sustain future profitability of the store. Likewise, the store could be a community center with summertime events, including a 4th of July celebration.

Third, the ECT effectively partnered with many agencies such as the PTV to obtain technical assistance and financial support, including funds to purchase the option agreement and building assessments along with a $100,000 NPS Paul Bruhn Revitalization Grant. PTV also helped mediate contract negotiations during the transition between operators.

Maple Corner Community Store

The Maple Corner Community Store dates to the mid-1800s with several private owners prior to its sale in 1945 to the Adamant Cooperative, which operated the store as well as their primary location in a neighboring community until the Maple Corner Store burned in 1949. They rebuilt the current building and quickly sold the store to a private owner, where it remained for another 60 years. The store's long and rich history in the small community of Calais, VT (pop. 1,661 in 2020) enabled 200 residents to form a C-corporation and purchase the store when the most recent private owners chose to sell in 2019. The main motivation was fear of losing a long-time establishment and the inconvenience of traveling to a neighboring community to purchase basic needs. See Figure 8.4.

FIGURE 8.4 Maple Corner Community Store.

Source: Maple Corner C-Corporation. Used with permission.

The general store is integrated into the community in various ways, such as providing ready access to food and drink items. Perhaps more importantly, it is a social center with services such as a long-standing Whammy Bar, described in more detail later. They allow residents to "work from home" or meet friends for lunch in the Whammy Bar space when the bar is not open. The store also has a small gathering place. Other essential items include providing postal services and access to the internet and community fiber. An apartment in the building helps pay fixed costs and provides a critical housing unit when the housing market is very tight.

The prepared food program has been a key element in the success. In 2023, the store hired a professional chef and kitchen manager, quickly followed with a large commercial kitchen that vastly expanded the Whammy Bar dinner menu, improved the daytime store deli and pizza business, and ensured a wide variety of prepared foods could always be offered.

Ownership Structure. A fascinating aspect about the small town of Calais, Vermont, is that while the population is small, it occupies 36 square miles and has three general stores, all of which are community-owned and -operated, yet each has a different legal structure. The Maple Corner Community Store is a for-profit C-corporation, co-owned by 200 local shareholders, overseen by a board of directors, and supervised day-to-day by a hired general manager. Community volunteers make up most of the labor force.

The C-corporation ownership has two types of shares. Each holder of the 200 A-voting shares ($500 each) has one vote and the number of these shares is limited. Anyone holding an A-voting share is also entitled to purchase additional B-shares, which accrue additional equity for the shareholder, but not additional voting power. Each investor, regardless of number of shares, has only one vote. In total, as many as 1,000 B shares are held by the 2000 voting shareholders. Investors do not receive an overall discount on purchases as is often possible with traditional cooperatives. The C-corporation is governed by a five-member board of directors and a six-member advisory group. PTV provided guidance and technical assistance but was not directly involved in establishing the corporation.

The Maple Corner Community Center, a 501(c)(3), bought shares so residents interested in helping to sponsor the effort could use a tax deduction rather than buying a share directly. This makes the Community Center the largest shareholder, further building community resilience. Large contributors and investors preferred that the venture avoid major debt that could impede the success of the venture. Consequently, a variety of silent auctions and similar local events were used to make the operation essentially debt-free.

A business venture such as this can be managed in several ways. One option is that the financing organization buy the property and then lease it to a person or LLC responsible for managing the overall operations. This approach lessens the burden on the financing group for making the operation succeed and is the model used by the East Calais Community Trust. A second alternative is for the financing group to take responsibility for operations and hire a manager as an employee. Maple Corner followed the second approach with the general manager as an employee rather than a contractor.

A board of directors meets monthly, and an annual meeting of shareholders/investors sets overall directions for the store, while the general manager is responsible for daily operations. There are three full-time paid staff and 10 or 12 part-time employees, including a rotating stream of local teenagers. The employees receive a discount on purchases. In addition, many volunteers help with various aspects of store operations.

Services Offered. A special and long-standing service is the Whammy Bar, which offers drinks and food events several nights each week. The Whammy Bar seats approximately 25 people due to space and facility capacity. Customers can eat in or take out dinners with additional space available for dining in the building or on an outside patio. A weekly "open mic" night attracts a wide variety of local musicians. The store carries a diverse selection of food items, and a deli with specialties such as local meats, wines, and produce depending on time of year. It also carries an assortment of local craft items and, depending on the day of the week, the store is open from 8 a.m. to 7 or 10 p.m. The store strives to be a welcoming place with a diversity of products that represent the varied tastes in the community.

Possible additional services could include a catering license to serve area groups and organizations. Lunch may be served in the Whammy Bar area, depending on the potential market opportunities and availability of adequate staff. Maintaining a quality staff in a rural community and in a very slim margin business has always been one of the largest challenges. The main interest will continue as a community-gathering place with access to essential basic items such as postal services and food supplies needed daily.

There is considerable interaction and cooperation with other nearby general stores in terms of sharing an order when the supplier has a minimum size that one store can't meet. This collaboration benefits both stores and residents alike by improving the selection available. It is especially important to small stores located in proximity and will likely continue.

Common Elements in Successful Transitions Using CSE Approaches

The business transitions discussed, while different in focus and operations, have several common characteristics that contributed to their success. The differences among strategies illustrate the potential for use in other settings, while the common elements reflect long-held key community development principles. Previous discussions have highlighted ways that nonprofit agencies provide technical assistance, guidance, and sometimes financial resources to support local efforts. Other states actively support similar efforts with equal success in different ways and should be explored.

Community Focus and Engagement

Key to each example discussed is a focus on providing readily accessible place(s) for residents to gather and socialize. While providing access to essential consumer goods or services is a prime motivation, project organizers emphasize ways to make residents part of a building process and "own the project" when completed. This approach helps build a steady clientele and ensures success in the activity. The venture is beyond a private business and becomes a broad-based social enterprise and community effort.

Broad Ownership Structure

Information on alternative approaches to business transitions in the private sector is available in other chapters but the examples here focus mainly on local groups financing the business enterprises using a CSE, C-corporation, and community trust. These options are available in many places, and it is important that local groups explore available opportunities and decide on the most effective approach.

Active Local Leadership

Each project has a set of local leaders committed to the project. They come from various sectors of the community and are motivated for different reasons but, nevertheless, are willing to engage in these efforts. It is important for local organizers to find residents or others willing to take the lead and then support them with time and resources. The leaders may not always be those who have led in the past, so an extensive search of the community for new people to engage is important.

Accessing Local and External Support

In each business transition example described, local leaders identified and pursued support not only from local agencies but also from other groups like the Preservation Trust of Vermont or a state or federal agency. In the Elmore Community Store example, local groups contacted federal representatives to help retain postal services in the community. The contacts were not only with economic development agencies but also with agencies dealing with other aspects of community development.

Perhaps a main takeaway from these discussions is that when confronted with a potential business closing, community groups must rally local support, create a consensus around suitable alternatives, and then move ahead to marshal available resources to bring the project to fruition. Especially important is to recognize and incorporate resources from beyond the community.

In looking ahead, the examples or models discussed here reflect changes that result from demographics such as population aging as well as economic changes that adversely affect rural areas, including the growth of internet shopping or the aging of the population. The growth of dollar stores has also affected markets for main street businesses in rural areas. These trends are likely to persist and will likely increase in the future as aging business owners consider retirement.

Thus, community leaders must continually look for innovative strategies and approaches to manage the transition. This chapter highlights the assistance and guidance available in nonprofits and other groups that can help local groups. Finding and accessing these resources may involve serious efforts by local leaders but, in the long run, they can provide essential support in making the local projects succeed.

Note

1 These discussions are based on personal interviews with personnel involved in each location in Fall 2023 and Spring 2024 with follow-up reviews. They reflect mainly the authors' interpretations and impressions of activities underway and accomplishments at the time of the interviews. The authors especially thank Denise Wheeler, an ECCT board member, for insights regarding the East Calais Store project and Jamie Moorby, general manager, for help with the Maple Corner Store discussion.

References

Agency of Commerce and Community Development. (2023, January 18). *Worker incentive relocation program: Interim report*. State of Vermont, United States. https://outside.vermont.gov/agency/ACCD/ACCD_Web_Docs/ED/Relocation/WORKER%20RELOCATION%20INCENTIVE%20PROGRAM%20INTERIM%20REPORT.pdf?_gl=1*1*k16wax*_ga*MTQyMjcxMTY0OC4xNzI5NjMyMzcy*_ga_V9WQH77KLW*MTcyOTYzMjM3Mi4xLjEuMTcyOTYzMjg0Mi4wLjAuMA

Auma, Q. (2024, January 24). *Ten reasons why Americans are choosing small-town living*. MSN.com. https://www.msn.com/en-us/travel/news/10-reasons-why-americans-are-choosing-small-town-living/ar-BB1hdywK

Austin, J. C., Weinstein, A., Hicks, M., & Wornell, E. (2022, January 26). *Improving quality of life—not just business—is the best path to Midwestern rejuvenation*. Brookings Institution. https://www.brookings.edu/articles/improving-quality-of-life-not-just-business-is-the-best-path-to-midwestern-rejuvenation/

Bailey, J. M. (2010, October). *Rural grocery stores: Importance and challenges* [Issue brief]. Rural Research and Analysis Program, Center for Rural Affairs. https://www.cfra.org/sites/default/files/publications/rural-grocery-stores-importance-and-challenges.pdf

Community Capital of Vermont. (2024, October 28). *Community Capital borrower East Calais General Store is featured on the cover of the Preservation Trust of Vermont Annual Report* [Image attached]. Facebook. https://www.facebook.com/community capitalofvermont

Deller, S. C. & Conroy, T. (2022). Regional economic trends across the rural urban divide. In N. Walzer & C. D. Merrett (Eds.), *Rural areas in transition: Meeting challenges & making opportunities* (pp. 19–44). Routledge. 10.4324/9781003280620

Elmore Community Trust. (2022). *Elmore Community Trust annual report 2022*. https://static1.squarespace.com/static/5e5184261461e703888c491d/t/6463887949819c7af8199101/1684244602680/ECT+Annual+Report.pdf

Johnson, K. M. (2022, Winter). *Rural areas lost population over the past decade for the first time in history* [National issue brief 160]. Carsey School of Public Policy, University of New Hampshire. https://scholars.unh.edu/cgi/viewcontent.cgi?article=1446&context=carsey

Lanham, M., & Pratt, E. (2024, February 28–29). *Revitalizing rural downtowns: A TIF-fueled transformation* [Conference presentation]. *Illinois Institute for Rural Affairs & Lt. Governor's Rural Affairs Council and Rural Partners 35th Annual Rural Community Economic Development Conference, Springfield, IL, United States.*

McCusker, S. (2021). Community-owned pubs in Great Britain: Hubs of community enterprise. In N. Walzer (Ed.), *Community owned businesses: International entrepreneurship, finance, and economic development* (pp. 58–81). Routledge.

Neilsburg Research. (2024, July 26). *Sheffield, IL: Population by age*. Neilsburg. https://www.neilsberg.com/insights/sheffield-il-population-by-age/

Plunkett UK. (n.d.). Case studies. https://plunkett.co.uk/case-studies/

Preservation Trust of Vermont. (2024, April 12). *Call to Vermont's small towns! Expertise and funding available to support community revitalization*. https://www.vtrural.org/village-trust/

Procter, D. E. (2021). St, Paul, Kansas' city-owned grocery store: A variation of the community supported enterprise approach. In N. Walzer (Ed.), *Community owned businesses: International entrepreneurship, finance, and economic development* (pp. 103–122). Routledge.

Saad, L. (2021, January 5). *Country living enjoys renewed appeal in the U.S.* Gallup. https://news.gallup.com/poll/328268/country-living-enjoys-renewed-appeal.aspx
United States Census Bureau. (2022). *American community survey 5-year estimates.* Census reporter profile page for Calais town, Washington County, VT. http://censusreporter.org/profiles/06000US5002311350-calais-town-washington-county-vt/
United States Census Bureau. (2023, July 25). *Delineating metropolitan and micropolitan statistical areas.* https://www.census.gov/programs-surveys/metro-micro/about.html
Walzer, N. (2019). Guidebook and resources for starting community supported enterprises. *Reports, Whitepapers, Articles, and Other Publications, 15.* Center for Government Studies, Northern Illinois University. https://huskiecommons.lib.niu.edu/ctrgovernment-reports/15
Walzer, N. (Ed.). (2021). *Community owned businesses: International entrepreneurship, finance, and economic development.* Routledge.
Winchester, B. S. (2010, December). *Regional recruitment: Strategies to retain and attract newcomers* [Report]. EDA Center, University of Minnesota Crookston. https://hdl.handle.net/11299/204340

9

CREATING RURAL WORKER COOPERATIVES IN IOWA

Stacy Mullinex

Background on Rural Business Succession

The 2020 U.S. Census confirmed data that many may have already suspected. The older population has spiked: approximately one in six residents in the U.S. are age 65 or older (United States Census Bureau, 2023b). In addition, baby boomers are reaching retirement age, with more than half of business owners aged 55 or older (United States Census Bureau, 2023a). The silver tsunami is upon us. It is commonly accepted that only 20%–25% of these mom-and-pop shops actually sell (Exit Planning Institute [EPI], 2023b), though definitive data is difficult to ascertain as small business transfers have been historically nonexistent. Regardless, an ongoing decline in these rural businesses directly affects the viability in each rural community as access to quality-of-life services diminishes. The question is then raised as to how this trend can be mitigated. One answer is found by looking internally to potentially the most practical group of buyers: employees.

Advance Iowa, housed at the University of Northern Iowa, was designed to help drive the Iowa economy forward by assisting small-to-medium-sized businesses. One component of this initiative involves guiding businesses through succession planning. Too often, staff arrive at the end of their journey with the business only to be asked, “Now, who should I sell it to?” The children, who the owners always thought would happily take over the business, have no intention of returning home because their own careers blossomed elsewhere. Advertising the business for sale locally is unnerving because that public knowledge may affect their current revenue.

DOI: 10.4324/9781003497462-9

A business broker may be an option but there can be concern the external buyer might not take care of the employees who have become like family. A successful company could be sold to a third party, but may ultimately be relocated to another area or strategically purchased for the client list where the local facility would eventually be closed. These options do not typically seem palatable to business owners whose community supported their livelihood. However, employee ownership may be a solution that provides a feasible buyer while alleviating other concerns posed by the aforementioned selling options. In fact, this option is so successful that the Iowa Center for Employee Ownership (IA-CEO) was created in May 2023 to guide business transitions to employee owners.

Importance of Business Succession in Rural Communities

Rural businesses are often integral to the economic vitality and social fabric of their communities. The importance of business succession in rural regions cannot be overstated as their continued existence is the cornerstone for economic stability, social cohesion, and the subsequent resilience in these areas. Ensuring business continuity after an owner exits maintains community stability by safeguarding jobs and residential quality of life. Without these elements, displaced workers may be forced to find employment outside of their current locale, which often leads to their income being spent away from home. Even worse, the new job may be too far for a reasonable drive, forcing the family's relocation to another area and resulting in an even greater negative local economic impact.

Businesses that close due to a lack of succession planning essentially leave a void in their community. Quality-of-life services offered by businesses, such as a barber, coffee shop, auto mechanic, bakery, or similar enterprise, help attract newcomers to the area. However, essential facilities such as a grocery store or pharmacy are vital for basic living standards. Moreover, reduction in tax revenue base can hinder future development and community services, furthering the dissuasion of new population growth.

Effective succession planning can help mitigate these issues by retaining employees within the community to nurture the community cohesiveness. A conducive environment is ultimately fostered for business sustainability growth and innovation. Essentially, the business owners collectively contribute to the sustainability of their rural economy with a well-developed succession plan.

Worker Cooperative as A Solution

The worker cooperative business model can provide a viable solution to the distinctive challenges commonly observed for small-to-medium-sized businesses. Rural communities tend to be especially close, with generational families and long-term friendships deeply rooted in the area. Shared traditions in their rich history create a strong social bond and connection among residents. The group identity, where everyone knows each other by name, nurtures an informal structure to offer assistance and cooperation whenever the need arises. In fact, the social network can be so strong it becomes difficult to leave, regardless of opportunities offered elsewhere.

This business model leverages that powerful social cohesion. A supportive work environment with trust and mutual understanding among residents has already been established by default. Moreover, community engagement is commonly extended by participation in local fundraisers, school functions, civic organizations, and similar activities that further strengthen customer relationships for unwavering patronage.

What Is a Worker Cooperative?

Worker Cooperative Definition

The Democracy at Work Institute (DAWI) and the United States Federation of Worker Cooperatives (USFWC) published a joint document defining cooperatives:

> Worker cooperatives are values-driven businesses that put worker and community benefit at the core of their purpose. In contrast to traditional companies, worker members at worker cooperatives participate in the profits, oversight, and often management of the enterprise using democratic practices. The model has proven to be an effective tool for creating and maintaining sustainable, respectable jobs; generating wealth; improving the quality of life of workers; and promoting community and local economic development, particularly for people who lack access to business ownership or sustainable work options.
>
> *(DAWI, 2015, p. 1)*

More specifically, six individual attributes must be met regarding class membership, worker–owner eligibility, patronage, controlling interest, Board of Directors election, and capital investment decisions (see Box 9.1).

Although this definition does not explicitly state the obvious, members of the worker cooperative must work at the business. The worker-owners receive a distribution of the company profits known as the patronage. The dollar amount is calculated in accordance with the company bylaws but can be based on metrics such as hours worked, seniority, amount of wages, or similar measures.

BOX 9.1 CRITERIA FOR WORKER COOPERATIVE (DAWI, 2015, P. 1).

Worker Cooperative Definition

The term "Worker Cooperative" means any enterprise that meets all of the following criteria:

a The enterprise is a business entity with one or more classes of membership
b All workers who are willing to accept the responsibilities of membership and who meet member eligibility criteria are eligible to become worker-owners
c A majority of allocated earnings and losses are allocated to worker-owners on the basis of patronage
d The class of worker-owners has a controlling ownership interest
e A majority of the Board of Directors or governing body is elected by the worker-owners on the basis of one-member–one-vote
f Decisions about return on capital investment are made by the worker-owner class or by the Board of Directors or governing body

The operational policy can also specify that not all surplus earnings are distributed if a portion is retained for capital investments, cash reserves, or other purposes. This democratic model allows each worker-owner a voice to elect the board of directors and vote on significant matters. The membership is non-portable so when employment is terminated for retirement, dismissal, resignation, etc., the worker cooperative membership also ceases. That said, it is important to note that the business model has inherent flexibility. For example, the selling business owner may choose to exit from company ownership over several years where the worker cooperative would initially be a minority interest with the intent of full transition to majority interest at a future date.

Cooperative Values and Principles

Cooperative statutes can differ by state, but the fundamental principles are universal. The International Cooperative Alliance (ICA) is a global organization begun in 1895 for the sole purpose of promoting the cooperative model to provide quality employment ensuring sustainable economic growth and stability. In 1995, the ICA amended the seven cooperative principles, which serve as a guideline of values by which each cooperative should abide (see Box 9.2).

BOX 9.2 COOPERATIVE PRINCIPLES (INTERNATIONAL COOPERATIVE ALLIANCE, N.D.).

Cooperative Principles

The cooperative principles are guidelines by which cooperatives put their values into practice.

1. **Voluntary and Open Membership**

   Cooperatives are voluntary organizations, open to all persons able to use their services and willing to accept the responsibilities of membership, without gender, social, racial, political or religious discrimination.

2. **Democratic Member Control**

   Cooperatives are democratic organizations controlled by their members, who actively participate in setting their policies and making decisions. Men and women serving as elected representatives are accountable to the membership. In primary cooperatives, members have equal voting rights (one member, one vote) and cooperatives at other levels are also organized in a democratic manner.

3. **Member Economic Participation**

   Members contribute equitably to, and democratically control, the capital of their cooperative. At least part of that capital is usually the common property of the cooperative. Members usually receive limited compensation, if any, on capital subscribed as a condition of membership. Members allocate surpluses for any or all of the following purposes: developing their cooperative, possibly by setting up reserves, part of which at least would be indivisible; benefiting members in proportion to their transactions with the cooperative; and supporting other activities approved by the membership.

4. **Autonomy and Independence**

   Cooperatives are autonomous, self-help organizations controlled by their members. If they enter into agreements with other organizations, including governments, or raise capital from external sources, they do so on terms that ensure democratic control by their members and maintain their cooperative autonomy.

5 **Education, Training, and Information**

Cooperatives provide education and training for their members, elected representatives, managers, and employees so they can contribute effectively to the development of their cooperatives. They inform the general public—particularly young people and opinion leaders—about the nature and benefits of cooperation.

6 **Cooperation among Cooperatives**

Cooperatives serve their members most effectively and strengthen the cooperative movement by working together through local, national, regional and international structures.

7 **Concern for Community**

Cooperatives work for the sustainable development of their communities through policies approved by their members.

Business Succession: The Employee Solution

Small Business Succession Red Flag

Collectively, small businesses are a substantial power that drives the rural economy. The Small Business Administration (SBA) reported in 2023 that 84.8% of rural establishments are operated by small businesses (Wilmoth, 2023). Moreover, 54.3% of employment in rural areas is provided by the small businesses, with an average of 8.5 employees at these enterprises. Thus, it is critical to ensure the continuity of these companies as they are essentially the lifeblood of their community vitality. However, that pulse may be weakening as many rural businesses are closing without a succeeding owner.

As noted in previous chapters, the silver tsunami is a label given to the demographic shift of the baby boomer generation reaching retirement age. The U.S. Census reports 55.8 million residents over the age of 65 in our country, reflecting a 38.6% increase from the data reported in 2010. The retirement aftershock wave will continue, given that those of age 45 years and older increased 15% to become 42% of the total population (United States Census Bureau, 2023b).

These statistics support the 2003 finding by the Exit Planning Institute (EPI) that "75% of business owners would like to exit their businesses within the next ten years" (EPI, 2023a, p. 8). The report continues to state that the baby boomer generation is the worst-prepared to transition their business. A finding of special concern is that 57% of the baby boomers have an accelerated timeline, wanting to exit within five years, and only 13% of this generation have a written plan (p. 52). The fact is that every business owner will eventually exit the company. The unspoken truth is that it is not always at the time of their choosing. It is critical to have a written succession plan so the business owner and family do not financially suffer, regardless of the exit time. Likewise, proper planning may also be considered a manner of recompensing the employees and community that supported the business over the years.

The Cooperative Advantage

The Selling Owner

When the selling owner is looking for a buyer, employees can provide a fair market transaction as well as other benefits not afforded with a traditional sale. Foremost, the workers offer a feasible buyer when other purchase interest may be limited due to the location. Rural life may afford a relaxed pace of life, reduced cost of living, and an enriched well-being, which the locals will never leave. Yet, it may prove difficult to lure an external buyer from an established life into an unfamiliar deep-rooted community for a business that may not be exceedingly lucrative.

In addition, worker cooperatives permit selling owners to reach value goals such as a lasting legacy. A third-party buyer may change the business name, consolidate into another location, or acquire it only for the assets. Knowing that the company could potentially exist perpetually can be as significant as the monetary value to some selling owners. Reassurance may also be found in awareness that the "new" owners truly care about the customers and already know important individualities. Likewise, extant vendors may continue to be patronized to ensure quality instead of seeking the cheapest price. Overall, the transition may be considerably smoother for all groups involved as the current culture, relationships, and values established by the selling owner will continue.

Moreover, the selling owner can exit the business on a timeline that is best suited for their lifestyle. A mandate does not exist where the business has to be sold to a worker cooperative in its entirety. A complete sale can be executed at once, or a phased-in approach is possible, where a certain percentage of the business is sold over time. A gradual transition can assist the business owner's personal readiness to leave the company. The selling owner may have extensive hours occupied by the business and may need an adjustment period to acclimate to the extra time now available. If needed, it also provides an opportunity for training and guidance to the employee owners. Regardless, the selling owner still has the ability to stay involved in the business without constant interaction, if desired, by stipulating a seat on the board of directors.

The Employees

Employee owners have benefits just as noteworthy as the selling owner advantages. Higher wages and improved job satisfaction are often associated with worker cooperative owners. In a 2021 report on the relationship between employee ownership and the worker's economic and psychological well-being, DAWI noted:

- Worker cooperatives prioritize employee compensation over business profits, as 86% of those surveyed modeled a top-to-bottom pay ratio of 2:1 or lower. By comparison, the average large corporation in the U.S. executed a 303:1 pay ratio (Schlachter & Prushinskaya, 2021, p. 10).
- Data analyzed by respondents reported a "cooperative wage boost" with a pay increase at a median $2 an hour and a mean $3.52 an hour over the wages earned at the previous job (p. 16).
- The majority of participants surveyed stated the overall working conditions, which included job security, confidence in company economic stability, work effort, and job satisfaction, were at least somewhat or much better than the previous employment. Workplace conflict resolution and a sense of common purpose were also described as being somewhat or much better than the relationship that existed with the boss or management at the prior employment. Moreover, the quality of supervision, feedback, and training, as well as the ability to pursue career goals, were also somewhat or much better when measured against the last employment (pp. 19–20).
- A high level of autonomy exists, where 70% of respondents reported either quite a bit or a great deal of involvement/direct influence at the individual level. In addition, the same ranking was also indicated on the team level at 57.3% and on the enterprise level at 50%. When comparing the autonomy to prior employment, a majority responded as having more control in workplace decision-making (pp. 20–21).

A higher sense of purpose, job security, profit distribution, and democratic governance may contribute to the personal fulfillment at work. Job satisfaction, whether realized on an emotional level, financial basis, or both, is crucial to the contentment of the employee, which directly relates to the production output, customer engagement, and loyalty to the company.

The Businesses

The business per se can also benefit from a transition to employee ownership. Clearly, the silver tsunami affects not only the business owners. It impacts other areas as well, including the available workforce, which ultimately contributes to the labor shortage. The benefits afforded to employees provide longevity to their employment at the company, reducing turnover rates. Moreover, the appeal of employee ownership, financial incentives, and a collaborative culture is a powerful magnet in attracting workers to join the company.

Furthermore, it addresses a lack of good workers because a self-policing system is instilled. Employees will have not only a heightened awareness of their own choices affecting profitability, but also an awareness of co-worker contributions, inactions, and/or decision-making. The overall social influence provides a foundation for accountability, leading to higher work quality and productivity.

Simultaneously, the organizational citizenship, which measures the willingness to help co-workers, is also enhanced. Workers with a disposition toward cooperation, such as assisting to ease a colleague's workload or sharing knowledge to improve task efficiencies, will improve profitability. The Democracy at Work Institute [DAWI] (2014) reported worker cooperatives, regardless of industry, had an average profit margin almost 8.5% higher than the average private firm. The manufacturing (10.1% vs. 5.0%) and retail (7.1% vs. 2.4%) trades surveyed found even higher profitability increases over U.S. averages at the same time (pp. 3–4).

Employee ownership also fosters economic resiliency for the business, as proven during the world-wide COVID-19 crisis. A study by Summers and Bratanova (2023) regarding employee-owned businesses' responses during the pandemic found these businesses placed a greater importance on non-economic over economic goals. This prioritization meant that jobs were more likely to be protected from layoffs than they were with other companies. Interestingly, a greater length and level of employee ownership proved more valuable to the business resiliency of the company than available financial resources.

The Communities

The goal of employee-owned businesses to support employees by providing stable employment and offering increased wealth creation has a direct impact on the local community. Business proceeds going to employees through paychecks and patronage dividends often stay in the same area in which they are earned since workers live and spend locally. Likewise, these businesses are also connected to their community, with a vested interest in its well-being. Often these small businesses support local events, fundraisers, charities, and the like due to the interconnected relationship between employees, customers, and vendors.

Furthermore, the worker cooperative democracy often transfers to the employee's personal lifestyle, with increased community involvement and heightened civic engagement. In 2017, DAWI compared individuals with the general population (Schlachter & Prushinskaya, 2021, pp. 26–28). The study reported cooperative workers had a greater volunteer rate, attended more civic activities, and had a slightly higher voter turnout. The contribution of their free time creates a more vibrant community by nurturing mutual support and collaboration.

Cooperative Myths

Employees are often overlooked as potential buyers. A business owner may not think workers have the ability to purchase or operate the company, or may be unwilling to share their upcoming exit plan. However, with proper planning, both the selling business owner and the employees can realize a stronger financial security. The first hurdle in employee ownership is mitigating misconceptions and false impressions about the worker cooperative for the selling owner to be interested in learning more about the business model. As described below, common myths can often be dispelled with general information on the worker cooperative structure.

My employees cannot afford to buy the business. FALSE

The employees do not need to mortgage their homes or deplete their savings accounts to buy the business. Instead, the business will be financed by leveraging the company itself with its ability to generate free cash flow from operations. The purchase capital is derived from three different sources.

1. Mission-driven financial organizations offer funding options without the personal guarantees or collateral that a traditional bank loan will typically require. A Community Development Financial Institution (CDFI) provides an opportunity to those who may otherwise lack access to financing. Likewise, nonprofit organizations exist to specifically fund worker cooperatives to positively impact the economic livelihood of workers and their communities. It is important to note that the business may need to meet certain criteria for the workers to be eligible for the nonconventional loans, such as historic profitability and stability, as well as fractional financing from the seller.
2. The selling owner may also offer funding for a company by holding the business note in its entirety. Partial financing by the seller, as aforementioned, may be required for the worker-owners to receive CDFI or nonprofit funding, as it indicates the belief in the business's ongoing profitability. Moreover, the exiting owner has a vested interest in its continued success and will likely provide consultation if requested.
3. The worker-owners also provide a monetary contribution toward the business acquisition, as they each purchase one share of the company. The share price will vary depending on the cooperative structure but will be sufficient to be meaningful, yet not so expensive as to be cost prohibitive. In some instances, the amount is deducted from the employee paycheck over an extended timeframe to ensure share attainability.

My employees won't be able to agree on how to run the business. FALSE

The management structure of the worker cooperative will, in most situations, resemble the hierarchy established by the selling owner. Although it is a democratic organization with a one member, one vote management system, the vote is not used in daily decision-making. Instead, it provides the ability to elect the board of directors, which governs the company. Each worker will still perform the duties assigned. For example, a shipping clerk cannot give themselves a pay raise. Moreover, employees with unsatisfactory performances can still be terminated.

My employees are not cut out to be business owners. FALSE

Workers who were previously employed by the selling owner most likely know how to do their jobs. If job roles change or expand, skills can be further developed when the workers are given an opportunity and time to learn. Employees can be motivated to take on more responsibility, knowing how it will directly impact their ownership and subsequent income. That said, it will be essential for employees to embrace the sense-of-ownership mentality. This mindset empowers each worker to take responsibility, which leads to the desired business outcomes.

My employees won't be able to make any money. FALSE

Statistics show across the board that employee-owners earn more money, receive better benefits, and experience higher job satisfaction (Schlachter & Prushinskaya, 2021, pp. 14–21). If the business is profitable with the selling owner, it should also make money when employee-owned. Likewise, if the business is insolvent, employees should not purchase it. External financing will typically require solid financials, positive cash pro forma, and similar evidence to verify the business's long-term sustainability before funding is provided.

My employees don't want to own the business. FALSE

An assumption should not be made until the workers have actually been approached with the proposition. An opportunity for employees to increase wealth and secure their future might be just the prospect they have been waiting for all their lives! Nonetheless, it can take time for the employees to understand the process to make an informed decision to proceed.

Selling to workers is complicated and expensive. FALSE

Selling a business will require professional services regardless of the buyer. Identifying employees as the buyer may actually be easier than selling the company independently, paying commission fees to a business brokerage, or liquidating for pennies on the dollar. Employee ownership is highly collegial, with low-cost (or potentially no-cost) guidance available in both the public and private sectors, including Employee Ownership Expansion Network (EOX) State Centers, United States Department of Agriculture (USDA), employee ownership mission-driven organizations, and other organizations.

Worker Cooperative Structure

Organization

A worker cooperative is an effective business model that retains a typical management structure where all personnel have defined roles. Employees with unsatisfactory performance can still be terminated and pay raises are implemented by supervisors. The notable difference in the organization is that each worker-owner has one vote to elect the board of directors, which governs the company in a democratic manner. The checks and balances system established allows for balanced power, as seen in the basic governance system illustrated in Figure 9.1. Adaptations to this model may be recommended by the cooperative developer depending on the company size and structure. The governance system will have organizational bylaws defining procedural matters which still allows flexibility for unique situations and its appropriate solution.

Worker Cooperative Sectors

Worker Members

While the member must work in the company to be a worker-owner, the person does not necessarily have to be a worker-owner. The worker becomes a member by purchasing a share of the company, although there may be certain

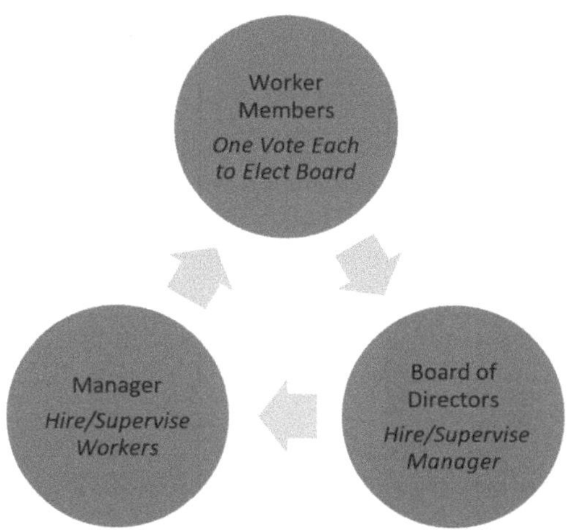

FIGURE 9.1 Basic Worker Cooperative Framework.

Source: Illustrated by author.

requirements mandated in the bylaws before the purchase can transpire. Typically, the only other ballot involves major decisions that affect the organizational existence or a primary characteristic of the worker cooperative. However, the organizational bylaws can include the right for worker-members to participate in other specific decisions. The governing policies will also stipulate the share repurchase procedure, as it will be bought back at the original purchase price should the worker-owner leave the company.

Board of Directors

The board is an elected position that should be comprised of worker-members but can include other people who have an affiliation with the organization such as the selling owner, lender, accountant, or other specialists. The board size is determined by the bylaws but should be kept small enough to be manageable. In larger cooperatives, subcommittees may also be necessary for efficiency to conduct business. The role of the board is to make decisions on policymaking matters that affect the company direction, business finances, or a majority of members.

Manager

A manager, or in some cases a management team, is appointed by the board and may also be a worker-owner. As expected, the responsibilities include managing daily operations and overseeing the employees assigned to complete these tasks. The position includes the authority to hire personnel when required as well as to terminate employees even if they are worker-owners.

Worker Cooperative Challenges

Employer–Employee Mindset

The first hurdle in the worker cooperative model is breaking down misconceptions between the selling owner and the workers. The aforementioned common myths can only be alleviated when the topic of employee ownership is being openly discussed. In other words, the issue cannot be mitigated if the subject is not even in the conversation. A lack of knowledge about worker cooperatives exists simply because it is not a traditional business model for rural localities. Selling owners, obviously, cannot consider this option if they are unaware of its existence.

A second obstacle arises when introducing a new business model since people tend to inherently fear the unfamiliar. A selling owner's thoughts doubting the success of an employee ownership transition may prevail. Without proper professional support to calm anxieties, the path to this conversion may seem too overwhelming to confront. The apprehension may be greatest for those who are first in the area to adopt the model without a known exemplar as proof of its success.

However, internal barriers do not exist only for the selling owner. Even if they would like to move forward with employee ownership, the workers themselves must also be interested in owning the company. The proposition to become a worker cooperative may require employees to absorb the overall concept, along with discussions to answer questions regarding its implementation, structure, governance, and other factors. Simply put, there must be a willing seller and a willing buyer for the model to proceed. The mindset must also shift that the employee is not simply a worker but a worker-owner. Financial education may be needed to understand market, revenue, expenses, etc. to build confidence as well as be able to recognize how small decisions can have a large impact on the company. It will be a clear pivot point towards the organizational success when this awareness emerges.

Ecosystem

Service Professionals

Just as the worker cooperative model is not well known in the business community, it is also atypical in the professional fields such as legal and accounting—especially in rural areas. Considering the practically non-existent demand for this niche specialty in these areas, there is little or no incentive to gain the knowledge and training to support this business model. Without such expertise, these trusted advisors are unlikely to suggest the worker cooperative model as a viable option to consider for a business succession plan.

Furthermore, lack of cooperative education can be even more detrimental as clients interested in employee ownership can be dissuaded from pursuing the business model with a recommendation for the more familiar, traditional model. It will be essential for the first adopters to be vigilant in locating professionals who are experienced with the worker cooperative model to receive objective advice.

Financing

Although each worker-owner has one share, the combined monetary value will not typically raise enough capital to purchase the business. (Even in this extremely unlikely situation, the share repurchase liability would be a major factor for consideration when developing the cooperative bylaws.) Simultaneously, the multi-owner structure becomes an obstruction to receive financing from a traditional lending institution because no single worker is obligated to provide personal assets or guarantees to secure the loan. Lack of collateral will, obviously, prohibit financing from being extended but so will perceived risk of the unfamiliar democratic management format.

Alternatively, the selling owner can hold either a partial or full note on the business purchase. Additional financing can also be pursued with organizations who recognize and value the unique characteristics of the worker cooperative. CDFIs, cooperative banks, nonprofits, and similar will be more open-minded to extend financing. In any case, a solid business plan and/or historical profitability will be required to demonstrate financial feasibility and credit worthiness to receive funding.

Other Cooperative Opportunities

Communities consistently face persistent challenges in workforce, housing, and childcare. Although employee ownership mitigates staffing deficits as previously discussed, traditional company labor shortages can also be eased by focusing on a resolution for the lack of housing and childcare. Workers would become more readily available in a community and/or company by resolving primary concerns of housing and childcare. One panacea for these pain points may be found by overlaying a cooperative model on these issues.

Real estate advertisements for mobile home park investments commonly note the capacity for the new landlords to raise the rent or other expenses. *Forbes* recently published a 2023 survey by Payroll.org showing that 78% of Americans live paycheck to paycheck (Batdorf, 2024). An unexpected rent increase is enough to cause relocation and a subsequent job change. The cooperative model would allow the residents to own their own neighborhood collectively instead of renting from an outside investor. A prevailing rebuttal heard regarding its success is that mobile park residents can neither afford, and nor do they have the capital to finance such a purchase.

However, Resident-Owned Communities (ROC) USA and its national network assists these resident-owned communities in purchasing their neighborhoods, offers ongoing training/support, and provides funding through its affiliate ROC USA Capital. Moreover, the profits previously generated for the investor can instead remain with the residents through lower housing payments, included utilities, updated public areas, or new amenities. Thousands of residents across the U.S. have made this transition, which encourages long-term residency (ROC USA, n.d.-a, n.d.-b, n.d.-c).

Lack of affordable and/or available childcare can also lock parents out of the workforce. A cooperative childcare can allow licensed daycares, parents, and local companies to partner in a way that benefits everyone. One variation of this model is explained in Table 9.1, noting that parameters such as paid/unpaid and number of hours provided would have to be established for all groups.

TABLE 9.1 Example of a Cooperative Childcare Arrangement

Group	*Receives*	*Provides*
Employer(s)	Dedicated workers who need daycare	Time off for parents to work at daycare
Licensed Daycare	Worker assistance and customers	Guaranteed spots for employer(s)' kids
Parents	Daycare/opportunity for involvement	Assist daycare on rotating basis

Source: Compiled by author.

These are the types of cooperative opportunities where a champion is needed in the community to bring residents and business owners together to discuss the possibilities. The positive impact made by just one person organizing a group to ask "What if?" can be everlasting.

Closing Reflections

Business owners have many traditional options for their business transition, including family members, key employees, business partners, third-party, or similar buyers. The worker cooperative model, although less known, should also be noted as a viable route to sell the company—especially when conventional methods are neither actionable nor achieve the value goals desired. As the silver tsunami deeply affects rural regions, the worker cooperative model is another strategy to keep the company open for the benefit of the selling owner, employees, and the community.

That said, worker cooperative succession may be one of the more difficult paths to follow if it is a new concept for the area. Guidance from cooperative developers or employee ownership centers will be essential to receive factual education, resources, and objective advice on a prospective worker cooperative conversion. Employees just may be the best option to transition company ownership, especially in rural communities. What follows is a case study of this process.

Case Study

Bean There, Done That: Nadav Mer's Brewing Success

Nadav Mer owned a successful IT company in Gainesville, Florida but desired more social interactions than the technology field could provide. Being a driven entrepreneurial businessman, he started another company to fulfill that interest. The Tree City Coffee Roasters was launched in 2011 with a homemade coffee roaster in his backyard and self-taught industry knowledge. The operation quickly upgraded to commercial equipment to keep up with demand at the farmer market sales. However, more changes were ahead as his spouse accepted a faculty position out of state. Tree City Coffee Roasters followed the traditional business transition of being sold to a third party.

It did not take long for the next venture, Morning Bell Coffee Roasters, to open for business in Arizona. Although the market in the new residence was already saturated with coffee roasters, the company received immediate attention as it offered a unique blend locally available. Green coffee beans were sourced directly from an organic farm in Nicaragua. Leveraging the value of an exclusive product, the owner also opened a tasting room to first attract coffee connoisseurs and then extend their experience with bean sales for home brewing. The marketing strategy was an overwhelming success, finding coverage in the *Phoenix New Times* within two weeks of opening.

The upward trajectory of Morning Bell Coffee Roasters was simultaneously paralleled by a family member's professional career, and another move was on the horizon. However, circumstances were different this time, as there was no opportunity for new owners to take over the existing rental space. Since the business could not essentially be sold, the owner took it with him. In 2015, the company was reopened in Ames, Iowa, with roasted coffee being shipped to the established customer base in Arizona. However, considering the likelihood of a potential home relocation in the distant future, a building was acquired to ensure the prospect that the business could be sold if necessary.

Mer also revised his business model to find a work–life balance that allowed more flexibility. Baristas were hired with a concept just as unique as his coffee flavor. He offered a company culture of trust where each worker was literally handed the keys to the store, entrusted to serve customers on their own, and valued for their opinions on business operations. The empowerment afforded to these college-age students was the beginning of a new narrative for the company, employees, and, eventually, the State of Iowa. The high-quality reputation of the coffee grew locally and then nationwide. The *Daily Coffee News*, the premier roasting magazine distributed nationally, featured an article on the company in 2016. Four years later, the *24/7 Wall St.* publication recognized Morning Bell Coffee Roasters as the "Best Independent Coffee Shop in Iowa."

The vision of the workers expanded with the company's recognition. One employee soon became intrigued with the concept of unionizing after learning about other coffee shops considering this formation. Although the owner was not against the idea, he had read about another business model that focused on the value introduced with human systems and the benefits to the company. Knowing he would eventually sell the company, he instead proposed forming a worker cooperative. In this structure, each employee would own a share of the company, which would not just determine employment conditions, but also share the profits.

The new concept was first met with a range of feelings by the staff. Enthusiasm was certainly in the air but the employees were mostly young, and several were college students who held a different vision for their future. Time was needed to absorb this proposition and understand how to move forward with the plan. Five of the eight employees ultimately came together to form a research committee to explore the feasibility of the concept. Fortunately, the owner had a strong belief in, and determination for, the success of a worker cooperative transition as obstacles were immediately revealed.

Although ag cooperatives and telephone cooperatives are quite common in Iowa, worker cooperatives were non-existent in the state. The concept seemed so foreign that the local accounting and legal professionals, who were needed to conduct the business transition, advised against it. Moreover, the current Morning Bell Coffee Roasters accountant would discontinue the company as a client if the business proceeded with these plans. Since the owner was a serial entrepreneur, it was instinctive to research and analyze all options before pursuing the employee-owner path. He knew the worker cooperative model was viable and so he continued the journey by locating service providers out of state who were willing and knowledgeable about the issues.

In the meantime, the owner's spouse had become a prominent scholar in the academic research field, receiving several distinguished honors and now being recruited to join other universities. So, the family would soon be moving to Texas. The worker cooperative evaluation stage had effectively ended with the relocation announcement. It was now time for the employees to commit to become a worker cooperative or have the business be sold to a third party. It was a clear and absolute decision as the five workers chose to move forward with the conversion.

Guidance and consultation on technical elements, governance, and similar activities was received from a worker cooperative developer. Details that are not necessary in a traditional business transition required careful consideration in this situation. Each worker could purchase one share at a set price of $1,000 that could be paid over one year through payroll deduction. The money is held in reserve and returned to the worker, without appreciation, whenever the employment ends. Patronage distribution is based on a seniority multiplier but veteran workers cannot receive a dollar amount higher than 50% of other worker-owner payments. Other specifics, such as the Board of Director members, vesting period, and organizational processes, had to be determined. Although the seller was a key component in developing the bylaws, the worker cooperative group would have the ability to modify the directives if the decision were brought to ballot and received a favorable vote.

A final consideration to complete the worker cooperative conversion was securing the necessary financing for the purchase. A significant hurdle that could impede any traditional acquisition is that this loan would be requested by young people, with college students among them, to operate a non-conventional business structure. However, the seller made this an easy process as he chose to self-finance the purchase. Furthermore, he went with "friendly financing," where the loan payment was not larger than the amount currently being drawn for his salary. This move ensures the loan will not negatively impact projected cash flow, leading to an even higher probability of success. Moreover, it provides flexibility in the event of potential revenue issues or other financial setbacks. To mitigate this risk, the seller sits on the worker cooperative board of directors until the loan has been satisfied.

On January 1, 2022, history was made as Morning Bell Coffee Roasters became the first worker cooperative in the State of Iowa (see Figure 9.2).

The journey took about one year to complete but was well worth the venture. The employees now have complete control of their own destiny with secure jobs in a democratic structure to govern the business. The model has proven successful as students transition out of the area to start careers without detriment to the business. The company is remarkably strong, with an estimated one-year wait for new employees to be hired—a significant achievement in today's economy where the workforce is in scarce supply. The seller laid the foundation for the business to flourish in the future by developing a workplace culture that empowered the workers even before they became owners.

FIGURE 9.2 Morning Bell Coffee Roasters: Selling Owners, Worker Cooperative Members, and Families Celebrate the Conversion. Photo credits: Morning Bell Coffee Roasters.

When Mer (personal communication, June 14, 2024) shared his thoughts about the conversion, he stated,

> Selling our business to our employees was an act of hope, and the worker-owners have risen to the challenge and have done an astoundingly good job running the business. Worker's cooperatives are the most optimistic structure I've found yet to allow businesses to support and enrich the lives of employees.

Today, the business is open daily, offering fresh roasted coffee beans with worldwide origination for both consumer and wholesale purchasing. The café allows an option to sip a cup in a relaxing atmosphere with a choice of four different brewing methods. Additionally, other beverages such as specialty drinks, teas, and cold brews are available alongside sweet treats prepared by local bakers to satisfy any craving. The business has already expanded the original bistro model adopted from the founder by offering a live music venue and a private rental space to host events. The company is an anchor on Main Street, bringing residents together to support not just the employees but the entire community (see Figure 9.3).

FIGURE 9.3 Café Interior of the Morning Bell Coffee Roasters Business. Photo credits: Morning Bell Coffee Roasters.

Takeaways for the Selling Business Owner

Find Support

Being a trailblazer for the first worker cooperative in Iowa, the owner discovered many obstacles to overcome for the successful conversion. Because the matured cooperative is just dawning within Iowa, it is essential for those wanting to pursue a worker cooperative to seek out and engage with those familiar with the structure. The employee-owner community is exceedingly collegial, providing insight as well as encouragement. Employee Ownership State Centers (eoxnetwork.org) can be contacted to provide guidance and locate professional assistance in many states. Likewise, the selling owner in this case study was inspired to launch another company, *Nadav Mer Consulting*, to advise business owners considering a worker cooperative conversion.

Transactional Differences

A stark difference exists between traditional and worker cooperative succession negotiations. The conventional third-party sale may conjure combative emotions or suspicion as opposing sides strive to subvert each other to attain the best financial outcome for themselves. Conversely, the worker cooperative transition is a unique situation where the owner sits on both sides of the transactional table, aiming for the overwhelming success of everyone involved. An alternate outlook prevails where the goal is to essentially place the equity interest of the company into trust of the community for the good of its residents as it simultaneously benefits the employees.

Value Goals

The previous owner in this case reached several value goals by selling the business to the workers, but three key points emerged as most significant. As his employees were an extension of family, he cared deeply for their well-being and was able to provide financial stability for their future. Morning Bell Coffee Roasters was his creation, ergo the business remains as his legacy even though he no longer owns it. The workers provided a viable buyer that evoked a sense of comfort and ease for transitioning the company.

References

Batdorf, E. (2024, April 2). *Living paycheck to paycheck statistics 2024*. Forbes Advisor. www.forbes.com/advisor/banking/living-paycheck-to-paycheck-statistics-2024/#:~:text=or%20lost%20income.-,How%20Many%20Americans%20Are%20Living%20Paycheck%20to%20Paycheck%3F,paying%20for%20their%20monthly%20expenses

Democracy at Work Institute. (2014). *US worker cooperatives: A state of the sector*. Research Publication Series. https://institute.coop/sites/default/files/resources/State_of_the_sector_0.pdf

Democracy at Work Institute. (2015). *Worker cooperative definition*. United States Federation of Worker Cooperatives. https://www.usworker.coop/wp-content/uploads/2018/02/Worker-Cooperative-Definition-2015.pdf

Exit Planning Institute. (2023a). *2023 national state of owner readiness*. https://exit-planning-institute.org/2023-national-state-of-owner-readiness

Exit Planning Institute. (2023b). *2023 state of owner readiness report*. https://exit-planning-institute.org/state-of-owner-readiness

International Cooperative Alliance. (n.d.). *Cooperative identity, values & principles*. https://ica.coop/en/cooperatives/cooperative-identity

Resident Owned Communities USA. (n.d.-a). *The communities*. https://rocusa.org/communities/

Resident Owned Communities USA. (n.d.-b). *Support*. https://rocusa.org/about-roc-usa/network-affiliates/

Resident Owned Communities USA. (n.d.-c). *Training and learning*. https://rocusa.org/training-learning/

Schlachter, L. H. & Prushinskaya, O. (2021). *How economic democracy impacts workers, firms, and communities: The census of individual workers in worker cooperatives*. Democracy at Work Institute, United States Federation of Worker Cooperatives. https://democracy.institute.coop/how-economic-democracy.impacts-workers-firms-and-communities

Summers, J., & Bratanova, B. (2023). Employee-owned businesses' responses during the pandemic: Economic, non-economic goal and democratic resilience and their link to ownership, control and benefit. *Journal of Entrepreneurial and Organizational Diversity*, *12*(2), 73–98. 10.5947/jeod.2023.011

United States Census Bureau. (2023a, March 8). *Business owners' ages: Over half of U.S. business owners were Age 55 and over*. www.census.gov/library/visualizations/2020/comm/business-owners-ages.html

United States Census Bureau. (2023b, May 25). *Census Bureau releases new 2020 census data on age, sex, race, Hispanic origin, households and housing* [Press release No. CB23-CN09]. www.census.gov/newsroom/press-releases/2023/2020-census-demographic-profile-and-dhc.html

Wilmoth, D. (2023, August). *Small business facts: Small businesses in rural areas*. U.S. Small Business Administration, Office of Advocacy. https://advocacy.sba.gov/wp-content/uploads/2023/08/Fact-Sheet-Small-Business-in-Rural-Areas-508c.pdf

10

BUYING PRIVATE BUSINESSES IN A SINGLE VERTICAL

A New Approach to Rural Investment

Dawn McGee, Kiah Hochstetler, and Michael Braun

After more than a decade of investing in startups in Montana, Goodworks Ventures launched a new enterprise in 2018—Goodworks Evergreen (GWE)—to purchase companies, the explicit purpose of which was to cultivate a prosperous and sustainable local economy through local ownership of businesses and self-reliance of communities (Shuman, 2015). The genesis of this work was an article in a local newspaper about a business owner who had recently died, resulting in 10 manufacturing jobs in a small community disappearing virtually overnight. Goodworks was a family office with an investment arm specifically designed to create good-paying jobs. The newspaper article brought to light a problem that many communities face—business owners who are older, retiring, or perhaps dying with no viable succession plan in place.

Additional research showed that Montana's baby boomer generation led the state in the creation of small businesses, and many were at a transitional point. A business owner who is 65+ years old and still working needs to identify the next generation of ownership, since many lack family members willing to take over their operations. An increasing number of these businesses struggle to transition as the purchase price is too large for local individuals and too small for institutional buyers.

The impact on local jobs across rural areas can be substantial, especially when a community loses its only local grocery or hardware store. In some cases, the owner chooses to close the business. In others, the owner becomes disabled or dies, and the family is left to manage the transition.

The family office of Goodworks worked with the governor of Montana's economic development office and prepared a landscape map that showed a more than billion-dollar opportunity to transition these kinds of businesses.

DOI: 10.4324/9781003497462-10

At that time, in Montana, jobs that paid $15 an hour plus benefits were hard to find. Fixed-income asset classes were returning less than 1%. Businesses that were making money without needing a turnaround were available for purchase.

So, GWE was created to provide transition opportunities to retiring owners by acquiring their local Montana businesses, with the goal to keep quality jobs within the community. The mission of GWE is to keep the business alive and well, while maintaining its community mindset during and after the transition. This approach differs markedly from the usual business exit strategy of finding a strategic buyer, either a competitor or a financial firm, planning to slash costs and quickly flip the company. Both options often involve lost jobs and stripped assets.

Specifically, by providing owner-operators with viable exit opportunities, GWE could help to maintain and even grow quality jobs in rural communities while concurrently providing investors with attractive returns, secured primarily via asset-backed business operations. What would make the investments especially attractive was a fixed-income impact strategy through a broad-based portfolio of companies that had already been making money in the low interest rate environment of the past 20 years (McGee et al., 2023).

Executing the strategy was relatively straightforward and was based on the following five priorities:

1 Acquire companies with established revenue streams and healthy profits that meet defined underwriting criteria.
2 Identify and hire general managers to replace the current owners and improve and enhance the operations of the business.
3 Make new investments in these businesses, such as capital improvements and staff.
4 Prove the investment thesis so that additional capital could flow into business preservation.
5 Determine an appropriate strategy for broad-based community ownership.

By way of background for this chapter, and as is described in more detail in McGee et al. (2023), an overview of how the current portfolio of businesses was obtained is provided next.

Background

Before purchasing the first business, the investment criteria had to be determined and included the following:

- The business had to be profitable at the time of acquisition and historically profitable aside from minor variances in economic downturns.

- The business had to employ five or more people (if the business is too small, it is too reliant on a few employees).
- The business was located within a reasonable distance from the Goodworks home office.
- The business owner had systemically underinvested in business assets, which allowed for some easy upside by implementing best business practices.
- The business had the possibility of growth with capital investment and smart business practices.
- Goodworks was able to acquire 100% of the business.

The first three business acquisitions were made from an initial $3.25 million investment placed in GWE by the founder. Businesses 4 and 5 were acquired with funds from cash flow generated in ongoing business activities. Businesses 6 and 7 were acquired with funds from cash flow, as well as outside capital raised through a preferred equity offering discussed later in this chapter.

The current discussion updates GWE's experiences in the early years, describes the implementation of the strategy to retain and grow local businesses in Montana, and evaluates some lessons learned to date. In a broad sense this is a middle chapter in a continuing story.

Of special note is the fact that the strategy was conceived and initially executed prior to COVID-19, which changed many assumptions about wages and jobs in rural economies. Prior to COVID-19, rural jobs paid less than $12 an hour in many cases, and those jobs were valued and hard to obtain. In the post-COVID-19 economy, fast food jobs regularly pay $20 an hour and it is difficult to find employees (Zip Recruiter, 2024). As shown in subsequent discussions, these experiences changed many ideas regarding our investment thesis and thoughts for the future.

Portfolio Investments

GWE made its initial investment in June 2018, in the form of a lumber yard and hardware home center retail store in a rural community with approximately 4,800 residents ("Business 1"). At the time of purchase, the business had eight employees with $1.78 million in gross sales generating $160,000 in profits. Terms of the acquisition included GWE retaining members of the owner's family to assist in the business transition, many of whom continue to work with GWE.

Prior to acquiring the first business, GWE did not have a specific sector focus or thesis about what *kind* of businesses it would acquire. It explored a variety of operations, from manufacturing to service industries. Once it bought the first business—a building supply center—it was a natural progression for the next business to also be in the wood products sector.

Business 1 has been the core business enterprise that has shaped and guided acquisitions of subsequent businesses. After an initial misstep of hiring someone as a general manager with retail sales, but not *industry-specific* experience, GWE quickly regrouped and hired a general manager with more than 20 years' experience in the wood products industry. That expertise has been critical to later successes with the overall GWE strategy. When this manager came on board, the intent was to make sure that the values were aligned so that during profitable times he would also benefit financially from the upside. In addition to a base salary, the manager's compensation package includes 10% of net profits on an annualized basis.

GWE's second acquisition was a lumber remanufacturing company that was bought via a stock purchase of a C corporation on May 13, 2019 ("Business 2"). This business specializes in value-added wood products and, at the time of purchase, employed 12 people, had $3.4 million in gross sales, and generated $157,000 in profits. Because this enterprise was significantly different in operations (although adjacent to a retail lumber yard and hardware store), and was its own C corporation, a general manager was hired for this enterprise with the same pay and bonus structure as Business 1. Although they are managed as separate businesses within the GWE structure, there have been many synergies in the ability of the two businesses to help each other prosper.

GWE's third acquisition, an asset purchase on January 6, 2020, was a lumber yard, paint, and small hardware store located in a former train station ("Business 3"). This business was the only lumber yard serving the immediate community of 830 residents and the surrounding area. At the time of acquisition, Business 3 had six employees and $2.5 million in gross sales, generating $100,000 in profits. Business 3 was rolled into the operating entity of Business 1 for financing and purchasing purposes but continued to use its historical name as the name of the business. It represents the first of many businesses that were merged with Business 1, bringing substantial economies of scale in buying power and vendor rebates. In addition, consolidating businesses into a single operating entity allows more efficient banking operations when using a line of credit or other credit facilities.

On June 10, 2020, GWE acquired another building center, an asset purchase, that had been on the market in a rural community (population 703) for more than four-and-a-half years ("Business 4"). While the marketplace for buying and selling businesses is imperfect—consisting of isolated business brokers, real estate agents, and the occasional Craigslist advertisement—trying to sell a business in a small rural community is even more difficult. These businesses are too small to attract the attention of private equity, but typically the purchase price is so large that an interested purchaser will likely not have the equity to make the investment work.

As the only lumber yard directly serving the community and the surrounding area, Business 4, like Business 3, was rolled into the Business 1 operating entity. Through economies of scale and increased buying power, the addition of this center to the investment portfolio allowed the combined buying power of all the businesses to compete more effectively with out-of-town big box stores. At the time of acquisition, the business had three employees and $1.43 million in gross sales generating $78,000 in profits.

On January 4, 2021, GWE bought a hardware store ("Business 5") as an asset purchase, in the same community (population 830) as Business 3. The store had been on the market for more than a year, with hardware as its sole line of business. Like Business 4, there were no likely buyers for this small enterprise in a small town. Moreover, while GWE was unaware of this at the time, the owner's reputation in the community limited the likelihood of an in-town buyer. This strategic purchase enabled GWE to replicate the hardware store's current lines of business such as an established equipment rental department and create additional vendor relationships. At the time of acquisition, Business 5 had six employees with $1 million in gross sales, generating $73,000 in profits.

Business 6 was purchased by GWE in September 2021. A local business known for installing cabinets and countertops, this acquisition led to the preservation of five jobs while subsequently adding three positions. Business 6 represented GWE's first primarily service-based business (cabinet design and installation), in contrast to the previous businesses that focused on selling products.

Due diligence regarding this business failed to identify several critical problems. First, there were several large multi-family contracts that would be in place post-acquisition at a fixed price. After closing, COVID-19 brought an extreme price escalation from suppliers that could not be passed on to contractor customers.

Second, the employee (who remained from the original business) to whom GWE offered the position of general manager started a competing business using company customers, contacts, and equipment. We were able to manage through price escalations, losing only a small amount of money. With respect to the competing former employee, it cost us business in the short term, but much has returned by delivering well-managed projects on time and at a favorable price.

Finally, Business 7, with expertise and craftsmanship in customer doors, architectural moulding, and picture frames, was purchased in December 2021 for $1.2 million with seven employees and $602,000 in sales, generating $76,000 in profits. The picture frame aspect of the business was sold in the second year to allow more focus on the core business of custom moulding and doors. Until a large fire forced the business closure, it generated roughly $100,000 in annual profits.

GWE Strategy and Approach

GWE used two main strategies for each asset purchase: (a) an LLC to purchase the land and for which the owner received a real estate-backed promissory note for part of the purchase price; and (b) a holding company structure for the operating entities themselves (see Figure 10.1).

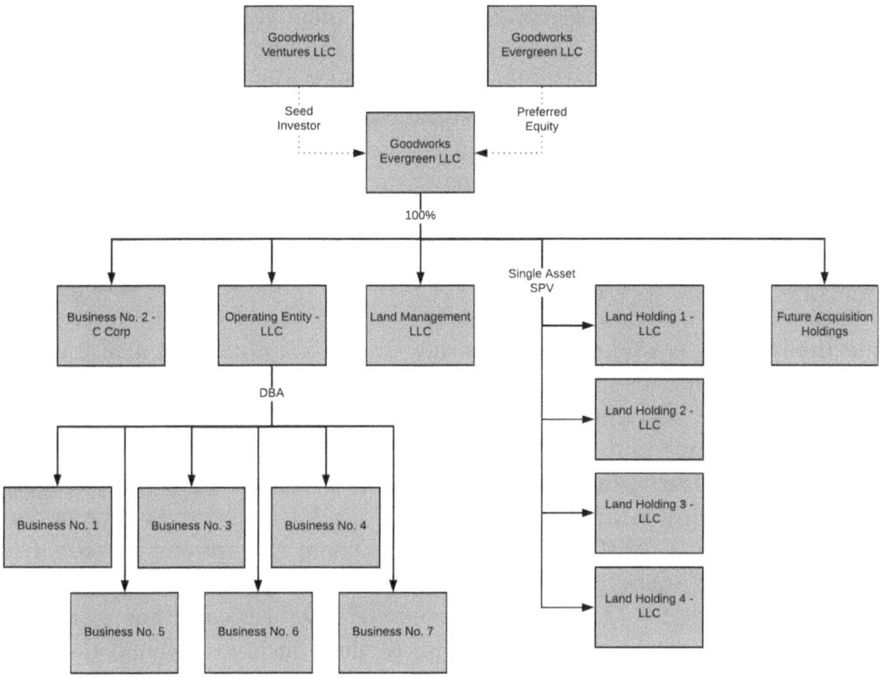

FIGURE 10.1 Investment Company Entity Structuring.

Source: Created by authors.

GWE financed the original purchase of assets with $2.9 million from the Goodworks Ventures Portfolio, plus cash flow generated by the combined entity. To complete the latter purchase of businesses, GWE raised external capital in the form of preferred equity, which from the point of view of investors works like a 10-year treasury note with quarterly interest payments and a balloon payment in 10 years.

The investment thesis by business, the equity raised, and current prognosis are described next.

Business Strategies

1 Acquire companies that meet defined underwriting criteria with established revenue streams and healthy profits

While GWE was extraordinarily lucky with its first four investments in terms of underwriting and due diligence, the purchase of the remaining three businesses required digging deeper and finding solutions for some unanticipated and difficult situations while striving to deliver on commitments to employees, customers, and investors. The initial inquiry during due diligence on Business

5 had not surfaced lingering community resentment toward the prior owner, the difficulty of operating a business in a competitive environment on a one-way street, the expense of then having to rebuild the sales pipeline in the fall, or the challenges of managing a small business that was neither making enough money nor losing enough to suggest a focus on other management tasks.

Eventually, lagging sales forced a harder review of operations and the difficult decision to close the business before entering the slow winter season. On August 30, 2024, the store was closed with the remaining usable assets transferred to other GWE businesses or sold at reduced prices. The true impact of this misstep on the balance sheet is unknown until the inventory is netted out and the building is sold or leased. In any event, this represents a case where better due diligence may have dissuaded the initial acquisition.

Due diligence also did not disclose the impact of COVID-19 on Business 6—the cabinets and countertop business. One of the contracts inherited with the purchase of the business was a 200-apartment complex, involving delivery of kitchens, bathroom vanities, and countertops during a specific time period at a fixed price. COVID-19-related supply chain disruptions for cabinets quickly doubled prices, but the contracts with the builder remained fixed at pre-COVID-19 prices. Much of the summer of 2023 was spent managing and restructuring the business at the expense of then having to rebuild the sales pipeline in the fall.

While in November 2023 a decision could have been made to close Business 6 as well, efforts were rededicated to build out a new showroom, hire a sales manager, and engage in managing overhead by deploying employees to other projects to fully utilize them. Fortunately, this strategy provided the necessary income to avoid layoffs. It has been a nine-month process of building back the sales pipeline and adding sub-businesses that can eventually contribute to the future success of the business.

2 *Identify and hire general managers to replace the current owners and to improve and enhance the operations of such investments*

Sourcing, acquiring, and retaining employee talent in the post-COVID-19 era remains challenging across industries, including GWE operations. Prior to the acquisitions, many employees made minimum wage without benefits. Post-acquisition, they were offered $15 an hour, a health insurance plan, and a 401(k).

Unlike many other states, Montana experienced a significant influx of remote employees during the pandemic, resulting in record home prices. These combined factors continue to make hiring employees difficult at best and, in smaller rural areas where our businesses are located, nearly impossible. Those conditions have rendered part of the GWE investment thesis—preserving good-paying rural jobs—largely obsolete.

Through these trials and tribulations, GWE nevertheless has secured and fostered managers at the operating entity level in all its businesses and supports them through investments that provide critical back-office support from GWE. Within GWE, a senior-level executive whose values did not fit with those of the organization left after a significant investment of time and effort to reconcile the differences. Lessons learned include not trying to make a cultural mismatch work, and recognizing that both parties can benefit from ending such a relationship early in the process.

3 *Make new investments in the companies*

While several additional investments are discussed in McGee et al. (2023), GWE continues to make contributions and necessary upgrades. Business 1 has cumulatively received more than $550,000 of capital investments toward trucks, software, and facilities improvements. To date, Business 1, acting as a holding company, has a 16% compound annual growth rate (CAGR) on its balance sheet equity value, notwithstanding new equity invested for acquisitions.

For Business 2, GWE prioritized substantially overhauling the manufacturing processes and systems while investing in deferred maintenance. As of September 1, 2024, GWE has invested more than $500,000 in capital investments in the business, ranging from manufacturing equipment to building upgrades.

GWE also had an opportunity to partner with a local nonprofit, whose wood products manufacturing segment was about to be discontinued. We leased their manufacturing space and contracted for their employees to determine whether adding this product line to our overall manufacturing mix made sense. GWE will continue operations with this business through fall of 2024 and then bring that manufacturing segment in-house.

GWE is also evaluating the relocation of Business 2 to allow for expansion of product lines and provide space to grow the business over time. Business 2 achieved a 14% CAGR with no further equity having been directly invested in the entity since its acquisition.

Business 3 continues to be a stalwart operation in the portfolio. To accommodate its growth potential, GWE anticipates building a facility with greater community visibility and a larger footprint to allow for growth. As such, it has been working with the City of Anaconda to acquire and develop a 10-acre parcel that will accommodate a new warehouse and lumber yard to serve the community. To date, capital investments include $168,000, with the new building expansion expected to cost approximately $5 million.

GWE remerchandised and brought in new vendors for Business 4 and made capital investments of $134,000. It will continue to invest in infrastructure, signage, and store enhancement.

As noted previously, Business 5 closed its retail operation in 2024, and transferred its inventory to other entities. Beyond opportunity costs, this closure does not represent a substantive risk to GWE since it had been purchased for slightly more than asset value. Business 3 will also absorb some of Business 5's previous product lines when it moves to its new retail operation in 2025.

Business 6 investments, totaling $282,000 in equipment and facilities and $1.65 million for a new facility, included a new showroom and the purchase of additional equipment, including a new CNC machine to make its operations more efficient. Under this entity, plans are to open a new line of business of AeroBarrier, used to seal buildings for energy efficiency. By diversifying the product offerings, GWE can keep its employees engaged during slow seasons for cabinet installs. Moreover, the opening of a larger showroom provides a better customer experience where clients can view multiple kitchen and bathroom styles.

While GWE had invested in specific upgrades to Business 7 since its purchase, the business experienced a catastrophic fire at the end of 2023. After investigation by both local authorities and the insurance company, its cause remains unknown. Because the fire destroyed the manufacturing equipment together with existing inventory, GWE spent the first quarter of 2024 considering the purchase of new or used equipment and rebuilding the facility. However, careful analysis indicated that these investments would require almost $500,000 of equipment and $1 million in a new facility, with an anticipated break-even point years down the road. In early 2024, a decision was made to shutter the business and to offer employees other opportunities within portfolio companies.

4 *Prove the investment thesis for additional capital flows into business preservation*

GWE has proven its investment thesis: purchasing existing local rural business enterprises not directly competing with Walmart or Amazon can offer viable business opportunities. While some missteps occurred along the way, the core of the business enterprises remains solid and robust. The combined GWE business currently employs 65 people, with an annual run rate of $22 million.

GWE invested the founder's capital of $2.9 million and had a successful increase of $2.55 million in preferred units, paying 5% per annum dividend in quarterly installments, with a redemption of the units in Year 10. It has made every coupon payment on time as of October 2024 and anticipates being able to build capital to repay principal during the coming years. Current investors have been pleased with their investment, with several electing to invest additional funds as the preferred yield has paid more than the benchmark 10-year treasuries for all but a few months. With the liquidation of Business 7 and receipt of the insurance proceeds, the founder's capital in the amount of $2.07 million has been repaid.

Because GWE has demonstrated that the thesis for investment in critical rural enterprises is both viable and attractive, it foresees significant opportunities for additional investment beyond just re-investing in its current businesses. Given Montana's ongoing challenges of finding and attracting employees and availability of affordable dwellings, the focus has shifted from acquiring new businesses to partnering with other community players to create attainable housing. One of the realizations gained in navigating through this equity strategy is that the GWE team has both the skill set and a passion for buying and optimizing businesses.

Yet of critical importance is that after businesses are acquired, they must be maintained, fostered, and nurtured. While GWE has the capacity for such work, this is not its forte and it is trying to determine the best possible stewardship going forward for what has been created. GWE maintains that the right type of investor embracing and pursuing rural private equity can do well while also doing good for communities.

5 Determine appropriate strategy for broad-based community ownership

While the initial strategy was broad-based community ownership of GWE's collection of businesses, the path forward is yet to be decided. Initially, only accredited investors could participate in GWE through a preferred equity offering. According to the U.S. Securities and Exchange Commission, an accredited investor is an individual earning income exceeding $200,000 (or $300,000 together with a spouse or spousal equivalent) or having a net worth over $1 million, excluding the value of the person's primary residence. Accredited investors are uncommon in Montana given the historically low pay structure in the state, as well as the lack of cashed-out startup entrepreneurs that often constitute accredited investor pools elsewhere.

While there is ample opportunity to continue to raise capital and acquire businesses, that will require a different management team and a determination of the type of capital strategy and subsequent exit strategy that the team seeks to pursue. Currently, the GWE focus is on continuing to make the businesses more profitable and successful through the build-out of new facilities and optimization of product and client mix. Also under consideration is a scenario of employee ownership, at least at the management level (management buy-out) if not for all employees (ESOP).

Where GWE is Now

The Goodworks Evergreen strategy began with high hopes and a commitment to keeping rural enterprises alive. This middle chapter of the business has proved challenging—managing through COVID-19, dealing with inflationary pressures, and trying to manage people and product for the best possible outcome. But business is cyclical and GWE must manage accordingly. Finding the right people to do the everyday work of managing and growing a business is hard. Continuing to build out retail sales in a softening environment is similarly difficult. Dealing with the unexpected catastrophe of fires and the decision to close a business that is just not working is humbling.

At the end of the day, business is a series of problems to be solved. Some of them are solvable and require the patience and strategy to continue to accelerate a business. Others require capital investment to relocate a business to a more favorable location or to make capital investments in equipment that will provide better net margins over the long term. Still others require a fierce examination of the business thesis and a commitment to taking action in the face of unwelcome findings.

Business 1 has suffered a slowdown in sales, which GWE is committed to rebuilding with continual improvements to the store, customer experience, and sales and marketing. Business 2 will move to a new location during the next couple of years and build out an additional product line. Business 3 and business 5 will be combined and moved to a new location in 2025–2026. Business 4 will require minor improvements in product mix and signage into next year. Business 6 will continue to expand its product offerings and services and continue targeted advertising to attract new customers. Business 7, as a result of the fire, has closed.

Lessons Learned in Implementing a Rural Private Equity Strategy

Every business experiences growing pains, and COVID-19 brought another level of challenges. Having learned useful lessons while acquiring and building this business, several insights might help others seeking to formulate and execute a rural acquisition strategy.

1 *Don't minimize due diligence.* Ask the unusual questions: Are employees and/or management interrelated? Are there contract terms or commitments that could affect the business in the future? And, critically important, are there stones left unturned simply because they seem too obvious to look under?

2 *Who will do the hard work of maintaining and growing a business going forward?* GWE has learned during the past several years that businesses have three cycles: creation, maintenance, and destruction. People also have strengths in each of these areas—there are people who are happy creating and building and those who excel at systems building and maintenance. While destruction can seem to be a difficult part of the cycle, making room for activities to come to an end or even for a business to close restarts the cycle of creation.

Not surprisingly, the GWE core team excels at the creation and building part while the managers thrive at maintaining. It has come to recognize and appreciate that to build out a larger portfolio of companies under the GWE umbrella requires more maintainers. What is now apparent is the delicate balance needed to find the right people to work at each point in the cycle and keep it going.

3 *What type of capital is required to grow the business and how will you source it?* Many states have economic development funds and excess capital available to acquire businesses that are community assets. Montana, unfortunately, does not. And, as noted earlier, the pool of accredited investors remains limited. While banks may provide some financing, there is usually a large equity component or personal guarantee required to access that type of funding.

Many of these businesses, however, are essential to maintaining the viability of rural communities and their amenities. A strong argument can be made for accessing philanthropic dollars via community foundations or other donors. For the most part, the cash required to maintain a business enterprise and create and maintain jobs is small, especially when the prior owner of the business is willing to help finance the transition.

4 *What is your future off-ramp*? Creating a portfolio of essential, lasting enterprises is one unique challenge, while maintaining those enterprises is another. But a third predicament arises when the businesses need to be transitioned again at some point in the future. Does a buyer exist? Is it an external investor? Or will existing employees step forward as viable, new owners? These are just the initial questions in a long list of issues that must be considered in an eventual exit of the business. Thinking through the end strategy early, however, even if there are no clear answers, is critical to help inform both the capital structure and the approach to rural private equity. Many of these issues are described in more detail in previous chapters.

References

McGee, D., Hochstetler, K. & Braun, M. (2023). Acquiring, building, and investing in private businesses: A new approach. In N. Walzer & C. D. Merrett (Eds.), *Rural areas in transition: Meeting challenges & making opportunities* (pp. 236–254). Routledge. 10.4324/9781003280620

Shuman, M. H. (2015). *The local economy solution*. Chelsea Green Publishing.

ZipRecruiter. (2024, October). *Fast food salary in Montana*. https://www.ziprecruiter.com/Salaries/Fast-Food-Salary--in-Montana

11

CAPITAL-DRIVEN BUSINESS SUCCESSION

Main Street Approach

Todd Barman and Errin Welty

Introduction

Public narratives often portray the outcomes of the sale of a business as a fortunate coincidence rather than the result of deliberate support and preparation, yet many successful transfers involve significant behind-the-scenes efforts that remain largely confidential. Often, both community leaders and business owners are unaware of the valuable role they played.

Organizations such as local Main Street Programs (www.mainstreet.org), particularly those with dedicated staff, can be instrumental in building individual and community capital. Even when other succession resources are lacking, that capital can contribute to the successful sale and ongoing viability of small businesses (Davidsson & Honig, 2003; Stam et al., 2014).

This chapter explores the role of community leaders and organizations trying to facilitate and support business succession as exemplified by local Main Street Programs. The result of that exploration is a more comprehensive capitals-driven framework for business succession process and support that has broad applicability for community leaders and organizations. The chapter closes with suggestions for future research and an introduction to the concept of, and need for, storefront succession.

Business Succession Need

In their 2017 review, Templin et al. highlighted a gap in the literature regarding the role of community leaders and organizations trying to facilitate and support business succession. Their research focused on the barriers to rural small business succession and how some rural business buyers overcame those

DOI: 10.4324/9781003497462-11

barriers. While the results of Templin et al.'s research may be known in academic circles, a recent survey in Minnesota showed that few business owners currently look to community leaders and organizations for help with succession efforts (Darger, 2024).

Even in communities facilitating and supporting business succession, the number of small businesses with a succession plan or owners who are otherwise prepared for succession is still low, placing these businesses at greater risk of closing (Darger, 2024). Failed business succession negatively impacts business districts and communities, as seen by vacant storefronts and disinvestment in commercial buildings due to loss of revenue. Loss of essential products, services, and gathering spaces impacts community quality of life (Forster-Holt, 2022). Loss of income for previous owners and their former employees and loss of local spending have multiplier effects on the local economy. Loss of local owners often results in the added loss of key volunteers and benefactors for local initiatives including crisis response (Forster-Holt, 2022). According to Welty (2022), women-owned businesses, in particular, tend to be highly engaged in the community, with 70% of those owners in Wisconsin Main Street districts serving on a municipal or civic board or committee.

Despite the role that succession plays in maintaining vibrant business districts and communities, there is a lack of clarity as to what constitutes business succession assistance. Eighty-seven percent of program directors who responded to Main Street America's 2024 Annual Trends Survey reported that they offer support for entrepreneurs and small business owners and 70% reported that they offer business and/or social networking events or support. However, only 14% reported that they offer business succession assistance, the least-reported service or program (Powe & Morita, 2024). While they don't believe they currently offer business succession assistance, 32% did report they would like to in the future—the most-desired addition to services or programs (Powe & Morita, 2024).

Business Succession, Social Capital/Networks, and Entrepreneurial Ecosystems

The terms succession and transition are often used interchangeably within a business context. Business transition is typically defined as significant and visible change to business ownership, management, or structure, with changes to structure including expansion/contraction, reposition, spinoff, or relocation.

Business succession definitions typically include transfer of management but often don't include transfer of ownership unless through inheritance (e.g., family business succession). Not including transfer of ownership through sale is a somewhat arbitrary distinction. A broader definition of business succession may be more useful: business succession is business transfer from predecessor to successor, including preparation pre-transfer and success post-transfer.

Community capitals include natural, cultural, political, built, human, financial, and social capital (Flora et al., 1997). Human and financial capital are commonly understood to be part of business succession, but social capital requires more explanation. Social capital includes resources inherent to and accessible through social networks (de Freyman et al., 2006), including business succession resources and business networks. Digging a little deeper, social capital is seen as being built from three elements: structural elements (e.g., the network structure, map of connections), relational elements (e.g., mutual trust, respected roles), and cognitive elements (e.g., shared norms, values, rules) (de Freyman et al., 2006). Individual social capital can be a business asset and community social capital can be an economic asset (Flora et al., 1997; Roxas & Azmat, 2014; Schulz & Baumgartner, 2013).

Social networks are a web of relationships. Today's entrepreneurs have access to offline and online social networks (Cisneros et al., 2022; Lee & Hallak, 2020). Within the context of business succession, the literature identifies value in both formal professional and informal personal social networks (Schulz & Baumgartner, 2013). Schulz and Baumgartner further distinguishes between economic (profit-driven) and community (people-driven) social networks.

Entrepreneurial ecosystems have been defined as "a set of inter-related actors and components, within a geographic region, that enable productive entrepreneurship" (Lux et al., 2020). There is an obvious overlap between community social networks and entrepreneurial ecosystems, and entrepreneurs need to be creative network managers and relationship builders to be successful (de Freyman et al., 2006; Tata & Prasad, 2010).

Entrepreneurship—a passionate, intuitive, innovative approach to business ownership—is important (Tata & Prasad, 2010), and evidence for the role of social capital/networks in entrepreneurship is growing (Cisneros et al., 2022; Davidsson & Honig, 2003; Stam et al., 2014). Focus on the entrepreneurial endeavor expands the discussion beyond business succession to encompass predecessor entrepreneurial exit and successor entrepreneurial entrance, or to encompass storefront succession—one entrepreneurial venture running its natural course and another ready to take its place.

The Main Street Network

The business succession experience of the authors is grounded in one specific social network, the national Main Street network. This network, while originating at the national level and supported at the state level, is implemented through local Main Street Programs practicing the Main Street Four Point Approach®. This asset-based economic development approach leverages historic capital (built and cultural) and human capital (entrepreneurs and an engaged public). Local Main Street Programs are most effective when integral to community capital and helpful to entrepreneurs developing their individual capital.

A key role of both paid and unpaid (volunteer) staff of local Main Street Programs is to become a resource inherent to, and accessible through, the social networks of the entrepreneurs they serve and a useful part of their web of relationships. This role requires relationship building through shared experience and partnership, forged on mutual trust and credibility. Within this context, local Main Street Programs strive to build trust by being transparent, respectful, and reliable (e.g., protecting confidentiality), and build credibility by providing valued technical, financial, and even emotional support.

Main Street is synonymous with small businesses and local Main Street Programs have a track record of helping create entrepreneurial communities/ecosystems and fostering entrepreneurial success in several ways:

- They serve as formal professional business networks that also facilitate informal personal social networks.
- They host social events to build both individual and community social capital/networks (Guercini & Ranfagni, 2022).
- They connect entrepreneurs with ambassadors, peers, mentors, cohorts, and to advisors, suppliers, and potential customers (through cooperative marketing/events).
- They serve as both an economic (profit-driven) social network and a community (people-driven) social network, generally having a community-driven mission (e.g., local amenity creation) and goals that include economic/business development (Miller et al., 2007; Schulz & Baumgartner, 2013).
- Their activities address the four facets of community social capital: participation in the local community, feelings of trust and safety, neighborhood connections, family and friends' connections (Roxas & Azmat, 2014).
- Local Main Street Program activities are often aimed at or result in increasing local investor confidence (entrepreneurial self-efficacy), which aids entrepreneurial intention and behaviors.
- They operate as an offline social network that can facilitate access to online social networks through state and national networks.
- At their most effective times, local Main Street Programs partner rather than compete with other economic social networks so as not to trigger diminishing or negative returns (Schulz & Baumgartner, 2013).

Concentrating on the entrepreneur, the person, rather than the business, aids in relationship building. Welcoming and celebrating a new entrepreneur, their story, and investment in the community builds more social capital than a simple ribbon cutting publicizing a new business. Entrepreneurs catch a glimpse of available resources (social capital) through social events and a mutual sharing of professional and personal stories (Guercini & Ranfagni, 2022). Continuing to celebrate the entrepreneur's milestones, including succession, strengthens the connection. A relationship or social capital-driven approach allows for pursuing and satisfying the dual community development goals of business retention along with broader support for the entrepreneurs involved.

Successful support requires not taking the business or the owner for granted after the opening and not taking the success of the predecessor or successor for granted after a transfer. For all these reasons, the concerns for business succession not only include predecessor and successor preparation pre-capital transfer, but also include successor and predecessor success post-transfer.

Business Succession Process

The business succession process will be divided into five concerns: predecessor preparation, successor preparation, capital transfer, successor success, and predecessor success (see Figure 11.1). While these concerns are presented here in a logical sequence, they can be addressed simultaneously. Across each of these concerns, there are business succession practices specific to human (HC), financial (FC), and social capital (SC) that we will highlight throughout our explanations and examples (Linder et al., 2020).

Before business succession truly begins, the owner needs to determine whether the business is a transferable entity. For business succession to be an option, the business must not depend on a specific individual with skills or relationships (HC/SC) that cannot be transferred. The business must also generate sufficient cash flow (FC) for both market compensation and return on investment, factoring in a successor's added cost of acquisition (Durham, 2021). If the business does not currently generate sufficient cash flow, strategies to increase cash flow must precede business succession strategies—a case for starting succession preparation early and for complementary business retention and expansion (BRE) strategies. If the business is not a transferable entity and won't be retained, the process will shift to harvest or liquidation and storefront succession.

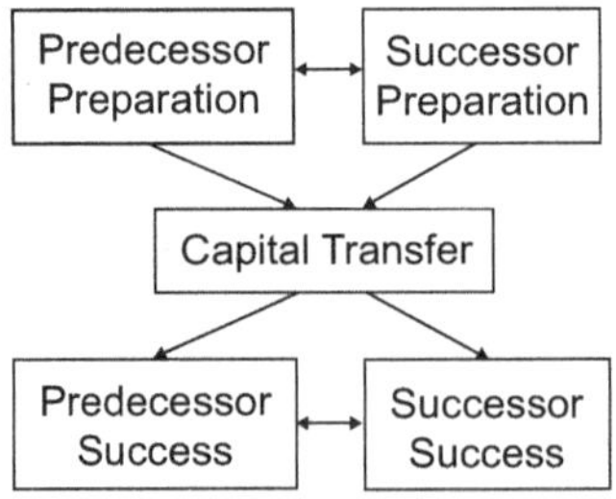

FIGURE 11.1 Business Succession Process Diagram.

Source: Diagramed by authors.

Predecessor Preparation

For years the most accepted business succession recommendation delivered to and through local Main Street Programs was to follow a set of business practices seen as key to predecessor preparation and overall business success. Each of the six best practices has ties to community capitals, although those ties weren't originally identified.

One, detail the business processes (HC)—the buyer is buying these processes, and the processes can't be transferred without being detailed; also, neither the current nor future owner can improve processes unless they are detailed (e.g., through written standard operating procedures (SOP) manuals, employee policies, retail floor strategy).

Two, engage employees (HC)—engaged employees (e.g., through communication, delegation, professional development) have more potential to be retained employees; engaged employees are also better employees for the current and future owner and are more likely to become successors.

Three, set financial goals and clean up financial statements (FC)—inaccurate or incomplete records won't communicate the value of the business to a potential successor or their lenders and investors; also, neither the current nor future owner can improve the bottom line if they don't know it. Remember, insufficient cash flow requires at least pausing the business succession process. If continuing, assign a dollar value to the business through an appraisal. Valuing a business may be more art than science, with the artist being the business appraiser. Valuations can be market-based (some businesses are more in demand and thus more valuable), asset-based (tangible and intangible), or earnings-based (multiplier method). Earnings-based valuation is popular because of its heavier reliance on science, a multiple of cash flow or EBITDA (earnings before interest, taxes, depreciation, and amortization).

However, EBITDA misses several factors. Consider two companies, ABC Company and XYZ Company, with the same EBITDA. ABC Company has high employee turnover, 46% of revenues tied to one customer, no contracts for future work, facilities at capacity, contracts with suppliers for raw materials, and a new in-town competitor. XYZ Company has low employee turnover, only 4% of revenues tied to any one customer, contracts in place for future work, facilities at 60% of capacity, no contracts with suppliers, and an unchanged competitive landscape. Despite the same EBITDA, XYZ Company clearly has more value (illustrative example from Durham, 2021).

It is worth noting that many of the factors EBITDA misses are social and human factors. This example illustrates the need for art in business valuation and demonstrates that value is more than a simple sum of the business parts or assets. However, the parts or assets are still important and include human and social capital in addition to financial capital. The average buyer wants to purchase a turnkey operation with all the business assets healthy and fully transferable.

Four, clean up and fix up (built capital)—besides the simple fact that the business assets need to be maintained and protected, the storefront and store interior are brand communication at the point of sale; for the current and future owner, design can sell, or not, and position the product or service effectively, or not. Quality design (or lack thereof) sends a message about brand and value. Built capital (BC) includes the business's facility, equipment, and inventory.

Five, capture customer information (SC)—customer lists are extremely valuable, especially when annotated (e.g., noting demographics and psychographics—buying patterns and preferences), and are sometimes the entire reason a business is purchased; also, the bigger and more detailed the list, the more customers the current and future owner can effectively direct market.

Six, invest strategically in marketing (SC)—marketing communicates, connects and if targeted, frequent, and effective/affective, can grow brand recognition and customer base; tracking return on marketing investment allows the current and future owner to retarget and improve marketing to increase that return.

With hindsight, there clearly should have been at least a seventh best practice: creatively manage social networks (de Freyman et al., 2006)—social networks can't be transferred without first being managed, including an inventory/mapping; also, neither the current nor future owner can evaluate and improve social networks unless they are inventoried/mapped. Relationships within a typical business social network include internal relationships with employees (best practice two) plus spouse/partner/family, and external relationships with customers (best practices five and six) plus friends/neighbors, colleagues/mentors, manufacturers/suppliers, tenants/landlords, competitors, business/trade associations and their members.

Professional and personal advisors are especially important components of social capital/networks for business succession. Darger (2024) found that for business owners in Minnesota, the most sought-out professional advisers were accountants (by 59.3%), attorneys (by 48.1%), and personal financial planners (by 30.2%). Top personal advisors include other business owners and spouses/partners (Darger, 2024; Kirkwood & Harris, 2011).

Other commonly recognized professional advisors to the business succession process include asset appraisers, business brokers, bankers, and insurance agents. Business owners are best served by first determining their intentions (Kirkwood & Harris, 2011), and then using professional advisors to find the best way(s) to fulfill those intentions; paid advisors should not dictate intentions.

Table 11.1 highlights the impact of a change in motivation on the business succession process. Whether an entrepreneur is driven more by financial capital

TABLE 11.1 Individual Versus Community Social Capital and Entrepreneurial Intention

Capital-driven Succession	*Financial Capital-driven*	*Human Capital-driven*
Individual Social Capital	Harvest/liquidation	Stewardship/business retention
Community Social Capital	Entrepreneurial ecosystem (entrepreneur exit/entrance, store front succession)	Social entrepreneurial ecosystem (triple bottom line)

Source: Compiled by authors.

or human capital can impact entrepreneurial intention as well as community priorities as they relate to the business (or commercial space). Thus, they impact the chosen metrics for measuring and therefore determining success. Darger (2024), for example, found that owners cared about the future of the business as much as maximizing their personal financial situation. Personal advisors (spouse/partner, family, friends/neighbors, colleagues/mentors) can help business owners clarify their intentions.

Missing from this discussion is a set of personal practices for the predecessor to follow as preparation for personal success post-business. As will become clear in the section on predecessor success, the first personal practice is to initiate their own retirement savings plan beyond reliance on potential proceeds from selling the business (Forster-Holt & Nagy, 2022). A second personal practice would be to balance work and life, to engage in activities outside the business.

Predecessor preparation includes selecting a successor, but that selection depends on finding or creating one or more prepared successors. There are advantages in having options and competition, but options necessitate choosing one over the others, which introduces the importance of fit. The predecessor, successor, and business will all benefit from a good fit between personalities and business concept (Linder et al., 2020).

Successor Preparation

Successor preparation strategies will obviously vary depending on the successor, but broadly include learning, training, and experience (HC); cleaning up personal finances and assembling business funds (FC); and strategically building and documenting personal and professional social networks (SC). The predecessor's business succession pathway will determine the pool of potential successors.

The traditional and still-lauded pathway is to retain family ownership and management control. For this pathway, financial capital transfer will likely need to address equitable treatment of non-participating family members, and human capital transfer will potentially need to address co-management (e.g., for a family corporation). A variation on this pathway is family ownership but non-family management.

EXAMPLE: DOWNTOWN DEPARTMENT STORE

This century-old business has successfully transitioned through several family generations. The transition was made possible by creating a family-run board of directors that owns the property and the business. This holding company partnership allows future generations to take over management roles within the firm without needing to secure bank loans to buy out previous generations. The combination of low overhead and stable ownership not only facilitates management transfer but also accommodates market adaptation. This model allows new generations of managers to innovate around day-to-day practices with the benefit of historic success and internal capital structures, ultimately making the business more customer-serving and successful.

Staying with internal social network succession pathways, businesses can be sold to an upper or middle manager or to a group of employees. While employee ownership specifics are covered in other chapters in this volume, it is important to briefly discuss differences in the role of human, financial, and social capital in successor preparation for employee ownership pathways.

With an employee stock ownership plan (ESOP), employee ownership takes the form of shares of company stock held in their retirement account with business profits distributed as additional shares. With an employee ownership trust (EOT), employee ownership takes the form of a beneficiary share of a trust with business profits added to the trust. With a worker cooperative, employee ownership involves one share, one vote, which allows them to elect a board of directors, make other corporate decisions, and receive a share of business profits each year.

Owner-employees are already integrated into the business's internal social network, though they may need to be integrated into external social networks if their responsibilities change (e.g., moving into a management position). Owner-employees are arguably engaged employees, although worker cooperatives allow for a more democratic governance than ESOPs or EOTs. All these employee ownership structures require strong social capital/networks in their creation and for sustainability, especially worker cooperatives.

EXAMPLE: RURAL ARTISAN CLOTHING MANUFACTURER

The impending retirement of the founding owners of this local manufacturer created uncertainty for the 75 employees. In addition to serving as a major employer in a small community, the business had a significant downtown retail presence and contributed to multiple community initiatives. Potential buyers of the company were exclusively out-of-town competitors and a sale to these entities would almost certainly result in a downsizing or closure of local operations. After consulting with advisors, company management was able to secure a favorable business loan and transition to an employee stock ownership plan. Under this model the management team purchased shares in the company, retaining the facility and staff in the community.

Switching to external social network succession pathways, businesses can be sold to friends/neighbors (personal network), to customers or other outside investors (professional network). For friends/neighbors, the social connection may be strong enough that the seller is willing to finance the sale through a down payment and installments or land contract.

Customers can become successors by creating a customer cooperative. While their ownership stake is like that of employees in a worker cooperative, customer-owners aren't employees so may need to prepare for their new responsibilities through learning, training, experiencing (HC), and by strategically building and documenting personal and professional social networks (SC). Customer cooperatives, community-owned ventures, and community-supported/crowdfunded enterprises also require strong social capital/networks in their creation and for sustainability. Crowdfunding/crowdlending is financial capital created through social capital.

EXAMPLE: WISCONSIN SUPPER CLUB

The long-time proprietor of a popular supper club restaurant created a five-year plan for retirement. Working with a business broker, he listed the business for sale. A local couple new to the community hoping to return to the restaurant industry saw the listing as an ideal opportunity to achieve their dream without the high costs of restaurant buildout and brand development. By purchasing a popular established business, they were able to rely on a proven income stream in the short term, while planning for future growth opportunities. Through diligent planning by the seller, the new owners were able to negotiate a transition period, and retain all existing staff, menu items, and space buildout.

EXAMPLE: LOCAL GROCERY

Family health issues required the owners of a downtown grocery to seek a buyer for the decade-old business sooner than originally intended. While the business had an established cash flow, supplier agreements and staff willing to remain, the new owners would need to purchase the property and the inventory and commit to working in the business. Because of the sudden nature of the departure, a prolonged listing was not possible, and a temporary closure would require renegotiating vendor relationships and building code improvements. The presence of a downtown grocery was a critical amenity to several nearby residential properties, who recruited two individuals to form a partnership to take over the business. A phased buyout was negotiated, and the new owners were able to use a Kiva crowdfunded loan (largely supported by local residents) to cover a majority of the initial transition costs.

Strategic buyers (competitors, similar nearby business, suppliers) often find candidate businesses through their external business networks and are looking for businesses that compete, complement, or partner with their existing businesses. For this pathway, value/price depends on duplication of equipment, employees, etc., and purchase may result in loss of local control, relocation or closure of the purchased business by the successor, ultimately necessitating storefront succession.

With an increase in the development and utilization of local venture capitalists to support local business startups, there may be more opportunities in the future for these venture capitalists to also purchase or finance the purchase of local small businesses. Access to venture capital is often facilitated through community social networks. No matter the business succession pathway, social capital/networks are a valuable and often necessary resource, and every potential successor must address social, human, and financial capital (Linder et al., 2020).

Training for any of these successors can be seen as social and human capital development and includes formal education on subject matter covering the specialty of the business, management, accounting, and, in the case of employee or customer successors, ESOP/EOT/cooperative structure. Training also includes gaining experience at a job outside the business and on the job inside the business (Cisneros et al., 2022; Linder et al., 2020).

Capital developed through formal education and at a job outside the purchased business is new capital that the successor(s) bring to the acquired business. On-the-job training can help the successor earn the trust and respect of current employees, customers, and other important groups. To get the most social and human capital from on-the-job training, the successor should have a job description, should be delegated responsibility and authority for certain tasks and relationships, should be supervised and evaluated the same as all employees, should be introduced into the predecessor's external network, and should be selected and integrated with help from valued, long-time key employees (de Freyman et al., 2006).

Preparation can result in a decision by a potential successor not to acquire the business, reintroducing the importance of fit. The business and a potential successor simply might not be a good fit based on business concept or personality, or the potential successor may be more intent on starting a business from scratch and looking for an open storefront (Linder et al., 2020). The community and a potential successor may also not be a good fit (Forster-Holt, 2022). Lack of desire on a successor's part reduces the pool of potential successors from which the predecessor can select.

Capital Transfer

It is during capital transfer that the plans of the predecessor and the plans of the successor come together. If both the predecessor and successor have prepared, the transfer should go more smoothly, but both parties must still formally transfer operations, complete the financial aspect of the sale, and integrate social networks (Cisneros et al., 2022). Transferring operations will ideally include the retention of valuable employees. Throughout the transfer, the predecessor should conduct business as usual, or better than usual, with the succession process relatively unseen by customers.

Arguably the most discussed aspect of business succession is financial capital transfer. The predecessor and the successor must give and gain "fair" value in the exchange. However, each likely assigns value differently (Durham, 2021). Value for the successor may be less than what the predecessor wants or needs to obtain from selling the business. For the highest financial return, if that is the predecessor's intention, social capital/networks and a business broker can create successor competition. For the successor, completing the sale may necessitate securing financing, investors and/or tapping local incentives.

Management transfer can be seen as both social and human capital transfer and should be included in SOP manuals and employee policies. Integrating social networks is a necessary part of management transfer and the fit between predecessor and successor may influence that transfer. The goal is to help the successor attain legitimacy within business social networks and critical business relationships (Steier, 2001; Tata & Prasad, 2010). This assumes that the types or content of network relationships have been identified and critical relationships have been determined and prioritized during earlier preparation.

Successful social capital transfer (de Freyman et al., 2006) calls for helping the successor earn the trust and confidence of the business's external social networks, especially customers—preparation for transferring the reputation and goodwill built up over the years. Transfer also calls for helping the successor earn the trust and respect of the business's internal social network, namely employees—preparation for transferring employee attachment and loyalty. Attaining legitimacy with network members such as customers and employees further affects the transfer of other tangible and intangible assets like business processes, customer loyalty, market share, and brand identity.

EXAMPLE: DOWNTOWN COFFEEHOUSE

An entrepreneur started a coffeehouse and roastery in a downtown storefront. Five years later, the roasting business had expanded into a full-time job, and managing the coffeeshop was taking away from this growing business. Because the roastery relies on the success of the coffeeshop for a percentage of sales, finding a suitable future owner was critical. This resulted in a year-long series of conversations with key customers, partners, and community leaders to identify a likely buyer. Ultimately, the spouse of a key customer was identified as seeking a new local opportunity, and a three-month transition plan was negotiated, retaining a key community hub in downtown and supporting the growth of two local businesses.

Successor Success

Successor success is assumed to be tied to business success, but the determination of business success may go back to entrepreneurial intentions (Table 11.1) and successor success may include elements of work–life balance. When both parties address business succession and capital concerns, prepare separately and collaborate to transfer capital, the transfer should succeed. However, success is not guaranteed (Kirkwood & Harris, 2011), and the successor will benefit from the previously introduced best practices for overall business success.

Post-transfer, the successor should improve business processes to fit their vision for the business (HC). They should quickly engage and further develop both retained and new employees and continue their professional development (HC). They should set their own financial goals for the business and maintain and use accurate financial statements (FC). It is never too early to strengthen the balance sheet. The successor should maintain and improve built assets and design to sell (BC).

The successor should use and add to captured customer information (SC), refine and likely increase strategic investment in marketing (SC), and manage their and the business's social networks (SC) (de Freyman et al., 2006). Cisneros et al. (2022) covered this topic thoroughly:

> Our results also reveal that, during the last two phases, successors expand their own [external social capital] not only by integrating contacts from previous experiences (university or previous jobs) but also by becoming active members of various business networking organizations... Upon my arrival, we called on recognized consulting firms and built a formal and independent board of directors with well-known entrepreneurs. It took us to another level. Many of these contacts I built when I was working outside"... Finally, the network is also strengthened through philanthropic actions.
>
> *(5.2.1 p. 10, 4.2 p. 8)*

According to Welty (2022), of the 225 Wisconsin Main Street District businesses that closed during the study period (2019–2021), only 12% of the owners had been actively involved in the community before the closure. It may be that owners of declining businesses were once engaged but had pulled back to focus on business challenges. However, for businesses that both opened and closed during the study period, only 30% of those owners were engaged in the community, suggesting that owner engagement is at least somewhat correlated with business success.

Post-transfer, the successor now becomes the new predecessor and needs to begin preparing for their own eventual exit from the business. That means not only following best business practices but also following the previously introduced best personal practices—to initiate a retirement savings plan beyond reliance on potential proceeds from reselling the business and to engage in activities outside the business to balance work and life. For successor and predecessor success post-transfer, the predecessor should be willing to mentor the successor (Cisneros et al., 2022).

Predecessor Success

Our final concern, predecessor success post-capital transfer, is arguably the most often neglected concern, by the business owners themselves (avoidance) and by community leaders and organizations (focused on startup entrepreneurs). According to the Exit Planning Institute (2023), 94% of private business owners have no personal post-business plan. Forster-Holt and Nagy (2022) believed rebalancing resources in an entrepreneurial ecosystem would be more age-friendly, and would not only serve later-stage entrepreneurs, but also benefit the community. A common theme among seasoned entrepreneurs was a desire to age in the community and for an identity after the business.

Determination of predecessor success may be a personal measurement of self-fulfillment along with mental, emotional, and physical well-being—their ability to maintain or remake their identity, stay active and involved in the community, and/or secure a legacy. The first best practice is for a predecessor to assume an advisory role to the successor while establishing new social networks (SC). Mentoring other entrepreneurs may be an additional opportunity.

Next, the predecessor will likely benefit from a new professional or personal venture (HC) such as starting another business, volunteering for a local cause, or running for public office. Last, but certainly not least, predecessor success is linked to receiving "fair" financial return (FC). However, the predecessor should not rely on the business as a retirement investment (Forster-Holt & Nagy, 2022).

Entrepreneurs with a sound financial plan for retirement; activities outside the business that provide social contact/influence and a mental challenge; goodwill toward and confidence in a successor (good fit); and access to and a willingness to listen to professional and personal advisors are more apt to have a personal post-business plan and success post-capital transfer. Participation in age-relevant peer cohorts and events provides a safe place to discuss aging and life after business ownership (Forster-Holt & Nagy, 2022). Celebrating predecessors as community champions facilitating the entrance of a successor shifts the narrative from endings and loss to beginnings and gain. Practices like these provide business succession support, so serve as a segue into the next section.

The compiled framework in Table 11.2 summarizes the discussion of the business succession process and the intersection of three key community capitals with five business succession concerns. It represents a more comprehensive understanding of the business succession process, especially for small businesses. It also serves as a jumping-off point for the next topic, which is more prescriptive regarding business succession support.

Business Succession Support

The authors have extensive experience in both supporting business succession and building the capacity of local Main Street Programs to support business succession. However, as obvious as it may now seem that social, financial, and human capital are all key business succession assets, it wasn't always the case—at least not using those specific terms and concepts.

For many years, accepted Main Street Program business succession support emphasized planning for business succession, basic training for sellers and buyers, confidential matchmaking, incentivizing business succession, and developing an entrepreneurial community (to increase the pool of potential buyers). More recently, accepted support has shifted to emphasize engaging business owners (to serve as liaisons, facilitate connections), engaging potential

TABLE 11.2 Capital-Driven Framework for Business Succession Process

Succession Concerns	*Social Capital (SC)*	*Financial Capital (FC)*	*Human Capital (HC)*
Predecessor preparation	Capture customer info; market; map, manage, prioritize, improve social networks; balance work/life; select successor	Clean up business financials, appraise business, invest in retirement, create successor competition	Document operations, engage/develop employees, delegate, select successor
Successor preparation	Strategically build and document social networks, evaluate SC fit	Clean up personal finances, assemble business FC, evaluate FC fit	Learn, train, experience on the job in and outside business, evaluate HC fit
Transfer	Plan SC transfer, integrate social networks	Plan FC transfer, complete sale, tap financial incentives	Plan HC transfer, business as usual or better, transfer operations, retain valuable employees
Successor success	Add customer info, increase marketing, manage & expand social networks, supplement through top management, balance work/life	Set $ goals, maintain books, increase/ diversify revenue, decrease expenses, invest in retirement	Finetune operations, engage and further develop employees/ self
Predecessor success	Assume advisory role, est. new social networks, mentor entrepreneurs	Receive "fair" financial return from sale	Start new venture (professional or personal)

Note: Regarding Built Capital (BC): Predecessor preparation and successor success to include improvement and maintenance of physical assets.

Source: Compiled by authors.

buyers (to matchmake, facilitate leasing), and establishing a community engagement plan (through incentives, mentorship). Building relationships is foundational to the success of these strategies, and relationships define social capital/networks, but there hasn't been a meaningful connection to social or other capital.

Main Street America's (MSA's) 2024 National Trends Survey asked local program directors how they assist with business succession (Powe & Morita, 2024). The following stand out among the 49 anonymous responses reported:

- "With my background in finance, I analyze their business, what their goals are, and help them with choices they could make. Then I connect them with a business broker if they choose to sell. I also show them how they can plan to sell their business to existing employees over time with life insurance policies so the employee can afford it, and the employer can get money from their business. Also, the biggest issue is always trust. It takes time to build those relationships and trust for them to open up about their fears and hopes."
- "We serve as a liaison with larger organizations' resources. In our case, we have personal conversations and relationships with our downtown businesses and can connect them with county resources."
- "We work to finance the transition of the business, engage both sides in best practices, and connect potential owners to in-house educational resources and business support conduits that fit their business type."
- "I counsel the business owner and actively recruit a suitable successor."

The full set of open-ended qualitative responses were analyzed for patterns. Sixteen local program directors used words such as connect and liaison to describe their business succession assistance. By far, most agreement found among respondents was serving in a social network capacity. Further, five used words such as relationships, trust, and engage, which reinforces this social capital role. Five respondents specifically referred to succession planning and five specifically referred to resources (Powe & Morita, 2024).

Welty (2019) found that businesses opening in communities with some sort of liaison helping them rated the experience 50% better than those without—an average score of 8 out of 10 versus 5. To summarize, local Main Street Program experiences with business succession support places connecting and relationships (social capital/networks) first and then, in the best cases, follows or complements those relationships with business succession technical, financial, and in some cases, emotional assistance and resources.

The framework in Table 11.3 is based on the authors' experiences with the Main Street Four Point Approach® (Organization, Economic Vitality, Design,

TABLE 11.3 Four-Point Approach to Business Succession

Four-Point Approach	*Organization*	*Economic Vitality*	*Design*	*Promotion*
Succession (assuming business retention goal)	Improve and transfer internal and external social networks	Improve value and salability of business, transfer business concept/ operations	Improve and transfer brand identity at the point of sale	Improve and transfer brand awareness, promote succession

Source: Compiled by authors.

and Promotion) and additional experience with business succession within that context. The comprehensive nature of Main Street Program efforts lends itself to comprehensive business succession assistance.

Capital-Driven Framework for Business Succession Support

For any approach to business succession support, treatment of financial, human, and social capital could benefit from being explicit and comprehensive. Support for predecessor preparation and financial and human capital transfer is common, while support for successor preparation is less so.

Furthermore, support for social capital transfer, and support for successor and predecessor success post-transfer, are too often neglected. Therefore, it would not be surprising if community leaders and organizations attempting to facilitate and support the succession process were not currently aware of, let alone addressing the full range of, business succession needs and opportunities.

The framework in Table 11.4 provides structure and logic to the many ways community leaders and organizations, Main Street Programs or otherwise, can facilitate and support the succession process, especially for small business owners. The framework makes it easier to uncover opportunities to be more capital-driven and comprehensive. It is important to note that the support framework takes a business coaching-networking approach for its ability to build more social capital than training alone (Squires et al., 2006).

For Main Street Programs, coaches are like personal trainers—they provide entrepreneurs who are looking to get into better shape (businesswise) with help setting goals, exercises (best business practices) to try, gentle (or not so gentle) pushes, feedback (reality checks), and pep talks (emotional support). They facilitate changes in business attitude and practice.

Future Capital-Driven Business Succession Research

While past research provides an evidence base for the business succession process and support applications suggested in this chapter, more research is still needed on the actual and best role of community leaders and organizations. The frameworks (Tables 11.2 and 11.4) help identify possible applied research on how to influence the frequency and quality of predecessor and successor preparation, aid in transferring business capital, and support post-succession success for both successor and predecessor. The first research questions might be: do practitioners agree with the frameworks and do the frameworks offer practical utility?

How can the acceptability of community social networks (community leaders and organizations) offering support be increased? Are community leaders and organizations better off building the capacity of local advisors to support

TABLE 11.4 Capital-Driven Framework for Business Succession Support

Succession Concerns	*Social Capital (SC)*	*Financial Capital (FC)*	*Human Capital (HC)*
Predecessor preparation	Build and promote community social network/ entrepreneurial ecosystem, coach predecessor on mapping and prioritizing pers./ prof. social networks and marketing, support successor search	Connect predecessor with accountants/ CPAs, appraisers/ brokers, bankers, and CFPs; coach predecessor on best pers. and prof. financial practices, including retirement preparation	Coach predecessor on detailing and improving business processes/ operations including retail floor strategy; coach predecessor on employee engagement and attachment practices
Successor preparation	Host conviviality events; connect successor with peers, mentors, cohorts; encourage successor to join trade association	Coach successor on personal finance; create new, target and promote all business succession financial incentives	Offer business/ entrepreneurship training including for ESOP, EOT, and co-op business models
Transfer	Celebrate succession, welcome successor into community social network/ entrepreneurial ecosystem; coach parties through SC transfer	Coach predecessor and successor on gap and nontraditional financing, including seller and crowd, coach parties through FC transfer	Coach successor on employee engagement and attachment practices; invest in community placemaking, local amenity creation
Successor success	Coach successor on mapping, managing and prioritizing pers./prof. social networks; coach on strategic marketing/ PR	Coach successor on best professional and personal financial practices	Offer more business/ entrepreneurship training and coaching, encourage successor to access training through their trade associations

(*Continued*)

Table 11.4 (Continued)

Succession Concerns	*Social Capital (SC)*	*Financial Capital (FC)*	*Human Capital (HC)*
Predecessor success	Welcome predecessor into new roles within community social network/ entrepreneurial ecosystem, support mentorships, offer emotional support	Connect predecessor with CFPs/wealth managers	Support seasoned and serial entrepreneurs; create roles for predecessors within community social network/ entrepreneurial ecosystem

Source: Compiled by authors.

Note: regarding Built Capital (BC): Assist predecessor and successor with improvement and maintenance of physical assets, offer technical assistance and financial incentives.

business succession as individual social capital? What are the best strategies for strengthening community social capital/networks?

Do social networks influence successor fit or is fit between predecessor and successor simply more observable while they socialize? Are communities with stronger or healthier social capital/networks more entrepreneurial? Do they have more entrepreneurs? Does a larger and/or more successful pool of entrepreneurs increase the pool of potential successors or do those entrepreneurs prefer starting their own business from scratch?

How does community social capital influence entrepreneurial intention and further influence the predecessor's chosen metrics and consequently affect determination of success? Does healthy community social capital shift entrepreneurial intentions toward being more socially conscious?

Storefront Succession

This chapter has shown how social capital is integral to business succession as a process and can shape business succession support. However, it is important to remember that the business must be a transferable entity. Many small businesses in practice depend on a specific individual with skills or relationships (HC, SC) that cannot be transferred. Also, many businesses do not currently, nor are ever expected to, generate sufficient cash flow (FC) for both market compensation and return on investment. This may be due to a once-viable business concept trending out of style or a business concept "experiment" that ultimately proved to have insufficient demand. If the business is not a transferable entity, storefront succession may be the best or only option.

It is also possible that an otherwise transferable business simply closes or liquidates—all too often the default option in the absence of predecessor preparation. Closure or liquidation shifts the community development need to storefront succession. With regards to succession pathways, remember that strategic or synergistic buyers may intend to close or relocate the purchased business, ultimately necessitating storefront succession. Finally, regarding successor fit, a potential successor or entering entrepreneur may be more intent on starting a business from scratch and looking for an open storefront, necessitating either storefront succession or new storefront development.

Storefront turnover is a normal and potentially healthy aspect of commercial districts over time, allowing districts to adapt to changing market conditions. Commercial districts struggle when there are no open, move-in ready, appropriately sized or priced storefronts to accommodate this market adaptation or to accommodate new entrepreneurs testing business concepts. The storefront per se, especially within older commercial districts, may sometimes be the issue behind relocation or storefront vacancy if disinvestment and decline have resulted in a marginal or undesirable commercial space. Unfortunately, businesses may also vacate a storefront when their tenant–landlord relationship breaks down.

Commercial districts have difficulties when exiting entrepreneurs aren't replaced with new entrepreneurs, so storefronts sit empty or are occupied by primarily hobby or part-time businesses. Vacancies including those caused by limited hours, or weaknesses in the sequence of storefronts/businesses within a commercial district, have been shown to cause customers to lose interest, stop, and turn around—resulting in shortened shopping trips, lost district sales, and storefronts/businesses beyond that location or interruption not receiving foot traffic (Underhill, 2004).

Failed storefront succession, as much as the previously discussed failed business succession negatively impacts business districts and communities. This condition may lead to community leaders and organizations panicking and over-investing in the retention of businesses that are not viable, and for the community at large, fretting over every closure. They all may need to become comfortable with change and instead invest in facilitating positive change.

Even healthy business districts will see businesses move from one location to another to grow or to cluster near-complementary or even competing businesses. There is a time and a place for both business succession strategies and storefront succession strategies within community development. Once again drawing upon Main Street Program experience, it may be a matter of diagnosing the best approach for each business and each storefront or the best support for each exiting and entering entrepreneur.

For example, if a diagnosis shows a business concept fits the market position of the commercial district (what the district is best at selling and to whom) and the business is successful, the treatment might be to celebrate, learn from, cluster around, and certainly support retention and succession of the business. If, instead, a diagnosis shows a business concept fits but the business is not successful, the treatment might be to coach the entrepreneur. If the business concept doesn't fit but the business is successful, the treatment could be to support relocation or view the business as a traffic generator or anchor and revise the market position. Finally, if a business concept doesn't fit the market position of the commercial district and the business is not successful, the treatment could be to help the entrepreneur see the writing on the wall sooner rather than later.

Each storefront impacts the success of its neighbors and the district. Just as fit between a business and a potential successor is important to successful business succession, fit between a storefront/business and its neighbors is important to storefront succession. Therefore, community leaders and organizations trying to facilitate and support the storefront succession process benefit from having a commercial district master or development plan (Miller et al., 2007). If storefront succession begins to receive more attention by researchers and practitioners, there may be value in a dedicated framework. For now, simply identifying potential differences between business and storefront succession may be sufficient.

The real estate may be the most valuable storefront asset, making cleanup and fixup a storefront succession best practice. Community leaders and organizations should conduct a storefront (building) inventory. Equipment and inventory may be a valuable asset in storefront succession if included in the transfer, and certainly when one high-investment business such as a restaurant, brewery, or medical office is followed by the same type or when the community development goal is for that to happen. For example, retaining a commercial kitchen may be a higher priority than retaining the current outgoing restaurant. Due to the need for appropriately sized and priced storefronts, supporting space subdivision, sub-leases and store-within-a-store concepts (a different entrepreneur owning each department) can help in storefront succession.

Rather than retaining employees, efforts may shift to preparing employees to find new employment (e.g., writing letters of recommendation, investing in workforce development programs) or helping employees start or buy their own venture. Beyond these identified differences, storefront succession process and support is mainly entrepreneurial ecosystem development support for new or serial entrepreneurial entrance, which could easily be the subject of a new chapter or book.

References

Cisneros, L., Deschamps, B., Chirita, G. M., & Geindre, S. (2022). Successful family firm succession: Transferring external social capital to a shared-leadership team of siblings. *Journal of Family Business Strategy*, *13*(3), Article 100467. 10.1016/j.jfbs.2021.100467

Darger, M. (2024, June 25). How well are business owners preparing for succession and transition? *Entrepreneur & Innovation Exchange*. 10.32617/1087-667ab73c71942

Davidsson, P., & Honig, B. (2003). The role of social and human capital among nascent entrepreneurs. *Journal of Business Venturing*, *18*(3), 301–331. 10.1016/S0883-9026(02)00097-6

Durham, C. (2021, February 12). *Succession planning: It all begins with understanding & increasing business value* [Presentation].

Exit Planning Institute. (2023). *2023 national state of owner readiness report*. https://exit-planning-institute.org/2023-national-soor-purchase

Flora, J. L., Sharp, J., Flora, C., & Newlon, B. (1997). Entrepreneurial social infrastructure and locally-initiated economic development. *Sociological Quarterly*, *38*(4): 623–645. http://www.jstor.org/stable/4121083

Forster-Holt, N. (2022). Main street business owners: Aging in plain sight. *Journal of Small Business and Enterprise Development*, *29*(6), 878–885. 10.1108/JSBED-11-2021-0452

Forster-Holt, N., & Nagy, N. (2022). From cradle to grave: Recommendations for age-friendly entrepreneurial ecosystems. *Journal of the International Council for Small Business*, *3*(4), 359–372. 10.1080/26437015.2022.2101162

de Freyman, J., Paturel, R., & Richomme-Huet, K. (2006, February 7–10). *Condition model for transferring social capital in family business succession* [Paper presentation]. *AGSE 3rd International Entrepreneurship Research Exchange, Auckland, New Zealand.*

Guercini, S., & Ranfagni, S. (2022). Animating business relationships through community social capital: An insight into conviviality. *Journal of Enterprising Communities: People and Places in the Global Economy*, *16*(4), 562–581. 10.1108/JEC-06-2020-0109

Kirkwood, L., & Harris, P. (2011). Beyond business: One local government's efforts to help business owners with succession planning. *Small Enterprise Research*, *18*(2), 130–142. 10.5172/ser.2011.18.2.130

Lee, C., & Hallak, R. (2020). Investigating the effects of offline and online social capital on tourism SME performance: A mixed-methods study of New Zealand entrepreneurs. *Tourism Management*, *80*, Article 104128. 10.1016/j.tourman.2020.104128

Linder, C., Lechner, C., & Pelzel, F. (2020). Many roads lead to Rome: How human, social, and financial capital are related to new venture survival. *Entrepreneurship Theory and Practice*, *44*(5) 909–932. 10.1177/1042258719867558

Lux, A. A., Macau, F. R., & Brown, K. A. (2020). Putting the entrepreneur back into entrepreneurial ecosystems. *International Journal of Entrepreneurial Behavior & Research*, *26*(5), 1011–1041. 10.1108/IJEBR-01-2020-0031

Miller, N. J., Besser, T., & Malshe, A. (2007). Strategic networking among small businesses in small US communities. *International Small Business Journal*, *25*(6), 631–665. 10.1177/0266242607082525

Powe, M., & Morita, E. (2024, April 2). *Main spotlight: Insights from the 2024 trends survey*. Main Street America. https://mainstreet.org/the-latest/news/main-spotlight-insights-from-the-2024-trends-survey

Roxas, H. B., & Azmat, F. (2014). Community social capital and entrepreneurship: Analyzing the links. *Community Development*, *45*(2), 135–150. 10.1080/15575330.2014.880495

Schulz, T., & Baumgartner, D. (2013). Volunteer organizations: Odds or obstacle for small business formation in rural areas? Evidence from Swiss municipalities. *Regional Studies*, *47*(4), 597–612. 10.1080/00343404.2011.587799

Squires, P., Cox, E., & Boyle, D. (Eds). (2006). *Who's the entrepreneur? The BizFizz story: Unleashing the passion, transforming communities*. New Economics Foundation; The Civic Trust. https://neweconomics.org/uploads/files/55400eb98c812d391d_ycm6vgefa.pdf

Stam, W., Arzlanian, S., & Elfring, T. (2014). Social capital of entrepreneurs and small firm performance: A meta-analysis of contextual and methodological moderators. *Journal of Business Venturing*, *29*(1), 152–173. 10.1016/j.jbusvent.2013.01.002

Steier, L. (2001). Next-generation entrepreneurs and succession: An exploratory study of modes and means of managing social capital. *Family Business Review*, *14*(3), 259–276. 10.1111/j.1741-6248.2001.00259.x

Tata, J., & Prasad, S. (2010). Social capital and next-generation succession in the family firm. *International Journal of Entrepreneurship and Small Business*, *11*(3), 322–337. 10.1504/IJESB.2010.035821

Templin, E., Chazdon, S., Muske, G., Barroso, F. D., Osborne, L., & Craig, W. (2017). The silver tsunami and rural small business retention: What can communities do? *Community Development*, *48*(2), 282–298. 10.1080/15575330.2017.1287110

Underhill, P. (2004). *Call of the mall: The geography of shopping*. Simon & Schuster.

Welty, E. (2019). *2019 Business climate study* [Unpublished].

Welty, E. (2022). *Wisconsin Main Street entrepreneurship trends 2022* [Unpublished].

INDEX

Pages in *italics* refer to figures, pages in **bold** refer to tables, and pages followed by n refer to notes

FSC
www.fsc.org
MIX
Papier | Fördert gute Waldnutzung
FSC® C083411

Kolibri 360 GmbH
Ferdinand-Jühlke-Straße 7
99095 Erfurt, Deutschland
produktsicherheit@kolibri360.de